Probability

An Introductory Guide for Actuaries and other Business Professionals

Fourth Edition

David J. Carr, BSc
Fellow of the Institute of Actuaries

Michael A. Gauger, Ph.D.
Associate of the Society of Actuaries

Robert Chadburn, Ph.D.
Fellow of the Institute of Actuaries

BPP Professional Education
Phoenix, AZ

BPP Professional Education
4025 S. Riverpoint Parkway
Phoenix, AZ 85040
Mail Stop: CF-K909

Manufactured in the United States of America

10 9 8 7 6 5 4 3 2 1

ISBN: 978-0-9816081-2-9

Preface

Welcome to this introductory guide to probability.

Based on our experience as professional educators, our aim when writing this text has been to produce a clear, practical and student-friendly guide in which theoretical derivations have been balanced with a helpful, structured approach to the material. We have supplemented the explanations with over 370 worked examples and practice questions to give students ample opportunity to see how the theory is applied. The result—we hope—is a thorough but accessible introduction to probability theory, which is suitable for college students from a wide variety of backgrounds.

This text is of particular relevance to actuarial students who are preparing for Exam P of the Society of Actuaries, and Exam 1 of the Casualty Actuarial Society. Where possible, examples are set in an insurance or risk management context, and selected practice questions have been taken from relevant past exams of the actuarial professions in the US and the UK. For more information about an actuarial career, visit www.beanactuary.org or www.soa.org. Aspiring actuaries in the UK should visit www.actuaries.org.uk.

This text could not have been completed without the helpful contributions of several outstanding individuals. Beverly Butler and Rachel Arnold deserve particular mention for their superb technical reviews, which have greatly improved the clarity and accuracy of each chapter. Any errors in this text are solely our own. Special thanks are also due to Denise Rosengrant, who took the final chapters and—with her usual great efficiency—produced the physical book that is now in your hands.

We hope that you find this text helpful in your studies, wherever these may lead you.

David Carr and Michael Gauger
November 2004

In the third edition of the textbook we have expanded Chapter 4 in light of comments from students.

June 2007

In this fourth edition we have taken the opportunity to correct some minor typographical errors and include some improvements suggested by BPP's students.

Robert Chadburn
November 2011

Table of contents

Introduction

Before we start the main subject matter in this text, we should take care of a little housekeeping.

Assumed knowledge

We do not assume that the reader has any prior knowledge of probability. We do, however, expect the reader to be familiar with high-school mathematics including basic calculus such as differentiation and integration (by parts and by substitution).

Since many of the examples in this book are presented in an insurance context, we have included an introduction to insurance in the next section. Once you understand the basic ideas and terminology, you'll be well placed to focus on the most important aspect of the worked examples and practice questions, *ie* the application of probability theory.

Notation and rounding

We have tried hard to ensure that all new notation is explained clearly. We sometimes use $\exp(x)$ in place of e^x, especially when this avoids complicated superscripts that might otherwise be difficult to read.

Rounding poses a particular dilemma. Our standard policy in this text has been to keep full accuracy within intermediate calculations even though an intermediate result may be shown as a rounded value. So, you may occasionally disagree with the last significant figure or two in a calculation if you calculate the result using the rounded values shown.

Past exam questions

Selected end-of-chapter practice questions have been taken from relevant professional actuarial exams. The abbreviation SOA/CAS refers to questions published by the Society of Actuaries and the Casualty Actuarial Society. The abbreviation IOA/FOA refers to questions published by the Institute of Actuaries and the Faculty of Actuaries in the United Kingdom. Past exam questions are reprinted with permission from the Society of Actuaries, the Casualty Actuarial Society, the Institute of Actuaries and the Faculty of Actuaries.

Solutions to practice questions

Short numerical solutions to all of the end-of-chapter practice questions can be found at the end of the book. Detailed worked solutions to these practice questions can be downloaded free of charge by going to the BPP Professional Education website at **www.bpptraining.com**, and selecting student resources under the SOA Exam P/CAS Exam 1 tab. Other useful study resources can also be found here.

Errors in this text

If you find an error in this text, we'll be pleased to hear from you so that we can publish an errata for students on our website and correct these errors in the next edition. Please email details of any errors to **info@bpptraining.com**. Thank you.

Introduction to insurance

In this short introductory section, we'll study how insurance works, describe common types of insurance policies, and explain some insurance jargon.

How insurance works

Insurance helps individuals and organizations to reduce the financial risk of an adverse event, *eg* the cost of rebuilding a house after a fire, or the cost of hospital care in the event of illness.

Insurance involves two parties:

- the **insurance company** (also known as the **insurer**)

- the **policyholder**.

The policyholder purchases an insurance policy by paying a **premium** to the insurance company. The premium is calculated by the insurance company and reflects the level of risk.

In return for the premium, the insurance company promises to pay the policyholder an amount of money (called a **benefit** or **claim payment**) if the policyholder were to suffer a financial loss due to a specified event.

For example, a policyholder might insure his house for $200,000 against the risk of fire. The policyholder would pay a premium to the insurance company. If the house were destroyed by fire, the insurance company would pay a benefit to the policyholder of $200,000 to meet the cost of rebuilding.

There are two very important ideas about insurance:

- The insurance company can afford to carry the risk because it sells a large number of similar policies.

- Each policyholder pays a premium greater than the expected amount of the benefit.

Let's look at these ideas with a numerical example.

Suppose that the Neon Insurance Company sells 10,000 identical insurance policies. Each policy insures the policyholder's house against the risk of fire, and will pay a claim benefit of $200,000 if a major fire were to occur.

The probability of a house being totally destroyed by fire in any one year is 0.003. So, Neon expects to make $10,000 \times 0.003 = 30$ claim payments during the year. This gives a total of $30 \times \$200,000 = \$6,000,000$ in claim payments.

The insurance company will need to charge a premium of $\$6,000,000 / 10,000 = \$600$ per policy in order to cover claims. In addition, the insurance company will need to meet the cost of running the company (*eg* salaries, marketing costs, and other business expenses) and make some profit.

So, Neon decides to charge a premium of $750 per policy.

Most individuals are **risk averse**, that is they avoid taking unncessary risks. Paying a premium of $750 and being fully protected in the event of a fire is preferable for most individuals to saving $750 (*ie* paying no premium) but being exposed to the possibility (albeit unlikely) of a loss of $200,000, which would cause significant financial hardship.

Is Neon guaranteed to cover expenses and make a profit? No. If there are 40 claims in the year, the total claim payments will be $8,000,000, which exceeds the total premium. However, by selling a large number of independent policies, the insurer spreads its risk and reduces the likelihood of making a loss.

In practice, the insurance company does not know the true probability of a claim. However, an actuary can estimate the probability by considering the number of claims in recent years.

The example above is rather artificial because we only considered one level of claim payment. In reality, the claim payment will depend on the severity of the fire — the cost of repairs after a minor fire will be much smaller than the cost of rebuilding after complete destruction of the house.

So, the actuary will need to consider two aspects to the expected claims:

- the **claims frequency** (*ie* how likely is a claim?)

- the **claims severity** (*ie* how large is a claim likely to be?)

In terms of probability theory, we combine a **frequency distribution** with a **severity distribution** to obtain a **loss distribution**, which describes the likelihood of a claim and the likely size of that claim.

Common types of insurance

It's useful to have a basic understanding of the most common types of insurance, but you do not need to know the details of each type of insurance to answer the questions in this text.

Automobile insurance covers the cost of repairing a car in the event of accidental damage (property damage) and any costs associated with causing injury to a third party (liability).

Homeowners insurance also covers property damage (*eg* the cost of repairing a house after it is damaged by a storm, and the cost of replacing personal possessions that are stolen or destroyed) and liability (*eg* injury caused to a third party while in the house).

Health insurance covers the cost of medical expenses, *eg* hospital care, and physicians' fees.

Life insurance, in its simplest form, provides a lump sum benefit when an insured policyholder dies.

Disability insurance typically provides regular income when an insured policyholder becomes disabled. This is intended to replace (in part or in full) any loss of earnings.

Insurance terminology

You'll meet the following insurance terms in this text.

Claim

Claim payments are the amounts paid by the insurance company to policyholders. If there is no deductible or policy limit, the claim payment will be equal to the loss. If there is a deductible or policy limit, the claim payment may be less than the amount of the loss.

Deductible

If an insurance policy has a deductible, the insurer will only pay that part of the loss in excess of the deductible. If an insurance policy has a deductible of $100, say, and the loss is X, then the insurer will pay:

- nothing if the loss is below $100

- $\$(X-100)$ if the loss exceeds $100.

Deductibles discourage policyholders from making small claims, which helps to reduce premiums.

Gross premium

The gross premium is the total premium, including the expected claims amount, expenses, profit *etc*. In this text, we're usually more interested in calculating the net premium.

Loss

A loss is the financial loss to a policyholder as the result of a specified (insurable) event. If there is no deductible or policy limit, the claim payment will be equal to the loss. If there is a deductible or policy limit, the claim payment may be less than the amount of the loss.

Net premium

The net premium is that part of the insurance premium that relates to the expected cost of claims. It excludes any allowance for the insurer's expenses or profit. In terms of probability theory, the net premium is the expected value of the loss distribution (after allowing for the effect of any deductibles or policy limits).

Policy limit

A policy limit is the maximum amount that an insurer will pay to the policyholder in the event of claim. So, if a policy has a limit of $10,000, the insurer would pay:

- the full amount of the loss if the loss is below $10,000

- $10,000 if the loss exceeds $10,000.

Pure premium

The pure premium is another name for the net premium, described above.

This page is intentionally left blank.

1

Introduction to Probability Theory

Overview

The concept of probability is commonly used in everyday life, and can be expressed in many ways. For example, there is a 50:50 chance of a "head" when a fair coin is tossed. There is a 1-in-6 chance of scoring a four when rolling a fair six-sided die. And a meteorologist may tell us that the chance of rain tomorrow is 80%.

In this introductory chapter, we'll define very precisely what we mean by a probability, and we'll study some important characteristics of probabilities. Throughout this book, we'll demonstrate the applications of probability theory in the areas of insurance and risk management. For example, we may wish to answer questions such as:

- What is the probability that a policyholder will file a claim in excess of $1,000 on his medical insurance policy this month?

- What is the probability that two machines fail on the same day?

- What is the probability that a policyholder with an automobile policy and a homeowners policy will renew at least one policy next year?

1.1 Set theory

Probability theory is founded on set theory. While we fully expect all readers to be familiar with basic set theory from high school, we will devote this initial section of the book to a short review of the main notation and concepts.

Sets and elements

A **set** is a well-defined collection of **elements** or **members**.

If the element x belongs to the set A, then we write $x \in A$. If the element x does not belong to the set A, then we write $x \notin A$.

For example, if $A = \{1,2,3,4\}$ then $2 \in A$ but $2.5 \notin A$ and $8 \notin A$.

The elements of a set may be **quantitative**, *eg* $A = \{0,1\}$ or $B = \{3.42, 5.66, 8.17\}$, or **qualitative**, *eg* $C = \{\text{white, red, blue}\}$ or $D = \{\text{good, average, poor}\}$, or a combination.

A set may contain a finite or infinite number of elements. When a set contains a large number of elements, it may be impractical or impossible to list all of the elements using the notation above. For example, if A is the set of all integers between 1 and 100 inclusive, then the set may be defined in any of the following ways:

$A = \{\text{All integers between 1 and 100 inclusive}\}$

$A = \{1,2,3,\cdots,99,100\}$

$A = \{x : x \in \mathbb{Z}, 1 \le x \le 100\}$ where $\mathbb{Z}$ denotes the set of integers

A set may also contain an uncountable number of elements. For example, if A is the set of all real numbers greater than 5 but less than 75, we have:

$A = \{x : x \in \mathbb{R}, 5 < x < 75\}$ where $\mathbb{R}$ denotes the set of real numbers

Subsets

The set A is a **subset** of set B if every element of set A is also an element of set B.

If A is a **subset** of B, then we write $A \subset B$.

If A is not a **subset** of B, then we write $A \not\subset B$.

For example, if $A = \{1,3,5\}$, $B = \{5,7\}$ and $C = \{1,2,3,4,5,6\}$ then $A \subset C$ but $B \not\subset C$.

The definition leads easily to the following result:

$A \subset B, B \subset A \Rightarrow A = B$

The universal set

In any particular situation it is useful to define the set of all possible elements of interest.

The set of all elements under consideration in any particular situation is called the **universal set**, which we will denote S.

For any set A, we have $A \subset S$.

For example, if we are interested in the score that might be obtained by rolling a fair die, the universal set would be $S = \{1,2,3,4,5,6\}$, and we would restrict our consideration to subsets containing some or all of these six elements.

The empty set

It is also useful to define a set with no elements.

The **empty set** or **null set** contains no elements, and is denoted $\varnothing$:

$$\varnothing = \{ \ \}$$

The empty set is considered to be a subset of every other set, *ie*:

$$\varnothing \subset A \quad \text{for all sets } A$$

Basic set operations

There are three basic set operations: intersection, union and complement.

The **intersection** of two sets A and B is the set of all elements that belong to both A and B. It is denoted $A \cap B$ and is pronounced "A intersection B."

$$A \cap B = \{x : x \in A \text{ and } x \in B\}$$

The **union** of two sets A and B is the set of all elements that belong to either A or B or both. It is denoted $A \cup B$ and is pronounced "A union B."

$$A \cup B = \{x : x \in A \text{ or } x \in B\}$$

The **complement** of the set A is the set of all elements that belong to the universal set S but do not belong to set A. It is denoted A'.

$$A' = \{x : x \in S \text{ and } x \notin A\}$$

Note: The complement is sometimes denoted $\overline{A}$ or A^c.

For example, let $S = \{1,2,3,4,5,6\}$, $A = \{1,3,5\}$, and $B = \{4,5,6\}$. Then:

$$A \cap B = \{5\}$$
$$A \cup B = \{1,3,4,5,6\}$$
$$A' = \{2,4,6\}$$
$$B' = \{1,2,3\}$$

Venn diagrams

A Venn diagram is a very useful graphical representation of sets. Skillful use of a Venn diagram can sometimes lead to a relatively simple solution to a problem that may look complicated at first sight.

In this book, the universal set S will be represented by the interior of the rectangular area in the diagram. All subsets of S will be represented by the interior of other enclosed areas (usually circles) within S.

Here are some examples of Venn diagrams. The shaded area in each diagram is described below each figure.

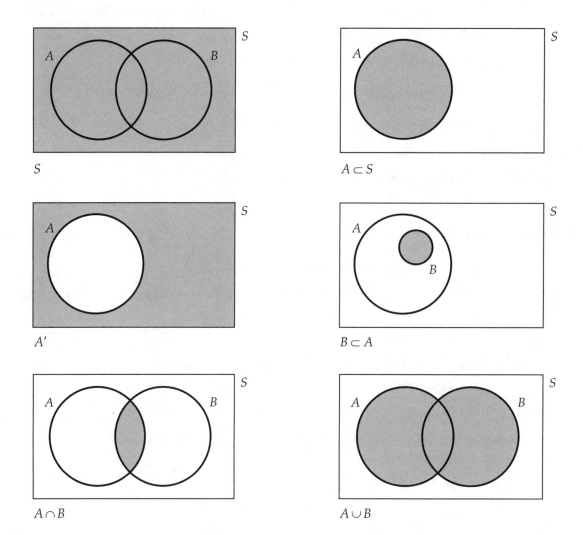

Basic laws of set operations

The following laws are useful when working with set theory algebra:

The **associative laws** state that:

$$(A \cup B) \cup C = A \cup (B \cup C)$$

$$(A \cap B) \cap C = A \cap (B \cap C)$$

The **distributive laws** state that:

$$A \cap (B \cup C) = (A \cap B) \cup (A \cap C)$$

$$A \cup (B \cap C) = (A \cup B) \cap (A \cup C)$$

De Morgan's laws state that:

$$(A \cup B)' = A' \cap B'$$

$$(A \cap B)' = A' \cup B'$$

Given the review nature of this section, we will not prove these results, but each of these laws can be proved from first principles, or can be illustrated using a Venn diagram.

For example, De Morgan's laws can be illustrated as follows:

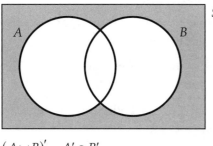

$$(A \cup B)' = A' \cap B'$$

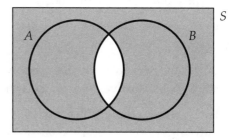

$$(A \cap B)' = A' \cup B'$$

1.2 Probability

We'll start with some basic definitions. These are based on the set theory concepts in Section 1.1 but have different nomenclature in probability theory, where we are interested in the possible outcomes of a random experiment.

Events

The set of all possible outcomes of a random experiment is called the **sample space**, and is denoted S.

A subset of the sample space is called an **event**. An event is said to have occurred if the outcome of the experiment is in the corresponding subset.

Events $A_1, A_2, \cdots$ are **mutually exclusive** or **disjoint** if:

$$A_i \cap A_j = \varnothing \text{ whenever } i \neq j$$

ie mutually exclusive events cannot occur simultaneously.

Events $A_1, A_2, \cdots$ are **exhaustive** if:

$$A_1 \cup A_2 \cup \cdots = S$$

ie the events $A_1, A_2, \cdots$ cover all the possible outcomes.

If events $A_1, A_2, \cdots$ are mutually exclusive and exhaustive, then events $A_1, A_2, \cdots$ are said to form a **partition** of the sample space.

For example, if the random experiment is the score obtained by rolling a fair die, the sample space is $S = \{1,2,3,4,5,6\}$. We can define the following events:

$$A_1 = \{\text{Score is odd number}\} = \{1,3,5\}$$
$$A_2 = \{\text{Score is even number}\} = \{2,4,6\}$$
$$A_3 = \{\text{Score is low}\} = \{1,2,3\}$$
$$A_4 = \{\text{Score is high}\} = \{4,5,6\}$$
$$A_5 = \{\text{Roll a 6}\} = \{6\}$$

Events A_1 and A_2 are mutually exclusive and exhaustive, so they form a partition of the sample space. The score must be either odd or even, but cannot be both.

Events A_3 and A_4 are also mutually exclusive and exhaustive, so they too form a partition of the sample space. The score must be either low or high, but cannot be both.

Events A_3 and A_5 are mutually exclusive, since the score cannot both be low and a 6. These events are not exhaustive, since they do not cover the possible outcomes of rolling a 4 or a 5.

Events A_2 and A_4 are neither mutually exclusive (a score of 4 or 6 is both even and high), nor exhaustive (they do not cover the possible outcomes of rolling a 1 or a 3).

Probability is a numerical measure of the likelihood of an event occurring. It is defined using a function that assigns a value to each subset of the sample space, subject to certain consistency conditions or axioms.

Probability is defined using the following axioms.

Axioms of probability

The probability of event A in the sample space S, denoted $\Pr(A)$, is a real number that satisfies the following:

(1) $\Pr(A) \geq 0$ for any event A

(2) $\Pr(S) = 1$

(3)   If $A_1, A_2, \cdots$ are mutually exclusive events, then:

$$\Pr(A_1 \cup A_2 \cup \cdots) = \Pr(A_1) + \Pr(A_2) + \cdots$$

So, a probability is a real number between 0 and 1 (where a value of 0 represents the probability that an impossible event occurs, and a value of 1 represents the probability that a certain event occurs). We can prove this and other important relationships from these axioms.

Theorem 1.1

$\Pr(\varnothing) = 0$

Proof

Events A and $\varnothing$ are mutually exclusive. From axiom (3), we have $\Pr(A \cup \varnothing) = \Pr(A) + \Pr(\varnothing)$ but since $A \cup \varnothing = A$, we have:

$$\Pr(A) = \Pr(A) + \Pr(\varnothing) \quad \Rightarrow \quad \Pr(\varnothing) = 0 \qquad\qquad \square$$

Theorem 1.2

For any event A:

$$\Pr(A') = 1 - \Pr(A)$$

Proof

Events A and A' are mutually exclusive. From axiom (3), we have $\Pr(A \cup A') = \Pr(A) + \Pr(A')$ but since $A \cup A' = S$, we have:

$$\Pr(S) = \Pr(A) + \Pr(A') \implies 1 = \Pr(A) + \Pr(A') \implies \Pr(A') = 1 - \Pr(A) \qquad \square$$

Theorem 1.3

For any event A:

$$0 \le \Pr(A) \le 1$$

Proof

From axiom (1), we know that $\Pr(A) \ge 0$, and similarly $\Pr(A') \ge 0$. From Theorem 1.2, we have:

$$\Pr(A) + \Pr(A') = 1$$

Since each quantity is non-negative, this implies that $0 \le \Pr(A) \le 1$ for any event A. $\qquad \square$

Theorem 1.4 *(The additive probability law)*

For any two events A and B:

$$\Pr(A \cup B) = \Pr(A) + \Pr(B) - \Pr(A \cap B)$$

Proof

Axiom (3) relates to mutually exclusive events, but events A and B do not necessarily satisfy this requirement. We proceed by expressing $A \cup B$ as the union of three mutually exclusive events (this relationship is simple to verify using a Venn diagram):

$$A \cup B = (A \cap B') \cup (A' \cap B) \cup (A \cap B)$$
$$\implies \Pr(A \cup B) = \Pr(A \cap B') + \Pr(A' \cap B) + \Pr(A \cap B)$$

We can also express events A and B as the union of mutually exclusive events:

$$A = (A \cap B) \cup (A \cap B') \implies \Pr(A \cap B') = \Pr(A) - \Pr(A \cap B)$$
$$B = (A \cap B) \cup (A' \cap B) \implies \Pr(A' \cap B) = \Pr(B) - \Pr(A \cap B)$$

Substituting into the main formula, we have:

$$\Pr(A \cup B) = \Pr(A) + \Pr(B) - \Pr(A \cap B) \qquad \square$$

This result has an important intuitive interpretation: when we consider the probability of the occurrence of event A **or** event B, we must not double count those outcomes for which events A **and** B both occur. Since the values of $\Pr(A)$ and $\Pr(B)$ both include $\Pr(A \cap B)$, we deduct $\Pr(A \cap B)$ in order to avoid counting these outcomes twice. Also, note that this rule reduces to Axiom (3) when events A and B are mutually exclusive.

The additive law can be extended to cover any three events, A, B, and C:

$$\Pr(A \cup B \cup C)$$
$$= \Pr(A) + \Pr(B) + \Pr(C) - \Pr(A \cap B) - \Pr(A \cap C) - \Pr(B \cap C) + \Pr(A \cap B \cap C)$$

Theorem 1.5   *(The law of total probability)*

If the events $A_1, A_2, \cdots$ are mutually exclusive and exhaustive, then:

$$\Pr(B) = \Pr(B \cap A_1) + \Pr(B \cap A_2) + \cdots$$

Proof

First, we will show that events $B \cap A_1, B \cap A_2, \cdots$ are mutually exclusive.

Since events $A_1, A_2, \cdots$ are mutually exclusive, $A_i \cap A_j = \varnothing$ whenever $i \neq j$. Using the associative laws, we have:

$$(B \cap A_i) \cap (B \cap A_j) = B \cap (A_i \cap A_j) = B \cap \varnothing = \varnothing \quad \text{whenever } i \neq j$$

Next, we show that $B = (B \cap A_1) \cup (B \cap A_2) \cup \cdots$

$$(B \cap A_1) \cup (B \cap A_2) \cup \cdots$$
$$= B \cap (A_1 \cup A_2 \cup \cdots) \qquad \text{(by the distributive laws)}$$
$$= B \cap S = B$$

Now it is a simple matter to use axiom (3) to provide the required result:

$$\Pr(B) = \Pr\big((B \cap A_1) \cup (B \cap A_2) \cup \cdots\big)$$
$$= \Pr(B \cap A_1) + \Pr(B \cap A_2) + \cdots \qquad\qquad \square$$

Let's summarize these results and then work through some numerical examples.

Further properties of probability

(1) $\Pr(\varnothing) = 0$

(2)   For any event A:

$$\Pr(A') = 1 - \Pr(A)$$

(3)   For any event A:

$$0 \leq \Pr(A) \leq 1$$

---

(4)   For any two events A and B:

$$\Pr(A \cup B) = \Pr(A) + \Pr(B) - \Pr(A \cap B)$$

(5)   If the events $A_1, A_2, \cdots$ are mutually exclusive and exhaustive, then:

$$\Pr(B) = \Pr(B \cap A_1) + \Pr(B \cap A_2) + \cdots$$

 ## Example 1.1

A manufacturing company operates two machines. The probability that the first machine breaks down in the next week is 0.14. The probability that the second machine breaks down in the next week is 0.17. The probability that both machines break down in the next week is 0.06. Calculate:

(i)   the probability that the first machine does not break down in the next week

(ii)   the probability that at least one machine breaks down in the next week

(iii)   the probability that exactly one machine breaks down in the next week.

Solution

(i)   Let $A = \{$First machine breaks down$\}$ and $B = \{$Second machine breaks down$\}$.

From the question we have:

$$\Pr(A) = 0.14, \quad \Pr(B) = 0.17, \quad \Pr(A \cap B) = 0.06$$

The probability that the first machine does not break down in the next week is:

$$\Pr(A') = 1 - \Pr(A) = 1 - 0.14 = 0.86$$

(ii)   The probability that at least one machine breaks down in the next week is:

$$\Pr(A \cup B) = \Pr(A) + \Pr(B) - \Pr(A \cap B) = 0.14 + 0.17 - 0.06 = 0.25$$

(iii)   This final calculation is the most difficult.

The required event is:

$$(\text{First machine fails} \cap \text{Second machine does not fail})$$
$$\cup (\text{First machine does not fail} \cap \text{Second machine fails}) = (A \cap B') \cup (A' \cap B)$$

Since these two outcomes are mutually exclusive, the required probability is:

$$\Pr(A \cap B') + \Pr(A' \cap B)$$

Using basic set theory, we have:

$$A = (A \cap B) \cup (A \cap B')$$
$$\Rightarrow \Pr(A) = \Pr(A \cap B) + \Pr(A \cap B')$$
$$\Rightarrow \Pr(A \cap B') = \Pr(A) - \Pr(A \cap B) = 0.14 - 0.06 = 0.08$$

and similarly:

$$B = (A \cap B) \cup (A' \cap B)$$
$$\Rightarrow \Pr(A' \cap B) = \Pr(B) - \Pr(A \cap B) = 0.17 - 0.06 = 0.11$$

Finally, the required probability is:

$$\Pr(A \cap B') + \Pr(A' \cap B) = 0.08 + 0.11 = 0.19 \qquad \blacklozenge\blacklozenge$$

We can also answer this question using a Venn diagram. The probability of each region can be calculated easily from the information in the question:

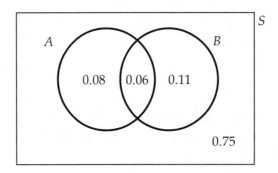

For part (i), we need to consider the shaded area in the following Venn diagram:

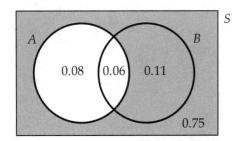

So, the required probability is:

$$0.11 + 0.75 = 0.86$$

For part (ii), we need to consider the shaded area in the following Venn diagram:

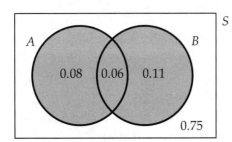

So, the required probability is:

$$0.08 + 0.06 + 0.11 = 0.25$$

For part (iii), we need to consider the shaded area in the following Venn diagram:

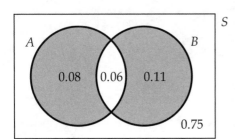

So, the required probability is:

$$0.08 + 0.11 = 0.19$$

Example 1.2

The probability that a policyholder will make a claim on his homeowners insurance policy during the next year is 0.44. The probability that a policyholder will make a claim on his automobile insurance policy during the next year is 0.36. The probability that a policyholder will make a claim on both his homeowners insurance policy and his automobile insurance policy during the next year is 0.21.

Calculate the probability that a randomly selected policyholder does not make a claim on either his homeowners insurance policy or his automobile insurance policy during the next year.

Solution

Let $A = \{\text{Claims on homeowners policy}\}$ and $B = \{\text{Claims on automobile policy}\}$.

From the question we have:

$$\Pr(A) = 0.44, \quad \Pr(B) = 0.36, \quad \Pr(A \cap B) = 0.21$$

Hence, the probability that a claim is made on either policy is:

$$\Pr(A \cup B) = \Pr(A) + \Pr(B) - \Pr(A \cap B) = 0.44 + 0.36 - 0.21 = 0.59$$

and the probability that a claim is made on neither policy is:

$$\Pr\big((A \cup B)'\big) = 1 - \Pr(A \cup B) = 1 - 0.59 = 0.41 \qquad\qquad \blacklozenge\blacklozenge$$

We can also answer this question using a Venn diagram. The probability of each region can be calculated easily from the information in the question:

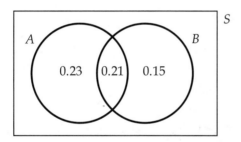

We need to calculate the probability of lying outside the circles. This is:

$$1 - 0.23 - 0.21 - 0.15 = 0.41$$

Example 1.3

Among a large group of patients suffering from Systemic Lupus Erythematosus (SLE), it is found that 26% suffer from both arthritis and kidney problems, whereas 8% suffer from neither of these. The probability that a patient suffers from kidney problems exceeds by 0.16 the probability that a patient suffers from arthritis. Determine the probability that a randomly chosen member of this group suffers from arthritis.

Solution

Let $A = \{$Suffers from arthritis$\}$ and $B = \{$Suffers from kidney problems$\}$.

From the question we have:

$$\Pr(A \cap B) = 0.26, \quad \Pr((A \cup B)') = 0.08, \quad \Pr(B) = \Pr(A) + 0.16$$

Using the property $\Pr(A') = 1 - \Pr(A)$, we have:

$$\Pr(A \cup B) = 1 - \Pr((A \cup B)') = 1 - 0.08 = 0.92$$

And using the property $\Pr(A \cup B) = \Pr(A) + \Pr(B) - \Pr(A \cap B)$, we have:

$$\Pr(A \cup B) = \Pr(A) + \Pr(B) - \Pr(A \cap B)$$
$$\Rightarrow 0.92 = \Pr(A) + \big(\Pr(A) + 0.16\big) - 0.26$$
$$\Rightarrow \Pr(A) = 0.51 \hspace{5cm} \blacklozenge\blacklozenge$$

We can also answer this question using a Venn diagram. The probability of some regions can be filled in from the information in the question:

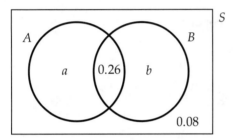

From the information in the question:

$$0.26 + b = 0.16 + (a + 0.26) \quad \Rightarrow \quad b - a = 0.16$$
$$a + 0.26 + b + 0.08 = 1 \quad \Rightarrow \quad b + a = 0.66$$

Subtracting the two equations, we get $2a = 0.5 \quad \Rightarrow \quad a = 0.25$, so that $\Pr(A) = 0.25 + 0.26 = 0.51$

Example 1.4

A survey of a group of college students finds that:

- 64% eat Chinese food
- 51% eat Indian food
- 48% eat Thai food
- 31% eat Chinese and Indian food
- 27% eat Indian and Thai food
- 34% eat Chinese and Thai food
- 23% eat Chinese, Indian and Thai food.

Calculate the probability that a randomly selected student eats Chinese food but does not eat Indian or Thai food.

Solution

This question is most easily solved using a Venn diagram.

From the question, $\Pr(C \cap I \cap T) = 0.23$.

Since $\Pr(C \cap I) = 0.31$, we have:

$$\Pr(C \cap I \cap T') = \Pr(C \cap I) - \Pr(C \cap I \cap T) = 0.31 - 0.23 = 0.08$$

Similarly, since $\Pr(C \cap T) = 0.34$, we have:

$$\Pr(C \cap I' \cap T) = \Pr(C \cap T) - \Pr(C \cap I \cap T) = 0.34 - 0.23 = 0.11$$

The other probabilities can be calculated in a similar fashion. From the diagram, we can see that the required probability (the shaded region) is 0.22.

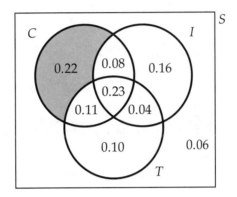

The question can also be solved algebraically:

$$\Pr(C \cap I' \cap T') = \Pr(C) - \Pr(C \cap I' \cap T) - \Pr(C \cap I \cap T') - \Pr(C \cap I \cap T)$$

$$= \Pr(C) - \big(\Pr(C \cap T) - \Pr(C \cap I \cap T)\big)$$

$$- \big(\Pr(C \cap I) - \Pr(C \cap I \cap T)\big) - \Pr(C \cap I \cap T)$$

$$= \Pr(C) - \Pr(C \cap T) - \Pr(C \cap I) + \Pr(C \cap I \cap T)$$

$$= 0.64 - 0.34 - 0.31 + 0.23 = 0.22 \qquad \blacklozenge\blacklozenge$$

1.3 *Equally likely events*

In many cases, it may seem appropriate to assume that each possible outcome of an experiment is equally likely to occur. For example, the probability of observing a head when a fair coin is tossed is equal to the probability of observing a tail. And there is an equal probability of scoring 1, 2, 3, 4, 5 or 6 when rolling a fair die.

Equally likely events

The sample space for an experiment comprises n possible outcomes, $S = \{o_1, o_2, \cdots, o_n\}$.

The n possible outcomes $\{o_1, o_2, \cdots, o_n\}$ are **equally likely** (or **equiprobable**) if:

$$\Pr(\{o_i\}) = \frac{1}{n} \quad \text{for } i = 1, 2, \cdots, n$$

For example, a date in January is chosen at random. There are 31 days in January, so there are 31 possible outcomes and:

$$\Pr(\text{Date chosen is January 1}) = \frac{1}{31}$$

$$\Pr(\text{Date chosen is January 2}) = \frac{1}{31}$$

$$\vdots$$

$$\Pr(\text{Date chosen is January 31}) = \frac{1}{31}$$

Compound events

A **compound event** corresponds to a set of possible outcomes $E \subset S$, with probability:

$$\Pr(E) = \sum_{o_i \in E} \Pr(\{o_i\})$$

When the n possible outcomes of an experiment $\{o_1, o_2, \cdots, o_n\}$ are equally likely, the probability of a compound event $E \subset S$ is given by:

$$\frac{\text{Number of outcomes in } E}{\text{Number of outcomes in } S} = \frac{\text{Number of outcomes in } E}{n}$$

For example, continuing our example of selecting at random a date in January, we have:

$$\Pr(\text{Date chosen is before January 13}) = \frac{12}{31}$$

$$\Pr(\text{Date chosen is before January 7 or after January 27}) = \frac{6+4}{31} = \frac{10}{31}$$

$$\Pr(\text{Date chosen is an odd number}) = \frac{16}{31}$$

 Example 1.5

An insurance company has 12,568 automobile policyholders, of which 3,088 live in California. What is the probability that a randomly selected automobile policyholder lives in California?

Solution

The phrase "randomly selected" is commonly used to indicate that each outcome (in this case that a given policyholder is selected) is equally likely.

So, if each policyholder is equally likely to be selected, then the probability that a randomly selected policyholder lives in California is:

$$\frac{\text{Number of policyholders who live in California}}{\text{Total number of policyholders}} = \frac{3,088}{12,568} = 0.2457 \qquad \blacklozenge\blacklozenge$$

Example 1.6

An urn contains 4 red balls, 6 yellow balls and 5 blue balls. Calculate the probability that a ball drawn at random is red or blue.

Solution

Each ball is equally likely to be drawn. The probability that a randomly selected ball is red or blue is:

$$\frac{\text{Number of balls that are red or blue}}{\text{Total number of balls}} = \frac{4+5}{4+6+5} = \frac{9}{15} = 0.6 \qquad \blacklozenge\blacklozenge$$

Example 1.7

A card is drawn at random from a standard pack of playing cards. Calculate the probability that the card drawn is a club or a 10.

Solution

Each of the 52 cards is equally likely to be drawn.

In total, 16 cards satisfy the condition of being a club or a 10 – these are the 13 clubs (including the 10 of clubs), the 10 of hearts, the 10 of diamonds, and the 10 of spades.

So, the probability that a randomly selected card is a club or a 10 is:

$$\frac{\text{Number of cards that are a club or a 10}}{\text{Total number of cards}} = \frac{16}{52} = 0.3077 \qquad \blacklozenge\blacklozenge$$

Note: In these examples, it is easy to count the number of possible outcomes within the specified event, and the total number of possible outcomes. In other situations, such calculations can be surprisingly complicated. We'll study more complicated counting problems in Chapter 2.

1.4 Independent events

The concept of statistical independence corresponds to the intuitive idea that two events are independent if the probability that the first event occurs is not influenced by the occurrence (or non-occurrence) of the second event, and vice versa. For example, it is intuitive that the scores obtained by rolling two fair dice should not be related in any predictable way.

Independence of two events

The formal definition of independence is as follows.

Independent events

Events A and B are **independent** if and only if:

$$\Pr(A \cap B) = \Pr(A)\Pr(B)$$

For example, two fair coins are tossed. The sample space is $S = \{HH, HT, TH, TT\}$, where H represents a head and T represents a tail. Each outcome is equally likely.

Let $A = \{$First coin is a head$\}$ and $B = \{$Second coin is a head$\}$. The probability that both coins are a head is $\Pr(A \cap B) = 1/4$, since there are four equally likely outcomes, and there is only one way in which both coins can be a head. The probability that the first coin is a head is $\Pr(A) = 1/2$, and the probability that the second coin is a head is $\Pr(B) = 1/2$.

The two events A and B are independent since:

$$\Pr(A)\Pr(B) = \frac{1}{2} \times \frac{1}{2} = \frac{1}{4} = \Pr(A \cap B)$$

In another experiment, two fair dice are rolled. There are 36 equally likely outcomes:

$$
\begin{array}{cccccc}
(1,1) & (1,2) & (1,3) & (1,4) & (1,5) & (1,6) \\
(2,1) & (2,2) & (2,3) & (2,4) & (2,5) & (2,6) \\
(3,1) & (3,2) & (3,3) & (3,4) & (3,5) & (3,6) \\
(4,1) & (4,2) & (4,3) & (4,4) & (4,5) & (4,6) \\
(5,1) & (5,2) & (5,3) & (5,4) & (5,5) & (5,6) \\
(6,1) & (6,2) & (6,3) & (6,4) & (6,5) & (6,6)
\end{array}
$$

Let $A = \{$First die is a 2 or a 4$\}$ and $B = \{$Second die is a 1 or a 3 or a 5$\}$. Then $\Pr(A) = 2/6 = 1/3$ and $\Pr(B) = 3/6 = 1/2$.

The event $A \cap B$ contains 6 outcomes: (2,1), (2,3), (2,5), (4,1), (4,3), and (4,5). So:

$$\Pr(A \cap B) = 6/36 = 1/6$$

The two events A and B are independent since:

$$\Pr(A)\Pr(B) = \frac{1}{3} \times \frac{1}{2} = \frac{1}{6} = \Pr(A \cap B)$$

When two events A and B are not independent, they are said to be **dependent** events.

To illustrate this, let's consider an experiment in which one fair die is rolled and the score is noted. Let $A = \{\text{Score is an odd number}\} = \{1,3,5\}$ and $B = \{\text{Score is low}\} = \{1,2,3\}$. Clearly, $\Pr(A) = 1/2$ and $\Pr(B) = 1/2$.

The event $A \cap B = \{1,3\}$, so $\Pr(A \cap B) = 2/6 = 1/3$.

We can see that events A and B are dependent since:

$$\Pr(A)\Pr(B) = \frac{1}{2} \times \frac{1}{2} = \frac{1}{4} \neq \Pr(A \cap B)$$

Independence of three or more events

So far we've considered the independence (or otherwise) of two events. We can extend this concept to three or more events.

Pairwise independence and mutual independence

Events A, B and C are **pairwise independent** if and only if:

$$\Pr(A \cap B) = \Pr(A)\Pr(B), \ \Pr(A \cap C) = \Pr(A)\Pr(C) \ \textbf{and} \ \Pr(B \cap C) = \Pr(B)\Pr(C)$$

Events A, B and C are **mutually independent** if and only if these events are pairwise independent and:

$$\Pr(A \cap B \cap C) = \Pr(A)\Pr(B)\Pr(C)$$

To illustrate this idea, let's consider an experiment in which a computer randomly selects an integer between 1 and 9 (inclusive). So, $S = \{1,2,3,4,5,6,7,8,9\}$.

Let $A = \{1,2,3\}$, $B = \{2,5,8\}$, and $C = \{2,4,6\}$.

The events A, B and C are pairwise independent because:

$$\Pr(A)\Pr(B) = \frac{1}{3} \times \frac{1}{3} = \frac{1}{9} = \Pr(A \cap B)$$

$$\Pr(A)\Pr(C) = \frac{1}{3} \times \frac{1}{3} = \frac{1}{9} = \Pr(A \cap C)$$

$$\Pr(B)\Pr(C) = \frac{1}{3} \times \frac{1}{3} = \frac{1}{9} = \Pr(B \cap C)$$

However, events A, B and C are not mutually independent since:

$$\Pr(A)\Pr(B)\Pr(C) = \frac{1}{3} \times \frac{1}{3} \times \frac{1}{3} = \frac{1}{27} \neq \Pr(A \cap B \cap C) = \frac{1}{9}$$

Other properties of independent events

It is intuitive that if event A is independent of the occurrence of event B, then it should also be independent of the non-occurrence of event B. In other words, whether or not event B happens, the probability of event A is unaffected.

This is restated formally as follows:

If events A and B are independent, then:

- events A and B' are independent, *ie* $\Pr(A \cap B') = \Pr(A)\Pr(B')$

- events A' and B are independent, *ie* $\Pr(A' \cap B) = \Pr(A')\Pr(B)$

- events A' and B' are independent, *ie* $\Pr(A' \cap B') = \Pr(A')\Pr(B')$.

Let us consider again the previous example in which a computer randomly selects an integer between 1 and 9. It is straightforward to confirm that:

$$\Pr(A)\Pr(B') = \frac{1}{3} \times \frac{2}{3} = \frac{2}{9} = \Pr(A \cap B')$$

$$\Pr(A')\Pr(B) = \frac{2}{3} \times \frac{1}{3} = \frac{2}{9} = \Pr(A' \cap B)$$

$$\Pr(A')\Pr(B') = \frac{2}{3} \times \frac{2}{3} = \frac{4}{9} = \Pr(A' \cap B')$$

Example 1.8

There are two urns. The first urn contains 4 red balls and 6 blue balls, and the second urn contains 7 red balls and 3 blue balls. One ball is drawn at random from the first urn and a second ball is drawn at random from the second urn.

Calculate the probability that both of the balls drawn are red.

Solution

Let $A = \{$Ball drawn from first urn is red$\}$ and $B = \{$Ball drawn from second urn is red$\}$. Then:

$$\Pr(A) = \frac{4}{10}, \quad \Pr(B) = \frac{7}{10}$$

Since the drawings are independent, the probability that both of the balls drawn are red is:

$$\Pr(A \cap B) = \Pr(A)\Pr(B) = \frac{4}{10} \times \frac{7}{10} = \frac{28}{100} = 0.28 \qquad\qquad \blacklozenge\blacklozenge$$

Example 1.9

A game is played by rolling a fair die and drawing a card at random from a standard pack of playing cards. Calculate:

(i)   the probability of scoring a 6 with a die and drawing the ace of spades

(ii)   the probability of scoring more than a 4 with the die and drawing a club

(iii)   the probability that the score on the die is equal to the number on the card (where an ace is equal to 1).

Solution

(i)   The two events (rolling the die, and drawing the card) are independent. So, the probability of scoring a 6 with a die and drawing the ace of spades is:

$$\Pr\left(6 \text{ with die} \cap \text{ace of spades}\right) = \Pr\left(6 \text{ with die}\right)\Pr\left(\text{ace of spades}\right)$$

$$= \frac{1}{6} \times \frac{1}{52} = 0.0032$$

(ii)   The probability of scoring more than a 4 with the die and drawing a club is:

$$\Pr\left(> 4 \text{ with die} \cap \text{club}\right) = \Pr\left(> 4 \text{ with die}\right)\Pr\left(\text{club}\right) = \frac{2}{6} \times \frac{13}{52} = \frac{1}{3} \times \frac{1}{4} = 0.0833$$

(iii)   The probability that the score on the die is equal to the number on the card is:

$$\Pr\left(\text{Score on die} = \text{Number on card}\right)$$

$$= \sum_{i=1}^{6} \Pr\left(\text{Score } i \text{ on die} \cap \text{Number } i \text{ on card}\right)$$

$$= \sum_{i=1}^{6} \Pr\left(\text{Score } i \text{ on die}\right)\Pr\left(\text{Number } i \text{ on card}\right)$$

$$= \sum_{i=1}^{6} \left(\frac{1}{6} \times \frac{4}{52}\right) = \frac{1}{13} = 0.0769 \qquad \blacklozenge\blacklozenge$$

 ### Example 1.10

A company employs two warehouse managers: Mr Allen and Ms Barclay. The probability that Mr Allen is unable to work due to illness is 0.04, and the probability that Ms Barclay is unable to work due to illness is 0.03. Assuming that the health statuses of the two managers are independent, calculate the probability that both managers are able to work.

Solution

Let $A = \{\text{Mr Allen is unable to work}\}$ and $B = \{\text{Ms Barclay is unable to work}\}$. Then:

$$\Pr\left(A\right) = 0.04, \quad \Pr\left(B\right) = 0.03$$

Since events A and B are independent, we have:

$$\Pr\left(A' \cap B'\right) = \Pr\left(A'\right)\Pr\left(B'\right) = \left(1 - \Pr\left(A\right)\right)\left(1 - \Pr\left(B\right)\right)$$

$$= \left(1 - 0.04\right) \times \left(1 - 0.03\right) = 0.96 \times 0.97 = 0.9312 \qquad \blacklozenge\blacklozenge$$

 ### Example 1.11

A hydraulic press produces machine parts. There is a probability of 0.06 that a machine part will be faulty. The quality of each machine part is independent of the quality of any other part. Calculate:

(i)   the probability that none of the first five machine parts is faulty

(ii)   the probability that at least one of the first ten machine parts is faulty.

Solution

(i)   Let $A_i = \{\text{Machine part } i \text{ is not faulty}\}$. Then $\Pr(A_i) = 1 - \Pr(A_i') = 1 - 0.06 = 0.94$.

Since $A_1, A_2, \cdots, A_5$ are independent, we have:

$$\Pr(A_1 \cap A_2 \cap A_3 \cap A_4 \cap A_5) = \prod_{i=1}^{5} \Pr(A_i) = 0.94^5 = 0.7339$$

(ii)   The probability that at least one of the first ten machine parts is faulty is:

$$1 - \Pr(A_1 \cap A_2 \cap \cdots \cap A_{10}) = 1 - \prod_{i=1}^{10} \Pr(A_i) = 1 - 0.94^{10} = 0.4614 \qquad \blacklozenge\blacklozenge$$

Example 1.12

A computer manufacturer provides a one-year warranty with all new computers. The number of computers that are repaired under warranty due to faults with the hard drive is 65% of the total number of repairs. The number of computers repaired under warranty due to faults with neither the monitor nor the hard drive is 21% of the total number of repairs.

The occurrence of faults with the monitor is independent of the occurrence of faults with the hard drive. Calculate the probability that a randomly selected computer that is repaired under warranty was repaired due to faults with both the monitor and the hard drive.

Solution

Let $A = \{\text{Faulty hard drive}\}$ and $B = \{\text{Faulty monitor}\}$. Then:

$$\Pr(A) = 0.65, \quad \Pr(A' \cap B') = 0.21$$

Since events A and B are independent, we have:

$$\Pr(A' \cap B') = \Pr(A')\Pr(B') = (1 - \Pr(A))(1 - \Pr(B))$$
$$\Rightarrow 0.21 = (1 - 0.65)(1 - \Pr(B))$$
$$\Rightarrow \Pr(B) = 0.4$$

And finally:

$$\Pr(A \cap B) = \Pr(A)\Pr(B) = 0.65 \times 0.4 = 0.26 \qquad \blacklozenge\blacklozenge$$

Chapter 1 Practice Questions

> **Free online solutions manual**
>
> You can download detailed worked solutions to every practice question in this book free of charge from the BPP Professional Education website at **www.bpptraining.com.** Select support for the SOA/CAS exams and click on the Probability (P) home page. You'll also find other useful study resources here.

Question 1.1

Let $A = \{2,3,5,7\}$, let $B = \{1,3,5,7,9\}$, and let the universal set $S = \{1,2,3,\cdots,9,10\}$. Determine:

(i) $A \cap B$

(ii) $A \cup B'$

(iii) $(A \cup B)'$

Question 1.2

Draw the sets A, B and S from Question 1.1 in a Venn diagram.

Question 1.3

If $\Pr(A) = 0.4, \Pr(B) = 0.3,$ and $\Pr(A \cap B) = 0.15$, calculate $\Pr(A \cup B)$.

Question 1.4

If $\Pr(A) = \Pr((A \cup B)')$ and $\Pr(A \cup B) = 1.5\Pr(A)$, calculate $\Pr(A)$.

Question 1.5

If $\Pr(A) = \Pr(B \cap A')$, $\Pr(A \cap B) = 0.1$, and $\Pr(A \cup B) = 0.8$, calculate $\Pr(B')$.

Question 1.6

The events A_1, A_2, A_3 are mutually exclusive and exhaustive, and:

$$\Pr(A_2 \cap B) = 2 \times \Pr(A_1 \cap B) \qquad \Pr(A_3 \cap B) = 2 \times \Pr(A_2 \cap B) \qquad \Pr(B') = 0.3$$

Calculate $\Pr(A_1 \cap B)$.

Question 1.7   *SOA/CAS*

You are given that $\Pr(A \cup B) = 0.7$ and $\Pr(A \cup B') = 0.9$. Determine $\Pr(A)$.

Question 1.8

The probability that a policyholder will make a claim on his homeowner's insurance policy during the next year is 0.46. The probability that a policyholder will make a claim on his automobile insurance policy during the next year is 0.32. The probability that a randomly selected policyholder does not make a claim on either his homeowner's insurance policy or his automobile insurance policy during the next year is 0.52.

Calculate the probability that a policyholder will make a claim on only his homeowner's insurance policy.

Question 1.9   *SOA/CAS*

The probability that a visit to a primary care physician's (PCP) office results in neither lab work nor referral to a specialist is 35%. Of those coming to a PCP's office, 30% are referred to specialists and 40% require lab work.

Determine the probability that a visit to a PCP's office results in both lab work and referral to a specialist.

Question 1.10

A survey of an insurance company's medical policyholders in the last three years revealed the following information:

- 31% made claims for dental care
- 27% made claims for optical care
- 21% made claims for other medical care
- 15% made claims for dental and optical care
- 13% made claims for optical and other medical care
- 11% made claims for dental and other medical care
- 7% made claims for all three sorts of care.

Calculate the percentage of the medical policyholders that made none of the three types of claims during the last year.

Question 1.11   *SOA/CAS*

A doctor is studying the relationship between blood pressure and heartbeat abnormalities in her patients. She tests a random sample of her patients and notes their blood pressures (high, low or normal) and their heartbeats (regular or irregular). She finds that:

(i)   14% have high blood pressure.

(ii)   22% have low blood pressure.

(iii)   15% have an irregular heartbeat.

(iv)   Of those with an irregular heartbeat, one-third have high blood pressure.

(v)   Of those with normal blood pressure, one-eighth have an irregular heartbeat.

What portion of the patients selected have a regular heartbeat and low blood pressure?

Question 1.12

An urn contains 15 balls: 4 red balls numbered 1-4, 5 blue balls numbered 1-5, and 6 yellow balls numbered 1-6.   A ball is selected at random from the urn.

Calculate the probability the random selected ball is yellow or red, and with an even number.

Question 1.13

An insurance company insures 2,400 policyholders in Ontario of whom 46% are female and 54% are male, and 3,150 policyholders in Quebec, of which 48% are female and 52% are male.

Calculate the probability that a randomly selected policyholder is male.

Question 1.14

A game is played in which a fair six-sided die is rolled, and a card is selected at random from a standard pack of playing cards.

(i)   Calculate the probability of rolling a 4 and choosing a heart.

(ii)   Calculate the probability of neither rolling a 6 nor choosing a spade.

(iii)   Calculate the probability of rolling no more than a 3 or choosing a red card.

Question 1.15

The local branch of Fudget Car Rentals owns 20 cars: 10 red, 6 blue, and 4 white. The local branch of Mavis Car Rentals owns 18 cars: 9 red, 2 blue, and 7 white. A car rented from Fudget is involved in a road traffic accident with a car rented from Mavis.

Calculate the probability that the two cars involved in the accident are not the same color.

Question 1.16

Events A and B are independent. If $\Pr(A) = 0.3$ and $\Pr(B) = 0.4$, calculate $\Pr(A \cap B')$.

Question 1.17

A fair six-sided die is rolled n times. Calculate the smallest value of n such that the probability of rolling at least one six is at least 95%.

Question 1.18

There are two urns. The first urn contains 6 red balls and 4 blue balls, and the second urn contains 5 red balls and 5 blue balls. One ball is drawn from the first urn and a second ball is drawn from the second urn.

Calculate the probability that the draw results in at least one blue ball.

Question 1.19

A printing company has three digital copiers. The probability that any copier will break down on a particular day is 0.05. Assuming that the copiers are independent, calculate the probability that the three copiers all break down on the same day at some point during the next 50 days.

Question 1.20

SOA/CAS

An urn contains 10 balls: 4 red and 6 blue. A second urn contains 16 red balls and an unknown number of blue balls. A single ball is drawn from each urn. The probability that both balls are the same color is 0.44. Calculate the number of blue balls in the second urn.

2

Counting
Techniques

At the end of Chapter 1, we studied how to calculate the probability of a particular event when each outcome is equally likely. We saw that if there are n equally likely outcomes, of which m are associated with a particular event, then the probability of the event is m/n.

While this concept is straightforward, in many situations it can be far from simple to calculate either the number of possible outcomes of an experiment or the number of outcomes that are associated with a particular event. For example, consider a lottery in which contestants must select 6 different numbers in the range 1-49. Astonishingly, there are 13,983,816 possible selections. We'll see how to calculate this number later in the chapter.

In an insurance and risk management setting, we can use the same techniques to calculate the probability that a policyholder files a claim in exactly 3 months out of 12, or the probability that 2 or more machines out of 6 malfunction in a given week.

2.1 The multiplication principle

Consider an insurance company that sells automobile insurance with three liability limits ($1m, $2m, and $5m) in four states (Connecticut, Massachusetts, New Hampshire, and Vermont). How many different combinations of liability limit and state are possible?

It is simple to see that there are 12 different combinations:

{MA, $1m}	{MA, $2m}	{MA, $5m}
{CT, $1m}	{CT, $2m}	{CT, $5m}
{NH, $1m}	{NH, $2m}	{NH, $5m}
{VT, $1m}	{VT, $2m}	{VT, $5m}

The multiplication principle

If event A_1 can occur in n_1 possible ways, and event A_2 can occur in n_2 possible ways, then the event $(A_1$ and $A_2)$ can occur in $n_1 n_2$ possible ways.

In the example above, there are $n_1 = 3$ liability limits and $n_2 = 4$ states, resulting in a total of $n_1 n_2 = 12$ possible combinations.

We can easily extend this principle to include a greater number of events. For example, we may also categorize the insurance company's policies according to the sex of the policyholder (male or female) and the age group of the policyholder (17-29, 30-39, 40-49, 50-59, 60-69, 70+). How many different combinations of liability limit, state, sex, and age group are possible?

There are $n_1 = 3$ liability limits, $n_2 = 4$ states, $n_3 = 2$ sexes, and $n_4 = 6$ age groups, resulting in a total of $n_1 n_2 n_3 n_4 = 3 \times 4 \times 2 \times 6 = 144$ possible combinations.

 Example 2.1

An automobile manufacturer offers a choice of 5 engine sizes, 12 exterior paint colors, 4 styles of interior trim, and 3 further options (air conditioning, CD player, and heated seats) which may be included or excluded. How many different specifications are possible?

Solution

There are $n_1 = 5$ engine sizes, $n_2 = 12$ colors of paint, and $n_3 = 4$ styles of trim. Since the 3 other options may be included or excluded, we have $n_4 = 2$, $n_5 = 2$, and $n_6 = 2$.

The total number of possible specifications is:

$$n_1 n_2 n_3 n_4 n_5 n_6 = 5 \times 12 \times 4 \times 2 \times 2 \times 2 = 1,920$$

◆◆

2.2 Ordered samples

Sampling with replacement

Suppose that an urn contains three balls, numbered 1, 2, and 3. A ball is drawn at random from the urn, the score is observed, and the ball is then replaced in the urn. The experiment is repeated twice, making a total of three drawings from the urn.

If we record the scores in the order in which they occurred, how many outcomes are possible?

We can write the possible outcomes as follows:

111	112	113	121	122	123	131	132	133
211	212	213	221	222	223	231	232	233
311	312	313	321	322	323	331	332	333

So, there are 27 possible outcomes in total.

This is an example of **sampling with replacement**, because any ball that is drawn from the urn is replaced before the next drawing occurs. As a result, each score can occur on each drawing.

It is also an example of an **ordered sample**, because the order in which the balls is drawn is significant. For example, the outcomes 122, 212, and 221 are considered to be distinct.

Let's now consider the general case. A set has n distinct elements. We choose an element at random from this set k times with replacement, *ie* the randomly chosen element is replaced before the next element is selected. The order in which the elements are chosen is noted. This experiment will produce an ordered sample of size k. How many ordered samples of size k are possible?

We can solve this problem using the multiplication rule.

The first drawing can occur in $n_1 = n$ possible ways, the second drawing can occur in $n_2 = n$ possible ways, *etc*, and the k-th drawing can occur in $n_k = n$ possible ways.

Hence, the number of possible ordered samples of size k is:

$$n_1 n_2 \cdots n_k = n \times n \times \cdots \times n = n^k$$

In the example above, we drew a sample of size $k = 3$ with replacement from a set of $n = 3$ balls.

Hence the number of possible outcomes was:

$$n^k = 3^3 = 27$$

Let's formalize our discussion with some definitions.

Ordered samples

An **ordered sample of size k** is a selection of k objects from a set of n objects, in which the order of selection is significant.

Sampling with replacement

A sample is constructed using **sampling with replacement** if any object that is selected is replaced before the next object is selected.

Number of possible ordered samples of size k from n (with replacement)

The number of possible ordered samples of size k from a set of n objects, when sampling with replacement, is:

$$n^k$$

The main significance of sampling with replacement is that all outcomes are possible every time we carry out the experiment. In our previous example, we described the physical replacement of the selected ball in the urn before the next drawing, so that a score of 1, 2, or 3 is always possible.

In many other situations, the concept of sampling with replacement can be applied, even if no physical replacement is involved. For example, consider an experiment in which a fair coin is tossed 3 times. On each toss, it is possible to score a head or a tail.

So, the number of possible ordered samples of size $k = 3$ from a set of $n = 2$ objects (H,T) is:

$$n^k = 2^3 = 8$$

The possible ordered samples are: HHH, HHT, HTH, HTT, THH, THT, TTH, TTT

Sampling without replacement

Let's now turn our attention to sampling without replacement, so that there can be no repetition.

Sampling without replacement

A sample is constructed using **sampling without replacement** if any object that is selected is not replaced before the next object is selected.

A set has n distinct objects. We choose an element at random from this set k times without replacement, *ie* the randomly chosen object is not replaced before the next object is selected. The order in which the objects are chosen is noted. This experiment will produce an ordered sample of size k. How many ordered samples of size k are possible?

Again, we can solve this problem using the multiplication rule.

There are n choices for the first object . Once this object has been selected, there are $(n-1)$ choices for the second object . We can continue this logic until $(k-1)$ objects have been chosen, leaving $(n-k+1)$ objects to be chosen in the final position.

Hence, the number of possible ordered samples of size k is:

$$n \times (n-1) \times \cdots \times (n-k+1) = \frac{n \times (n-1) \times \cdots \times 1}{(n-k) \times (n-k-1) \times \cdots \times 1} = \frac{n!}{(n-k)!}$$

Note: $n!$ (pronounced "n factorial") is defined as $n! = n \times (n-1) \times \cdots \times 1$ for any positive integer n.

The number of possible ordered samples of size k (using sampling without replacement) is denoted $_nP_k$. The letter P is short for the word **permutation**, which means an ordered arrangement of distinct objects.

Number of possible ordered samples of size *k* from *n* (without replacement)

The number of possible ordered samples of size k selected from a set of n objects using sampling without replacement is:

$$_nP_k = \frac{n!}{(n-k)!}$$

Note: $_nP_k$ may also be written as $P(n,k)$.

For example, how many ordered samples of size 2 can be obtained from the set $\{1,2,3,4,5\}$? We have $n = 5$ and $k = 2$, hence the number of ordered samples is:

$$\frac{n!}{(n-k)!} = \frac{5!}{3!} = \frac{120}{6} = 20$$

We can quickly write down the possible arrangements to verify this:

12	13	14	15	21	23	24	25	31	32
34	35	41	42	43	45	51	52	53	54

The final case to consider is an ordered sample of size n selected from a set of n objects, using sampling without replacement. In this case there is no repetition (because there is no replacement) and all objects are included in the sample. This, then, is equivalent to a simple ordering of the set of n objects.

Using the multiplication rule, the number of ways in which n distinct objects can be ordered is:

$$n \times (n-1) \times \cdots \times 1 = n!$$

This is consistent with our definition above, since we define $0! = 1$. Hence:

$$_nP_n = \frac{n!}{(n-n)!} = \frac{n!}{0!} = n!$$

For example, the numbers 1, 2, 3, and 4 can be ordered in $_4P_4 = 4! = 24$ ways.

The possible arrangements are:

1234	1243	1324	1342	1423	1432
2134	2143	2314	2341	2413	2431
3124	3142	3214	3241	3412	3421
4123	4132	4213	4231	4312	4321

We've covered many important ideas here, so let's work through some numerical examples.

Note: Many modern calculators can evaluate the permutation function $_nP_k$ directly. It is shown on my calculator as $n\mathrm{P}r$.

 Example 2.2

A bank vault has a 6-character security code. Calculate the number of possible codes if:

(i)   each character is a letter of the alphabet, and repetition is permitted

(ii)   each character is a digit from 0-9 and repetition is not permitted

(iii)   the first 4 characters are letters of the alphabet, the final 2 characters are digits from 0-9, and repetition is permitted

(iv)   the first 3 characters are letters of the alphabet, the final 3 characters are digits from 0-9, and repetition is not permitted.

Solution

(i)   Since repetition is permitted, we are effectively choosing an ordered sample of size $k = 6$ from a set of $n = 26$ ($A, B, \cdots, Z$), using sampling with replacement.

Hence the number of possible codes is:

$$n^k = 26^6 = 308,915,776$$

(ii)   Since repetition is not permitted, we are effectively choosing an ordered sample of size $k = 6$ from a set of $n = 10$ ($0, 1, \cdots, 9$), using sampling without replacement.

Hence the number of possible codes is:

$$_{10}P_6 = \frac{10!}{(10-6)!} = \frac{10!}{4!} = 151,200$$

(iii)   The first 4 characters can be selected in $26^4 = 456,976$ ways.

The final 2 characters can be selected in $10^2 = 100$ ways.

Using the multiplication rule, the number of possible codes is:

$$456,976 \times 100 = 45,697,600$$

(iv)   The first 3 characters can be selected in $_{26}P_3 = 15,600$ ways.

The final 3 characters can be selected in $_{10}P_3 = 720$ ways.

Using the multiplication rule, the number of possible codes is:

$$15,600 \times 720 = 11,232,000$$

♦ ♦

Example 2.3

A photography club with 11 members decides to choose its President, Treasurer, and Secretary by drawing names at random out of a hat. If each member of the club is able to hold no more than one position, calculate the number of possible ways in which the positions can be filled.

Solution

We are effectively choosing an ordered sample of size $k = 3$ from a set of $n = 11$ members using sampling without replacement.

Hence the number of possible ways of filling the positions is:

$$_{11}P_3 = \frac{11!}{(11-3)!} = \frac{11!}{8!} = 990$$

♦ ♦

Example 2.4

Four prizes (for reading, arithmetic, sports and good behavior) are to be awarded to a class of 18 children. Calculate the number of possible ways in which the prizes can be awarded if:

(i)   there is no limit on the number of prizes that can be awarded to a single child

(ii)   each prize must be awarded to a different child

(iii)   no more than 3 prizes can be awarded to a single child.

Solution

(i) We are effectively choosing an ordered sample of size $k = 4$ from a set of $n = 18$ children using sampling with replacement.

Hence the number of possible ways of awarding the prizes is:

$$n^k = 18^4 = 104,976$$

(ii) We are effectively choosing an ordered sample of size $k = 4$ from a set of $n = 18$ children using sampling without replacement.

Hence the number of possible ways of awarding the prizes is:

$$_{18}P_4 = \frac{18!}{(18-4)!} = \frac{18!}{14!} = 73,440$$

(iii) Note that there are 18 ways in which a single child can win all 4 prizes, since there are 18 children in the class. We can exclude the possibility of a single child winning all 4 prizes by simply subtracting 18 from the answer to part (i). Hence the number of possible ways of awarding the prizes if no more than 3 prizes can be awarded to a single child is:

$$104,976 - 18 = 104,958$$

♦♦

2.3 *Unordered samples*

We've studied ordered samples with and without replacement. Let's now consider the concept of an unordered sample, in which the order of the objects does not matter.

Unordered samples

An **unordered sample of size *k*** is a selection of k distinct objects from a set of n objects, in which the order of selection is not significant.

For example, consider an experiment in which an urn contains four balls: A, B, C, and D. We will draw two balls from the urn and observe their letters, but we will assign no importance to the order in which the balls were drawn from the urn. So, we will treat the outcome AB as being equal to the outcome BA.

There are now 6 distinct outcomes to this experiment. These are:

AB (=BA)	AC (=CA)	AD (=DA)
BC (=CB)	BD (=DB)	CD (=DC)

The number of possible unordered samples of size k from a set of n objects using sampling without replacement is denoted $_nC_k$. The letter C is short for the word **combination**, which means an unordered arrangement of distinct objects.

Number of possible unordered samples of size k from n (without replacement)

The number of possible unordered samples of size k selected from a set of n objects using sampling without replacement is:

$$_nC_k = \frac{n!}{k!(n-k)!}$$

Note: $_nC_k$ may also be written as $C(n,k)$ or as $\binom{n}{k}$.

In the above example, there are $n = 4$ balls in the urn, of which $k = 2$ are selected, so the number of possible combinations is:

$$_4C_2 = \frac{4!}{2!(4-2)!} = \frac{4!}{2!2!} = \frac{24}{2 \times 2} = 6$$

The general formula has an intuitive explanation. We have seen that the number of possible *ordered* samples of size k from a set of n objects using sampling without replacement is:

$$_nP_k = \frac{n!}{(n-k)!}$$

And since each of these samples of size k can be ordered in $k!$ ways, the number of *unordered* samples of size k selected from a set of n objects using sampling without replacement is:

$$\frac{_nP_k}{k!} = \frac{n!}{k!(n-k)!} = {}_nC_k$$

The numbers defined by the function $_nC_k = \binom{n}{k}$ are often referred to as **binomial coefficients**. This is because of their role in the binomial expansion:

$$(a+b)^n = \sum_{k=0}^{n} \binom{n}{k} a^k b^{n-k}$$

To understand this, let's express the expansion as follows:

$$(a+b)^n = \underbrace{(a+b)(a+b)\cdots(a+b)}_{n \text{ times}}$$

The coefficient of the term $a^r b^{n-r}$ is the number of ways in which we can choose an unordered sample of size r from a set of n objects.

Finally, note the symmetrical result:

$$_nC_k = {}_nC_{n-k}$$

Let's work through some numerical examples.

Note: Again, many modern calculators can calculate the combination function $_nC_k$ directly. It is shown on my calculator as nCr.

Example 2.5

A quiz team of 4 people must be selected from a group of 10 individuals. How many different quiz teams are possible?

Solution

The order in which individuals are picked for the team does not matter, so we need to calculate the number of unordered samples of size $k = 4$ selected from a set of $n = 10$ individuals, using sampling without replacement.

Hence, the number of possible teams is:

$$_{10}C_4 = \frac{10!}{4!(10-4)!} = \frac{10!}{4!6!} = \frac{3,628,800}{24 \times 720} = 210$$ ♦♦

Example 2.6

A poker player is dealt a hand of 5 cards from a standard deck of playing cards. How many different hands of cards are possible?

Solution

The order in which cards are dealt does not matter, so we need to calculate the number of unordered samples of size $k = 5$ selected from a set of $n = 52$ cards, using sampling without replacement.

Hence, the number of possible hands of 5 cards is:

$$_{52}C_5 = \frac{52!}{5!(52-5)!} = \frac{52!}{5!47!} = 2,598,960$$ ♦♦

Example 2.7

In a weekly lottery game, contestants must select 6 different numbers in the range 1-49. A contestant wins the jackpot if his/her numbers match those 6 numbers drawn at random by the lottery computer. The order of the numbers does not matter. Calculate the number of possible sets of winning numbers.

Solution

We need to calculate the number of unordered samples of size $k = 6$ selected from a set of $n = 49$ cards, using sampling without replacement.

So, the number of possible sets of winning numbers is (as described in the overview):

$$_{49}C_6 = \frac{49!}{6!(49-6)!} = \frac{49!}{6!43!} = 13,983,816$$ ♦♦

Example 2.8

A meteorologist records the number of tornadoes occurring each month. A month is classified as "tornado-free" if no tornadoes were reported during that month. Calculate the number of possible ways in which 10 or more "tornado-free" months may occur in one year.

Solution

We may observe $k = 10$ "tornado-free" months in $_{12}C_{10}$ ways, or $k = 11$ "tornado-free" months in $_{12}C_{11}$ ways, or $k = 12$ "tornado-free" months in $_{12}C_{12}$ ways.

So, the number of possible ways in which 10, 11, or 12 "tornado-free" months can occur is:

$$_{12}C_{10} + _{12}C_{11} + _{12}C_{12} = \frac{12!}{10!2!} + \frac{12!}{11!1!} + \frac{12!}{12!0!} = 66 + 12 + 1 = 79$$ ◆◆

Example 2.9

Members of a pension plan are required to select 3 equity funds and 2 bond funds in which to invest their retirement savings. If there are 10 equity funds and 6 bond funds available, how many choices are possible?

Solution

Although the method of sampling is not stated explicitly, it seems reasonable to use sampling without replacement, *ie* to assume that members are required to select 3 *distinct* equity funds and 2 *distinct* bond funds.

The equity funds can be chosen in $_{10}C_3$ ways, and the bond funds can be chosen in $_6C_2$ ways.

Using the multiplication rule, the number of possible choices is:

$$\left(_{10}C_3\right)\left(_6C_2\right) = \left(\frac{10!}{3!7!}\right)\left(\frac{6!}{2!4!}\right) = 120 \times 15 = 1,800$$ ◆◆

2.4 Multinomial coefficients

So far we've considered ordered and unordered samples from a set of distinct objects. We'll now extend the theory to cover situations where some of the objects may be indistinguishable.

For example, how many distinct anagrams can be made from the word TREE?

We can easily write down the possible anagrams:

    EERT   EETR   ERET   ERTE   ETER   ETRE
    REET   RETE   RTEE   TEER   TERE   TREE

So, the answer to this question is 12. Note that if the four letters in the word were distinct, there would be $4! = 24$ possible anagrams.

In the general case, there are $n!$ possible permutations of a set of n objects. However, if n_1 of these objects are alike, then the number of distinguishable permutations is:

$$\frac{n!}{n_1!}$$

because for every possible permutation, there are $n_1!$ ways to arrange the objects that are alike.

In the example above, there are $n = 4$ letters of which $n_1 = 2$ are alike (the E's). Therefore the number of distinguishable permutations is:

$$\frac{4!}{2!} = 12$$

If we label the E's as E_1 and E_2, then we can see that every distinct anagram can be made in two ways, eg E_1E_2RT is indistinguishable from E_2E_1RT when the subscripts are dropped.

We can generalize this theory for one or more sets of identical objects.

Number of possible arrangements when some objects are identical

The number of distinct arrangements of n objects of which n_1 are identical, n_2 are identical, ..., n_r are identical is:

$$\frac{n!}{n_1!\,n_2!\cdots n_r!}$$

For example, let's calculate the number of distinct anagrams of the word REINSURER. There are $n = 9$ letters in this word, of which $n_1 = 3$ are R's and $n_2 = 2$ are E's.

Hence the number of distinct anagrams is:

$$\frac{9!}{3!2!} = 30,240$$

Notice that if the group of n objects can be split into two groups, of which k are alike and $(n-k)$ are alike, then the number of distinct arrangements is:

$$\frac{n!}{k!(n-k)!} = {}_nC_k$$

For example, the number of distinct arrangements of the letters AAABB is:

$${}_5C_3 = \frac{5!}{3!2!} = 10$$

This general result can be interpreted intuitively as the process of selecting the k positions (out of n possible positions) to be filled by the identical objects in the first group.

 ## Example 2.10

An Australian insurance company receives 12 claims from automobile policies on a particular day, of which 7 are from policyholders in Sydney, 3 are from policyholders in Perth, and 2 are from policyholders in Melbourne. Calculate the number of ways in which the claims could have been received, if they are classified only by city of origin.

Solution

There are $n = 12$ claims, of which $n_1 = 7$ are from Sydney, $n_2 = 3$ are from Perth, and $n_3 = 2$ are from Melbourne.

Hence the number of possible orders in which the claims could have been received is:

$$\frac{n!}{n_1!\,n_2!\cdots n_r!} = \frac{12!}{7!3!2!} = 7,920 \qquad \qquad \blacklozenge\blacklozenge$$

Example 2.11

A fair die is rolled 15 times, and the following scores are observed:

Score	1	2	3	4	5	6
Frequency	3	1	4	0	2	5

Calculate the number of ways in which these scores could have been obtained.

Solution

The die was rolled $n = 15$ times. Let n_i be the number of times that a score of i was obtained.

Then the number of ways in which these scores could have been obtained is:

$$\frac{n!}{n_1! n_2! n_3! n_4! n_5! n_6!} = \frac{15!}{3! 1! 4! 0! 2! 5!} = 37,837,800$$ ♦♦

2.5   *Counting techniques and probability*

We've now studied many counting techniques that can help us to count the number of possible ways in which a particular event can happen in some rather complicated situations. Let's now study how this relates to the concept of probability.

In Chapter 1, we saw that when the m possible outcomes of an experiment $\{o_1, o_2, \cdots, o_m\}$ are equally likely, the probability of a compound event $E \subset S$ is given by:

$$\frac{\text{Number of outcomes in } E}{\text{Number of outcomes in } S}$$

So, if the outcomes of an experiment are equally likely, we can calculate the probability of a particular event by counting the number of ways in which that event can occur, and dividing this result by the number of possible outcomes.

For example, consider an experiment in which a fair die is rolled 3 times. What is the probability of scoring (in order) a 6, then a 5, then a 4?

Let event $E = \{\text{Score of 6, then 5, then 4}\}$.

The order of the scores is important, so we need to calculate the number of possible ordered samples of size $k = 3$ from a set of $n = 6$ scores, using sampling with replacement. Hence:

$$\text{Number of outcomes in } S = n^k = 6^3 = 216$$

There is only one outcome of interest in event E. Therefore:

$$\Pr(E) = \frac{\text{Number of outcomes in } E}{\text{Number of outcomes in } S} = \frac{1}{216}$$

Note that we could also have solved this problem using independence:

$$\Pr(E) = \Pr(6 \text{ on first roll}) \times \Pr(5 \text{ on second roll}) \times \Pr(4 \text{ on third roll})$$
$$= \frac{1}{6} \times \frac{1}{6} \times \frac{1}{6} = \frac{1}{216}$$

However, there are many other problems for which our counting techniques provide a much more efficient and elegant solution.

For example, what is the probability that a hand of 5 cards dealt at random from a standard deck of playing cards contains a pair of aces?

Let event $E = \{$Exactly 2 of the 5 cards are aces$\}$.

The order of the cards is not important, so we need to calculate the number of possible unordered samples of size $k = 5$ from a set of $n = 52$ cards, using sampling without replacement. Hence:

$$\text{Number of outcomes in } S = {}_{52}C_5 = 2,598,960$$

Event E occurs if the hand of cards includes 2 out of the 4 aces in the deck, and 3 out of the 48 cards in the deck that are not aces.

Hence, using the multiplication rule, the number of outcomes in event E is:

$$\text{Number of outcomes in } E = \left({}_4C_2\right)\left({}_{48}C_3\right) = 6 \times 17,296 = 103,776$$

So, the probability that a hand of 5 cards contains a pair of aces is:

$$\Pr(E) = \frac{\text{Number of outcomes in } E}{\text{Number of outcomes in } S} = \frac{103,776}{2,598,960} = 0.03993$$

We can also use counting techniques to calculate probabilities when the outcomes are not equally likely.

For example, assume that the probability of rain on any particular day is 0.2, and that the probability of rain is independent from one day to another. What is the probability that it rains on exactly two days in a given week? We could write out the possible outcomes for the full seven-day period, using R to represent rain and N to represent no rain:

    RRRRRRR   NRRRRRR   NNRRRRR   NNNRRRR   *etc*

but the probabilities of the possible outcomes are not equal. For example, the probability of seven dry days is $0.8^7 = 0.2097152$ and the probability of seven rainy days is $0.2^7 = 0.0000128$.

However, we can easily calculate the probability of a particular sequence of seven days, of which two are rainy, using independence:

$$\Pr(\text{RRNNNNN}) = 0.2^2 \times 0.8^5 = 0.0131072$$

And to calculate the probability that any two days are rainy in a seven-day period, we need to multiply this figure by the number of ways in which two rainy days and five dry days can occur.

This is simply ${}_7C_2 = 21$. We can easily write out the 21 possible arrangements as follows:

RRNNNNN	RNRNNNN	RNNRNNN	RNNNRNN	RNNNNRN
RNNNNNR	NRRNNNN	NRNRNNN	NRNNRNN	NRNNNRN
NRNNNNR	NNRRNNN	NNRNRNN	NNRNNRN	NNRNNNR
NNNRRNN	NNNRNRN	NNNRNNR	NNNNRRN	NNNNRNR
NNNNNRR				

Hence the probability that it rains on exactly two days in a given week is:

$$0.2^2 \times 0.8^5 \times {}_7C_2 = 0.275251$$

Let's use this method to calculate the probability of k rainy days, for $k = 0, 1, \cdots, 7$.

The probabilities are as follows:

k	Probability of exactly k rainy days in a seven-day period
0	$0.8^7 = 0.209715$
1	$0.2^1 \times 0.8^6 \times {}_7C_1 = 0.367002$
2	$0.2^2 \times 0.8^5 \times {}_7C_2 = 0.275251$
3	$0.2^3 \times 0.8^4 \times {}_7C_3 = 0.114688$
4	$0.2^4 \times 0.8^3 \times {}_7C_4 = 0.028672$
5	$0.2^5 \times 0.8^2 \times {}_7C_5 = 0.004301$
6	$0.2^6 \times 0.8^1 \times {}_7C_6 = 0.000358$
7	$0.2^7 = 0.000013$

Of course, we should find that these probabilities (which cover all possible outcomes) sum to one:

$$\sum_{k=0}^{7} \Pr\left(\text{Exactly } k \text{ rainy days}\right)$$

$$= 0.209715 + 0.367002 + 0.275251 + 0.114688 + 0.028672 + 0.004301 + 0.000358 + 0.000013$$

$$= 1$$

Note: This particular model is an example of the **binomial distribution**, which we'll study in much more detail in Chapter 5.

Let's now work through a wide selection of numerical examples to show how these techniques can be used to calculate probabilities.

Example 2.12

A gambler bets on the outcome of three horse races. There are seven horses in each race, and each horse is equally likely to win its race. If the gambler bets on one horse in each race, calculate the probability that exactly one of the three chosen horses will win its race.

Solution

Using the multiplication rule, the number of possible outcomes from the three races is:

$$7 \times 7 \times 7 = 343$$

The gambler must choose the winning horse in one of the races, and any of the six losing horses in the other two races.

The number of ways in which the one winning race can be picked from the three races is:

$${}_3C_1 = 3$$

If we write "W" to denote a winning horse and "L" to denote a losing horse, then the possible outcomes of interest are:

WLL   LWL   LLW

So, the number of ways of selecting the winning horse in one of the races, and any of the six losing horses in the other two races is:

$$_3C_1 \times 1 \times 6 \times 6 = 108$$

Finally, the probability that exactly one of the three chosen horses will win its race is:

$$\frac{108}{343} = 0.314869$$ ♦♦

Example 2.13

An urn contains four balls numbered 1-4. The balls are randomly drawn one-by-one with no replacement. Calculate the probability that ball 2 is drawn before balls 3 and 4.

Solution

The number of possible outcomes is:

$$_4P_4 = 4!/0! = 24$$

The possible outcomes are shown below. We can see that there are 8 outcomes in which ball 2 is drawn before balls 3 and 4:

1234	1243	1324	1342	1423	1432
2134	2143	2314	2341	2413	2431
3124	3142	3214	3241	3412	3421
4123	4132	4213	4231	4312	4321

So, the probability that ball 2 is drawn before balls 3 and 4 is:

$$\frac{8}{24} = \frac{1}{3}$$ ♦♦

Example 2.14

In a weekly lottery game, contestants must select 6 different numbers in the range 1-49. A contestant wins the jackpot if his/her numbers match those 6 numbers drawn at random by the lottery computer. The order of the numbers does not matter.

An individual plays the lottery once each week for 30 years. Calculate the probability that the individual wins the jackpot at least once during this time.

Solution

The number of possible combinations of $n = 49$ numbers, taken $k = 6$ at a time is $_{49}C_6$.

Each set of numbers is equally likely, so the probability of winning in any given week is:

$$\frac{1}{_{49}C_6} = \frac{1}{13,983,816}$$

The probability of losing each week for 30 years ($\approx 30 \times 52 = 1,560$ weeks) is:

$$\left(1 - \frac{1}{13,983,816}\right)^{1,560} = 0.99989$$

The probability of winning at least once during this time is:

$$1 - 0.99989 = 0.00011 \qquad \qquad \blacklozenge \blacklozenge$$

 ## Example 2.15

A hand of 13 cards is dealt at random from a standard deck of playing cards. Calculate:

(i)   the probability that the hand includes 5 hearts, 3 diamonds, 4 clubs, and 1 spade

(ii)   the probability that the hand includes no picture cards (*ie* no jacks, queens, or kings)

(iii)   the probability that the hand includes at least one ace.

Solution

We need to calculate the number of unordered samples of size $k = 13$ selected from a set of $n = 52$ cards, using sampling without replacement.

Hence, the number of possible hands of 13 cards is $_{52}C_{13}$, and each hand is equally likely.

(i)   The number of possible hands that include 5 hearts, 3 diamonds, 4 clubs, and 1 spade is:

$$\left(_{13}C_5\right)\left(_{13}C_3\right)\left(_{13}C_4\right)\left(_{13}C_1\right)$$

So, the probability that the hand includes 5 hearts, 3 diamonds, 4 clubs, and 1 spade is:

$$\frac{\left(_{13}C_5\right)\left(_{13}C_3\right)\left(_{13}C_4\right)\left(_{13}C_1\right)}{_{52}C_{13}} = 0.005388$$

(ii)   There are 12 picture cards (the 4 jacks, 4 queens, and 4 kings) and 40 non-picture cards. The number of possible hands that include no picture cards and 13 non-picture cards is:

$$\left(_{12}C_0\right)\left(_{40}C_{13}\right)$$

Hence the probability that the hand includes no picture cards is:

$$\frac{\left(_{12}C_0\right)\left(_{40}C_{13}\right)}{_{52}C_{13}} = 0.018950$$

(iii)   There are 4 aces and 48 other cards. So, the number of possible hands that include no aces is:

$$\left(_4C_0\right)\left(_{48}C_{13}\right)$$

Hence the probability that the hand includes no ace is:

$$\frac{\left(_4C_0\right)\left(_{48}C_{13}\right)}{_{52}C_{13}} = 0.303818$$

Hence the probability that the hand includes at least one ace is:

$$1 - 0.303818 = 0.696182 \qquad \qquad \blacklozenge \blacklozenge$$

Example 2.16

A South African insurance company insures policyholders in Durban, Cape Town and Johannesburg. The probability that a randomly selected claim is from a policyholder in Durban is 0.2, in Cape Town is 0.3, and in Johannesburg is 0.5. All claims are considered to be independent.

The insurance company receives 12 claims on a particular day. Calculate the probability that exactly 4 are from policyholders in Durban, 3 are from policyholders in Cape Town, and 5 are from policyholders in Johannesburg.

Solution

The number of ways in which the $n_1 = 3$ claims from Cape Town, $n_2 = 4$ claims for Durban, and $n_3 = 5$ claims from Johannesburg could have been received is:

$$\frac{n!}{n_1! n_2! n_3!} = \frac{12!}{3! 4! 5!} = 27,720$$

Hence the probability that there are 3 claims from Cape Town, 4 from Durban, and 5 from Johannesburg is:

$$0.3^3 \times 0.2^4 \times 0.5^5 \times 27,720 = 0.037422 \qquad \blacklozenge\blacklozenge$$

Example 2.17

An insurance company is about to sell a one-year term life insurance policy to 100 individuals, each age 80. Each policyholder will pay a premium of P. The insurance company will pay $10,000 to the beneficiary of each policyholder that dies within one year.

An actuary assumes that the 100 lives are independent, and that the probability that an 80 year-old will die within one year is 0.02. She computes the smallest fund F that is needed so that there is at least a 90% chance of being adequate to pay the death benefits. The premium P is then calculated by dividing the fund F equally between the policyholders.

Calculate P.

Solution

The probability that exactly k of the 100 lives die within one year is:

$$0.02^k \times 0.98^{100-k} \times {}_{100}C_k$$

So, we have:

Number of deaths (k)	Probability of exactly k deaths	Probability of at most k deaths
0	0.132620	0.132620
1	0.270652	0.403272
2	0.273414	0.676686
3	0.182276	0.858962
4	0.090208	0.949170

From the table, we can see that there is a 94.92% chance of 4 or fewer deaths, so there is at least a 90% chance that a fund of $40,000 will be sufficient to pay the death benefits for the group of 100 policyholders.

This fund could be obtained by charging each policyholder a premium of:

$$P = \frac{F}{100} = \frac{40,000}{100} = \$400$$

Notice that there is an 85.90% chance of 3 or fewer deaths. So, the probability that a fund of $30,000 is adequate to pay benefits is less than our required goal of 90% certainty. ◆ ◆

Chapter 2 Practice Questions

Free online solutions manual

You can download detailed worked solutions to every practice question in this book free of charge from the BPP Professional Education website at **www.bpptraining.com.** You'll also find other useful study resources here.

Question 2.1

A newly formed baseball team must choose its uniform. Baseball caps are available in four colors (white, red, blue, and black). Shirts are available in six colors (white, red, blue, green, yellow, and black). Pants are available in two colors (white and black).

(i)   How many different uniforms (comprising shirt, pants, and cap) are possible?

(ii)   How many different uniforms are possible if the team chooses white pants and shirts that are neither red nor yellow?

(iii)   How many different uniforms are possible if the shirt, pants, and cap must be different colors?

Question 2.2

An urn contains ten balls numbered 0-9. Balls are randomly selected from the urn one at a time and the score is noted (in order).

(i)   Calculate the number of possible outcomes if three balls are selected from the urn, and each ball is replaced before the next ball is drawn.

(ii)   Calculate the number of possible outcomes if three balls are selected from the urn, and each ball is not replaced before the next ball is drawn.

(iii)   Calculate the number of possible outcomes if three balls are selected from the urn, and any even numbered ball is replaced before the next ball is drawn, but any odd numbered ball is not replaced.

Question 2.3

Calculate the number of ways in which the gold medal, silver medal, and bronze medal can be awarded if 30 runners enter a marathon. Assume that all runners finish the race.

Question 2.4

A coin is tossed five times and the outcomes are noted (in order). Calculate the number of possible outcomes that include three or more heads.

Question 2.5

Calculate the number of possible distinct arrangements of the letters in the following words:

(i)   WYOMING

(ii)   ARIZONA

(iii)   MASSACHUSETTS.

Question 2.6

The 18 participants in a clinical trial for a new drug are classified in three possible ways, according to the level of dosage they will receive: high dose, low dose and placebo. Calculate the number of ways in which it is possible to select the three groups of six patients to receive each level of dosage.

Question 2.7

A game is played in which a fair coin is tossed several times until the third occurrence of a tail, when the game stops. Calculate the probability of observing three or more heads before the game stops.

Question 2.8

You have $1,000 to invest at the start of the year. There are 100 investment funds in which you can invest. You randomly select ten different funds and allocate $100 to each. At the end of the year a table is published, which ranks the funds by performance over the year. The top 25 funds are described as "Top Quartile" funds and the bottom 25 are described as "Bottom Quartile" funds. Calculate the probability that your ten funds contain exactly three Top Quartile and two Bottom Quartile funds.

Question 2.9

In a weekly lottery game, contestants must select 6 different numbers in the range 1-48. A contestant wins the jackpot if his/her numbers match those 6 numbers drawn at random by the lottery computer. The order of the numbers does not matter.

(i)   Calculate the probability that exactly two of the winning numbers are single-digit numbers.

(ii)   Calculate the probability that two of the winning numbers are single digit, one is between 10 and 19, one is in the twenties, one is in the thirties and one is in the forties.

Question 2.10

An insurance company monitors the largest claim paid each week. Claims may be paid on three types of insurance policies: automobile, homeowners, and medical. The probability that the largest claim is from an automobile policy is 0.3, that it is from a homeowners policy is 0.1, and that it is from a medical policy is 0.6. Calculate the probability that over a four-week period, the largest claim is from a medical policy on at least 2 more occasions than from an automobile policy.

Question 2.11

A construction company takes out an insurance policy to cover accidents on its construction sites. The probability that one or more accidents will occur during any month is 0.24. The number of accidents that occur in any month is independent of the number of accidents that occur in all other months. Calculate the probability that six or more accident-free months will occur before two months with accidents.

Question 2.12 *SOA/CAS*

Workplace accidents are categorized into three groups: minor, moderate and severe. The probability that a given accident is minor is 0.5, that it is moderate is 0.4, and that it is severe is 0.1. Two accidents occur independently in one month. Calculate the probability that neither accident is severe and at most one is moderate.

Question 2.13

The Cleveland Cadavers basketball team are a notoriously weak road team. They win just 35% of the games that they play as the road team. Just before a seven-game road trip, team management informs the coach that unless the team wins at least three of these seven games he will be fired at the conclusion of the road trip. Assuming that the outcomes of different games are independent, calculate the probability that the coach is fired at the end of this trip.

Question 2.14

You win your tennis match with a certain friend 40% of the time. If you play 5 matches with this friend, what is the probability that you will win consecutive matches?

Question 2.15

You have seat 4B on flight 2134 from Hartford to Milwaukee. There are 60 seats on this flight and today there will be 48 passengers, of whom 15 are members of a college soccer team. Assuming that individuals are randomly assigned to randomly chosen seats, calculate the probability that at least one of the adjacent seats 4A and 4C will be occupied by a member of the college soccer team.

Question 2.16

George is taking a Sociology class with 4 of his friends. The class has 24 students. For a group project the class is randomly divided into 8 equal size groups of 3. Calculate the probability that none of George's friends are in his group.

Question 2.17

George is taking a Sociology class that has 24 students. For a group project the class will be randomly divided into 8 equal size groups of 3. What is the least number of friends he must have in the class so that there is at least a 50% chance of having at least one of his friends is in his group?

Question 2.18

Mr. Moneymaker is playing poker. His first three cards are the jack of hearts, the two of clubs, and the nine of diamonds. What is the probability that he will have at least one pair of matching cards after two more cards are dealt?

Question 2.19

Consider a lottery in which contestants must select six different numbers in the range 1-49. What is the probability that a contestant who purchases one ticket will match at least three of the six numbers in the winning six-number combination?

Question 2.20   *SOA/CAS*

A large pool of adults earning their first driver's license includes 50% low-risk drivers, 30% moderate-risk drivers and 20% high-risk drivers. Because these drivers have no prior driving record, an insurance company considers each driver to be randomly selected from the pool.

This month, the insurance company writes four new policies for adults earning their first driver's license. What is the probability that these four will contain at least two more high-risk drivers than low-risk drivers?

3

Conditional Probability & Bayes' Theorem

Overview

In this chapter, we'll consider the probability that an event *A* occurs given that an event *B* has occurred. For example, we may be interested in the probability that a medical insurance policyholder requires hip replacement surgery during the current calendar year given that the policyholder suffers from osteoarthritis.

What makes this issue of particular interest is that while most people will never need to undergo hip replacement surgery, it is much more frequently required by those who suffer from osteoarthritis. So, knowing that a policyholder suffers from this condition will lead us to significantly increase our estimate of the probability that the policyholder will need this surgery. The concept of using additional information to adjust a probability calculation is at the heart of conditional probability.

Bayes' Theorem allows us to consider this problem the other way around. We can use Bayes' Theorem to calculate the probability that an event was the result of a particular cause. For example, we can calculate the probability that a medical insurance policyholder who requires hip replacement surgery during the current calendar year suffers from osteoarthritis (and not from some other condition that necessitates such treatment).

3.1 Conditional probability

In our study of probability so far, we have assumed that we have no pertinent information about the outcome of interest. We'll now introduce the idea of a **conditional probability**, which measures the probability of an event given certain knowledge.

Conditional probability

The **conditional probability** of event A given that the event B has occurred is denoted $\Pr\left(A|B\right)$ and is defined as:

$$\Pr\left(A|B\right) = \frac{\Pr\left(A \cap B\right)}{\Pr\left(B\right)} \qquad \text{where } \Pr\left(B\right) > 0$$

For example, we roll a fair die and observe the score. We define the following events:

$A = \{\text{Score is less than 4}\} = \{1,2,3\}$ and $B = \{\text{Score is odd number}\} = \{1,3,5\}$

Then we have:

$A \cap B = \{\text{Score is less than 4 and odd number}\} = \{1,3\}$

and:

$$\Pr\left(A|B\right) = \frac{\Pr\left(A \cap B\right)}{\Pr\left(B\right)} = \frac{2/6}{3/6} = \frac{2}{3}$$

This answer is intuitive. After all, if we know that Event B has occurred, then the sample space is immediately restricted from $\{1,2,3,4,5,6\}$ to $\{1,3,5\}$. These three possible outcomes are equally likely, and Event A occurs if the score on the die is one of two values (1 or 3).

We can also explain conditional probability using a Venn diagram. Let's represent events A and B as follows, with the probability of each region as w, x, y or z (with $w + x + y + z = 1$).

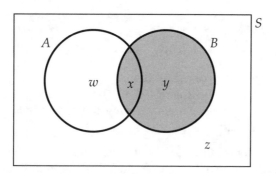

If we know that Event B has occurred, then the outcome must be within the shaded area in this diagram. (We can think of this shaded area as a restricted sample space.) The conditional probability $\Pr\left(A|B\right)$ can then be expressed as:

$$\Pr\left(A|B\right) = \frac{\Pr\left(A \cap B\right)}{\Pr\left(B\right)} = \frac{x}{x+y}$$

Example 3.1

You are given that $\Pr(A) = 0.52$, $\Pr(B) = 0.44$ and $\Pr(A \cap B) = 0.12$.

Calculate $\Pr(A|B)$.

Solution

From the definition of conditional probability, we have:

$$\Pr(A|B) = \frac{\Pr(A \cap B)}{\Pr(B)} = \frac{0.12}{0.44} = 0.2727$$

The probabilities can be represented in the following Venn diagram:

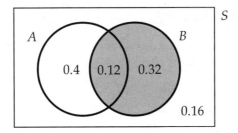

Since we know that event B has occurred, our sample space is restricted to the shaded area.

Intuitively, the probability that event A occurs given B is $0.12/(0.12 + 0.32) = 0.2727$.

Note that we did not use the fact that $\Pr(A) = 0.52$ to solve this question, and that the value of $\Pr(A|B)$ differs significantly from $\Pr(A)$.   ♦♦

Example 3.2

A college calculus class comprises 32 male students and 28 female students. 8 of the male students and 5 of the female students are considering an actuarial career. Calculate the probability that a randomly selected female student is not considering an actuarial career.

Solution

Intuitively, since 23 of the 28 female students are not considering an actuarial career, the probability of selecting such a student is $23/28 = 0.8214$. But let's look at the formal approach using the definition of conditional probability.

There are 60 students in total. Of the 28 female students, 23 are not considering an actuarial career.

Let $A = \{\text{Not considering actuarial career}\}$ and $B = \{\text{Female}\}$.

Then:

$$\Pr(A|B) = \frac{\Pr(A \cap B)}{\Pr(B)} = \frac{23/60}{28/60} = \frac{23}{28} = 0.8214$$ ♦♦

Example 3.3

Suppose that a survey of 10,000 individuals over the age of 65 yields the following results:

	Family history of heart disease	No family history of heart disease
High blood pressure	1,828	1,596
Normal blood pressure	2,033	4,543

Calculate the probability that a randomly selected individual has high blood pressure, given that the individual has a family history of heart disease.

Solution

Let $A = \{$High blood pressure$\}$ and $B = \{$Family history of heart disease$\}$.

The probability that a randomly selected individual has high blood pressure, given that the individual has a family history of heart disease is:

$$\Pr(A|B) = \frac{\Pr(A \cap B)}{\Pr(B)} = \frac{0.1828}{0.1828 + 0.2033} = \frac{0.1828}{0.3861} = 0.4735$$

For an intuitive explanation, let's add row and column totals to the table:

	Family history of heart disease	No family history of heart disease	**Total**
High blood pressure	1,828	1,596	**3,424**
Normal blood pressure	2,033	4,543	**6,576**
Total	**3,861**	**6,139**	**10,000**

There are 3,861 individuals with a family history of heart disease. Of these, 1,828 have high blood pressure.

So, the probability that an individual with a family history of heart disease also has high blood pressure is:

$$\frac{1,828}{3,861} = 0.4735$$

◆◆

3.2 *Properties of conditional probability*

We studied the axioms of probability in Chapter 1. We can restate the axioms for conditional probability.

Axioms of conditional probability

If $\Pr(B) > 0$, we have:

(1) $\Pr(A|B) \geq 0$

---

(2) $\Pr\left(B\middle|B\right)=1$

(3)   If $A_1, A_2, \cdots$ are mutually exclusive events, then:

$$\Pr\left(A_1 \cup A_2 \cup \cdots \middle|B\right) = \Pr\left(A_1\middle|B\right) + \Pr\left(A_2\middle|B\right) + \cdots$$

From axiom (3), we also have:

$$\Pr\left(A'\middle|B\right) = 1 - \Pr\left(A\middle|B\right)$$

Let's use these results to solve a more complicated problem.

 Example 3.4

Two balls are drawn at random from an urn containing 7 red balls, 6 blue balls and 4 yellow balls. Calculate the probability that the second ball drawn is blue or yellow given that the first ball drawn was blue.

Solution

Let $A_1 = \{\text{Second ball is blue}\}$, $A_2 = \{\text{Second ball is yellow}\}$, and $B = \{\text{First ball is blue}\}$.

If the first ball drawn is blue, the urn will now contain 16 balls (7 red, 5 blue, and 4 yellow), and we have:

$$\Pr\left(A_1 \cup A_2 \middle|B\right) = \Pr\left(A_1\middle|B\right) + \Pr\left(A_2\middle|B\right)$$
$$= \frac{5}{16} + \frac{4}{16} = \frac{9}{16}$$

We can also calculate this probability by considering the complementary event that the second ball drawn is neither blue nor yellow, *ie* that it is red.

Let $A = \{\text{Second ball is red}\}$ and $B = \{\text{First ball is blue}\}$. Then we have:

$$\Pr\left(A'\middle|B\right) = 1 - \Pr\left(A\middle|B\right) = 1 - \frac{7}{16} = \frac{9}{16}$$

This alternative approach uses the fact that event A (the second ball is red) is the complement of event $A_1 \cup A_2$ (the second ball is blue or yellow), *ie* $A' = A_1 \cup A_2$. ◆◆

3.3   *The multiplication rule*

We can rearrange the terms in the definition of conditional probability to obtain an expression for $\Pr\left(A \cap B\right)$, *ie* the probability that events A and B both occur. This result is commonly known as the **multiplication rule**.

Multiplication rule

The probability that events A and B both occur is given by:

$$\Pr\left(A \cap B\right) = \Pr\left(B\right)\Pr\left(A\middle|B\right)$$

Using symmetry, we can also see that the multiplication rule can alternatively be written as:

$$\Pr(A \cap B) = \Pr(A)\Pr(B|A)$$

We can also extend the rule to calculate the probability that three or more events occur:

$$\Pr(A \cap B \cap C) = \Pr(A)\Pr(B|A)\Pr(C|A \cap B)$$

This result follows from the definition of $\Pr(C|A \cap B)$.

Example 3.5

An urn contains 8 red balls and 5 blue balls. Calculate the probability that three balls drawn at random from the urn without replacement are (in order) red, blue, red.

Solution

Let $A = \{$First ball is red$\}$, $B = \{$Second ball is blue$\}$, and $C = \{$Third ball is red$\}$. Then:

$$\Pr(A) = \frac{8}{13}$$

If the first ball drawn is red, then there will be 7 red balls and 5 blue balls left in the urn. Hence:

$$\Pr(B|A) = \frac{5}{12}$$

If the first ball drawn is red and the second ball drawn is blue, then there will be 7 red balls and 4 blue balls left in the urn. Hence:

$$\Pr(C|A \cap B) = \frac{7}{11}$$

So, the probability that three balls drawn from the urn are (in order) red, blue, red is:

$$\Pr(A \cap B \cap C) = \Pr(A)\Pr(B|A)\Pr(C|A \cap B) = \frac{8}{13} \times \frac{5}{12} \times \frac{7}{11} = 0.1632 \qquad \blacklozenge\blacklozenge$$

3.4 Independence – revisited

In Chapter 1, we defined events A and B to be independent if and only if:

$$\Pr(A \cap B) = \Pr(A)\Pr(B)$$

The multiplication rule states that:

$$\Pr(A \cap B) = \Pr(B)\Pr(A|B) = \Pr(A)\Pr(B|A)$$

Hence we can deduce that the independence of events A and B also implies that:

$$\Pr(A|B) = \Pr(A) \quad \text{and} \quad \Pr(B|A) = \Pr(B)$$

This expresses mathematically the idea at the heart of independence, *ie* that knowing the outcome of event B does not affect the probability that event A occurs, and vice versa.

For example, consider a card drawn at random from a standard pack of 52 playing cards.

Let $A = \{\text{Card is a heart}\}$, $B = \{\text{Card is a 10}\}$, and $C = \{\text{Card is red}\}$.

Then we have:

$$\Pr(A) = 13/52 = 1/4$$
$$\Pr(B) = 4/52 = 1/13$$
$$\Pr(C) = 26/52 = 1/2$$

We can see that events A and B are independent since:

$$\Pr(A|B) = \frac{\Pr(A \cap B)}{\Pr(B)} = \frac{\Pr(\text{Card is 10 of hearts})}{\Pr(\text{Card is a 10})} = \frac{1/52}{1/13} = 1/4 = \Pr(A)$$

and:

$$\Pr(B|A) = \frac{\Pr(A \cap B)}{\Pr(A)} = \frac{\Pr(\text{Card is 10 of hearts})}{\Pr(\text{Card is a heart})} = \frac{1/52}{1/4} = 1/13 = \Pr(B)$$

However, events A and C are not independent since:

$$\Pr(A|C) = \frac{\Pr(A \cap C)}{\Pr(C)} = \frac{\Pr(\text{Card is red and a heart})}{\Pr(\text{Card is red})} = \frac{1/4}{1/2} = 1/2 \neq \Pr(A)$$

and:

$$\Pr(C|A) = \frac{\Pr(A \cap C)}{\Pr(A)} = \frac{\Pr(\text{Card is red and a heart})}{\Pr(\text{Card is a heart})} = \frac{1/4}{1/4} = 1 \neq \Pr(C)$$

3.5 *The law of total probability – revisited*

As we saw in Chapter 1, the law of total probability states that if the events $A_1, A_2, \cdots, A_n$ are mutually exclusive and exhaustive, then:

$$\Pr(B) = \Pr(B \cap A_1) + \Pr(B \cap A_2) + \cdots + \Pr(B \cap A_n)$$

Using the multiplication rule, we can restate the law of total probability as follows:

Law of total probability

If the events $A_1, A_2, \cdots, A_n$ are mutually exclusive and exhaustive, then:

$$\Pr(B) = \Pr(A_1)\Pr(B|A_1) + \Pr(A_2)\Pr(B|A_2) + \cdots + \Pr(A_n)\Pr(B|A_n)$$

Let's work through some numerical examples.

 Example 3.6

There are two urns. The first urn contains 6 red balls and 6 blue balls. The second urn contains 8 red balls and 5 blue balls. An urn is randomly selected, and one ball is then drawn at random from this urn.

Calculate the probability that the ball is red.

Solution

Let $A_1 = \{$First urn selected$\}$, $A_2 = \{$Second urn selected$\}$ and $B = \{$Ball drawn is red$\}$.

Then A_1 and A_2 are mutually exclusive and exhaustive, hence:

$$Pr(B) = Pr(A_1)Pr(B|A_1) + Pr(A_2)Pr(B|A_2)$$

$$= \frac{1}{2} \times \frac{6}{12} + \frac{1}{2} \times \frac{8}{13}$$

$$= 0.5577 \qquad\qquad \blacklozenge\blacklozenge$$

Example 3.7

An insurance company specializes in writing automobile insurance. 65% of the policyholders are classified as "low risk," 20% are "moderate risk," and the rest are "high risk." During any year, 70% of the low risk policies do not generate any claims, 50% of the moderate risk policies do not generate any claims, and 25% of the high risk policies do not generate any claims.

Calculate the probability that a randomly selected policy generates at least one claim this year.

Solution

Let $A_1 = \{$Low risk$\}$, $A_2 = \{$Moderate risk$\}$, and $A_3 = \{$High risk$\}$. Then since A_1 , A_2 and A_3 are mutually exclusive and exhaustive, we have:

$$Pr(A_1) = 0.65$$
$$Pr(A_2) = 0.2$$
$$Pr(A_3) = 1 - Pr(A_1) - Pr(A_2) = 0.15$$

Let $B = \{$At least one claim this year$\}$. Then:

$$Pr(B|A_1) = 1 - Pr(B'|A_1) = 1 - 0.7 = 0.3$$
$$Pr(B|A_2) = 1 - Pr(B'|A_2) = 1 - 0.5 = 0.5$$
$$Pr(B|A_3) = 1 - Pr(B'|A_3) = 1 - 0.25 = 0.75$$

Hence:

$$Pr(B) = Pr(A_1)Pr(B|A_1) + Pr(A_2)Pr(B|A_2) + Pr(A_3)Pr(B|A_3)$$

$$= 0.65 \times 0.3 + 0.2 \times 0.5 + 0.15 \times 0.75$$

$$= 0.4075$$

As with most problems of this sort, there is an alternative approach based on the expected breakdown of a group of policies. In this case, for every 10,000 policies, we will have 6,500 "low risk" policies, 2,000 "moderate risk" policyholders, and 1,500 "high risk" policyholders.

Multiplying these numbers by the appropriate probability of no claims (*eg* 0.7 for low risk policies), the expected breakdown of the 10,000 policies is as follows:

	Low	Moderate	High	Total
No claim	4,550	1,000	375	5,925
One or more claims	1,950	1,000	1,125	4,075
Total	6,500	2,000	1,500	10,000

Hence, we expect 4,075 out of the 10,000 policies to generate at least one claim this year. So, the probability that a randomly chosen policy generates at least one claim this year is:

$$\frac{4,075}{10,000} = 0.4075$$

This "counting" approach will also be helpful as we solve more complex problems using Bayes' Theorem, which we study in the next section.   ◆◆

3.6 Bayes' Theorem

Since $\Pr(A \cap B) = \Pr(B)\Pr(A|B) = \Pr(A)\Pr(B|A)$, the definition of conditional probability can be rewritten as:

$$\Pr(A|B) = \frac{\Pr(A)\Pr(B|A)}{\Pr(B)}$$

This is the simplest version of **Bayes' Theorem** (named after the Reverend Thomas Bayes, an 18th century English mathematician).

The quantity $\Pr(A)$ is known as the **prior probability** (prior to having knowledge of the occurrence of B). The quantity $\Pr(A|B)$ is known as the **posterior probability** (after we know that event B as occurred).

Bayes' Theorem quantifies how knowledge of the occurrence of B changes our views on the probability of A, from the prior probability $\Pr(A)$ to the posterior probability $\Pr(A|B)$.

Bayes' Theorem is often used to calculate the probability that event B occurred as a result of a particular cause A_k out of a possible n causes $A_1, A_2, \cdots, A_n$ which are mutually exclusive and exhaustive.

Replacing the term $\Pr(B)$ in the denominator with the alternative form of the law of total probability, we obtain the general form of Bayes' Theorem.

Bayes' Theorem

If $A_1, A_2, \cdots, A_n$ are mutually exclusive and exhaustive, then:

$$\Pr(A_k|B) = \frac{\Pr(A_k)\Pr(B|A_k)}{\displaystyle\sum_{i=1}^{n}\Pr(A_i)\Pr(B|A_i)}$$

Example 3.8

There are two urns. The first urn contains 4 red balls and 10 blue balls. The second urn contains 6 red balls and 8 blue balls. An urn is randomly selected with equal probability, and one ball is then drawn at random from this urn. Given that the ball drawn is red, calculate the probability that it was drawn from the second urn.

Solution

Let $A_1 = \{$First urn selected$\}$, $A_2 = \{$Second urn selected$\}$ and $B = \{$Ball drawn is red$\}$.

We have:

$$\Pr(A_1) = \frac{1}{2} \qquad\qquad \Pr(A_2) = \frac{1}{2}$$

$$\Pr(B|A_1) = \frac{4}{14} \qquad\qquad \Pr(B|A_2) = \frac{6}{14}$$

Then, using Bayes' Theorem, we have:

$$\Pr(A_2|B) = \frac{\Pr(A_2)\Pr(B|A_2)}{\Pr(A_1)\Pr(B|A_1) + \Pr(A_2)\Pr(B|A_2)}$$

$$= \frac{(1/2)(6/14)}{(1/2)(4/14) + (1/2)(6/14)}$$

$$= 0.6$$

Notice that our posterior probability of selecting the second urn is:

$$\Pr(A_2|B) = 0.6$$

which is higher than our prior probability:

$$\Pr(A_2) = 0.5$$

This is because a red ball is more likely to be drawn from the second urn than from the first urn. So, since we know that the ball drawn was red, we infer that it is more likely that the drawing was made from the second urn.

In fact, we can go further than this. Notice that there are 10 red balls in total (4 in the first urn, and 6 in the second). Intuitively, since we know that a red ball was selected, the probability that it came from the second urn is simply 0.6.　　　　　　　　　　　　　　　　　　　◆◆

Example 3.9　　　　　　　　　　　　　　　　　　　　　　　　　　　　　SOA/CAS

Ten percent of a company's life insurance policyholders are smokers. The rest are nonsmokers. For each nonsmoker, the probability of dying during the year is 0.01. For each smoker, the probability of dying during the year is 0.05.

Given that a policyholder has died, what is the probability that the policyholder was a smoker?

Solution

Let $A_1 = \{\text{Smoker}\}$, $A_2 = \{\text{Nonsmoker}\}$ and $B = \{\text{Policyholder dies}\}$.

Then:

$$\Pr(A_1) = 0.1, \quad \Pr(A_2) = 0.9, \quad \Pr(B|A_1) = 0.05, \quad \Pr(B|A_2) = 0.01$$

And using Bayes' Theorem, we have:

$$\Pr(A_1|B) = \frac{\Pr(A_1)\Pr(B|A_1)}{\Pr(A_1)\Pr(B|A_1) + \Pr(A_2)\Pr(B|A_2)}$$

$$= \frac{0.1 \times 0.05}{0.1 \times 0.05 + 0.9 \times 0.01}$$

$$= 0.3571$$

We can also solve problems like this using the "counting" approach that we studied in Example 3.7.

We'll start by calculating the expected breakdown for 1,000 policyholders, of whom 10% are smokers and 90% are non-smokers. So, this group comprises 100 smokers (of whom 5% die during the year) and 900 non-smokers (of whom 1% die during the year).

	Smoker	Non-smoker	Total
Policyholder dies	5	9	14
Policyholder survives	95	891	986
Total	100	900	1,000

This table shows that we expect 14 policyholders to die during the year, of whom 5 are smokers and 9 are non-smokers.

Hence, the required probability that a policyholder who dies was a smoker is:

$$\frac{5}{14} = 0.3571 \qquad \qquad \blacklozenge\blacklozenge$$

Example 3.10

A newly developed genetic test is used to indicate whether an individual suffers from a particular condition. The test gives a positive result 90% of the time when the condition is actually present. The same test indicates the presence of the condition 0.8% of the time when the condition is not present (this is known as a "false positive"). 1.8% of the population actually has the condition.

Calculate the probability that a person has the condition given that the test indicates the presence of the condition.

Solution

Let $A_1 = \{\text{Person has condition}\}$, $A_2 = \{\text{Person does not have condition}\}$ and $B = \{\text{Positive test}\}$.

Then:

$$\Pr(A_1) = 0.018 \qquad \Pr(A_2) = 1 - \Pr(A_1) = 0.982$$

$$\Pr(B|A_1) = 0.9 \qquad \Pr(B|A_2) = 0.008$$

And using Bayes' Theorem, we have:

$$\Pr(A_1|B) = \frac{\Pr(A_1)\Pr(B|A_1)}{\Pr(A_1)\Pr(B|A_1) + \Pr(A_2)\Pr(B|A_2)}$$

$$= \frac{(0.018)(0.9)}{(0.018)(0.9) + (0.982)(0.008)}$$

$$= 0.6734$$

Notice how low this probability is. It means that even after a positive test result, an individual has around a 1/3 probability of not having the condition. ◆◆

Example 3.11   *SOA/CAS*

An actuary studied the likelihood that different types of drivers would be involved in at least one collision during any one-year period. The results of the study are presented below:

Type of driver	Percentage of all drivers	Probability of at least one collision
Teen	8%	0.15
Young adult	16%	0.08
Midlife	45%	0.04
Senior	31%	0.05
Total	100%	

(i)   Given that a driver has been involved in at least one collision in the past year, what is the probability that the driver is a young adult driver?

(ii)   Given that a driver has been involved in at least one collision in the past year and that this driver is not a senior, what is the probability that the driver is a young adult driver?

Solution

(i)   Let $A_1 = \{\text{Teen}\}$, $A_2 = \{\text{Young adult}\}$, $A_3 = \{\text{Midlife}\}$, and $A_4 = \{\text{Senior}\}$.

Let $B = \{\text{At least one collision in the past year}\}$.

Then, using Bayes' Theorem, we have:

$$\Pr\left(A_2 | B\right) = \frac{\Pr\left(A_2\right)\Pr\left(B|A_2\right)}{\displaystyle\sum_{i=1}^{4} \Pr\left(A_i\right)\Pr\left(B|A_i\right)}$$

$$= \frac{(0.16)(0.08)}{(0.08)(0.15) + (0.16)(0.08) + (0.45)(0.04) + (0.31)(0.05)}$$

$$= 0.2196$$

(ii) Since we know that the driver is not a senior, we must recalculate the percentages for the other groups (which currently account for $8\% + 16\% + 45\% = 69\%$ of the total) to find the associated probabilities:

$$\Pr\left(A_1\right) = \frac{8\%}{69\%} = 0.1159, \quad \Pr\left(A_2\right) = \frac{16\%}{69\%} = 0.2319, \quad \Pr\left(A_3\right) = \frac{45\%}{69\%} = 0.6522$$

Let $B = \{\text{At least one collision in the past year} \cap \text{Not a senior}\}$.

Then, using Bayes' Theorem, we have:

$$\Pr\left(A_2 | B\right) = \frac{\Pr\left(A_2\right)\Pr\left(B|A_2\right)}{\displaystyle\sum_{i=1}^{3} \Pr\left(A_i\right)\Pr\left(B|A_i\right)}$$

$$= \frac{(0.2319)(0.08)}{(0.1159)(0.15) + (0.2319)(0.08) + (0.6522)(0.04)}$$

$$= 0.2991 \qquad\qquad\qquad \blacklozenge\,\blacklozenge$$

Chapter 3 Practice Questions

Free online solutions manual

You can download detailed worked solutions to every practice question in this book free of charge from the BPP Professional Education website at **www.bpptraining.com**. Select support for the SOA/CAS exams and click on the Probability (P) home page. You'll also find other useful study resources here.

Question 3.1

If $\Pr(A \cup B) = 0.75$, $\Pr(B) = 4\Pr(A \cap B)$ and $\Pr(A) = 0.39$, calculate $\Pr(A|B)$.

Question 3.2

Events A and B are independent, with $\Pr(A) = 0.5$ and $\Pr(B) = 0.3$. Calculate $\Pr(B|A')$.

Question 3.3   *IOA/FOA*

Two students are selected at random, one after the other and without replacement, from a group of ten students of whom six are men and four are women. Calculate the probability that the first student selected is a man, given that the second student selected is a man.

Question 3.4

A study of individuals who suffer from severe migraines shows that 63% suffer from impaired vision and 59% suffer from nausea. Of those surveyed, 32% suffered from both impaired vision and nausea. Calculate the probability that an individual in the study who does not suffer from nausea does suffer from impaired vision.

Question 3.5

A survey of a group of college students finds that:

- 64% eat Chinese food
- 51% eat Indian food
- 48% eat Thai food
- 31% eat Chinese and Indian food
- 27% eat Indian and Thai food
- 34% eat Chinese and Thai food
- 23% eat Chinese, Indian and Thai food.

Calculate the probability that a randomly selected student who eats Chinese food does not eat Indian or Thai food.

Question 3.6   *IOA/FOA*

In a large collection of life insurance policies, 60% are for male lives, and 15% of sums assured on these lives exceed $500,000. The percentage of sums assured on female lives which exceed $500,000 is 6%. A policy is selected at random. The sum assured on the life concerned is $350,000. Calculate the probability that the selected policy is for a female life.

Question 3.7

A game is played with two fair dice. You roll the first die and note the score. You then roll the second die. The game ends if the score on this die is equal to or less than the score on the first die. Otherwise, you continue to roll the second die until the game ends. Calculate the probability that the final score on the second die is a 3.

Question 3.8

There are two urns. The first urn contains 10 red balls and 12 blue balls. A second urn contains 6 red balls and 4 blue balls. Two balls are drawn from the first urn. Any red balls chosen are placed into the second urn, while any blue balls chosen are discarded. At the end of this process, a ball is drawn from the second urn.

Calculate the probability that the ball drawn from the second urn is red.

Question 3.9

An actuary analyzes information relating to a group of 1,895 women who gave birth in Boston in 2002 and discovers that 61 of the women gave birth to twins. The actuary also discovers that 174 of the 1,895 women had at least one grandparent who had a twin brother or sister, and, of these 174 women, 10 gave birth to twins.

Determine the probability that a woman randomly selected from this group gave birth to twins, given that none of her grandparents had a twin brother or sister.

Question 3.10

An insurance company sells two types of insurance: automobile and homeowners. Of the 1,000 policyholders, 88 have both automobile and homeowners policies with the company. There are three times as many policyholders with automobile insurance than policyholders with homeowners insurance.

Calculate the probability that an automobile policyholder randomly selected from this group does not have a homeowners insurance policy with the company.

Question 3.11   *SOA/CAS*

Upon arrival at a hospital's emergency room, patients are categorized according to their condition as critical, serious or stable. In the past year:

- 10% of the emergency room patients were critical;

- 30% of the emergency room patients were serious;

- the rest of the emergency room patients were stable;

- 40% of the critical patients died;

- 10% of the serious patients died;

- 1% of the stable patients died.

Given that a patient survived, what is the probability that the patient was categorized as serious upon arrival?

Question 3.12 *SOA/CAS*

An actuary is studying the prevalence of three health risk factors, denoted by A, B, and C, within a population of women. For each of the three factors, the probability is 0.1 that a woman in the population has only this risk factor (and no others). For any two of the three factors, the probability is 0.12 that she has exactly these two risk factors (but not the other). The probability that a woman has all three risk factors, given that she has A and B, is $1/3$.

What is the probability that a woman has none of the three risk factors, given that she does not have risk factor A?

Question 3.13

60% of the policyholders of a company writing auto insurance are low risk, 25% are moderate risk and the rest are high risk. During any year, 80% of the low risk policies do not generate any claims, 60% of the moderate risk policies do not generate any claims, and 40% of the high risk policies do not generate any claims.

Calculate the probability that a randomly selected policy that generated no claims in the last year belonged to a moderate risk policyholder.

Question 3.14 *SOA/CAS*

The probability that a randomly chosen male has a circulation problem is 0.25. Males who have a circulation problem are twice as likely to be smokers as those who do not have a circulation problem. What is the conditional probability that a male has a circulation problem, given that he is a smoker?

Question 3.15 *SOA/CAS*

A study of automobile accidents produced the following data:

Model year	Proportion of all vehicles	Probability of involvement in an accident
1997	0.16	0.05
1998	0.18	0.02
1999	0.20	0.03
Other	0.46	0.04

An automobile from one of the model years 1997, 1998 and 1999 was involved in an accident.

Determine the probability that the model year of this automobile is 1997.

4

Introduction to Random Variables

So far, we've studied how to calculate the probability of an event in the sample space. A random variable is a function that converts each possible outcome into a real number.

For example, if we toss a fair coin 100 times, we could define the random variable X to be the number of heads observed. The value of X is not known in advance of the experiment, but the range of values that it can take is known to be $\{0, 1, 2, \cdots, 100\}$. Intuitively, we might reasonably expect the value of X to be close to 50, and very likely in the range from 30 to 70.

In this chapter we'll study the key characteristics of random variables, including the probability distribution (*ie* the probability that it takes a particular value), the expected value, and measures of the likely range of outcomes.

The important theory in this chapter is presented in a general way, with many numerical examples to illustrate the main ideas. In Chapters 5, 6, and 7 we will use this theory to analyze the key characteristics of standard models of random variables.

4.1 Random variables

In simple terms, a **random variable** is a rule for associating a real number with each element in a sample space (the set of all possible outcomes of an experiment).

In mathematical terms, a random variable X is a function whose domain is the sample space S and whose range is some set of real numbers. So, for every element of the sample space $s \in S$, there is a real number $x \in \mathbb{R}$ such that $X(s) = x$. The range of the random variable is the set:

$$\{x : X(s) = x, s \in S\}$$

For example, consider an experiment in which a coin is tossed three times. The sample space S (the set of possible outcomes) is $S = \{HHH, HHT, HTH, THH, HTT, THT, TTH, TTT\}$.

Let the random variable X represent the total number of heads observed. The random variable takes the following values:

$$X(HHH) = 3$$
$$X(HHT) = X(HTH) = X(THH) = 2$$
$$X(HTT) = X(THT) = X(TTH) = 1$$
$$X(TTT) = 0$$

Hence the range of X is $\{0, 1, 2, 3\}$.

This is an example of a **discrete** random variable, because the range of the function is a finite set. Other random variables may be **continuous**. Let's define these terms formally and then we'll consider a wide range of examples.

Random variables

A **random variable** X is a function whose domain is the sample space S and whose range is some set of real numbers. For every element of the sample space $s \in S$, there is a real number $x \in \mathbb{R}$ such that $X(s) = x$.

A **discrete random variable** is a random variable for which the range of the function is a finite set or an infinite countable set, *eg* $\{1, 2, 3, 4, 5, 6\}$ or $\{\cdots, -3, -2, -1, 0, 1, 2, 3, \cdots\}$.

A **continuous random variable** is a random variable for which the range of the function is an interval (or union of intervals) on the real line, *eg* $\{x : x > 0\}$ or $\{x : 2 < x < 10\}$.

Note: The range of a random variable X is also known as the **space** or **support** of X.

Examples of random variables

1. The random variable X represents the score observed when a fair die is rolled. The sample space is $S = \{1, 2, 3, 4, 5, 6\}$ and X is a discrete random variable defined as:

    $$X(s) = s \text{ for all } s \in S$$

2.   The random variable X represents the number of days in a randomly chosen year in the 1980s. The sample space is $S = \{1980, 1981, 1982, \cdots, 1989\}$ and X is a discrete random variable with:

$$X(s) = 365 \qquad s = 1981, 1982, 1983, 1985, 1986, 1987, 1989$$
$$X(s) = 366 \qquad s = 1980, 1984, 1988 \text{ (leap years)}$$

3.   A game is played using a computer, which is programmed to randomly select a real number in the interval $[0,10]$. The player loses \$10 if the number is in the range $[0,3]$, wins \$10 if the score is in the range $[7,10]$, and wins nothing otherwise. The random variable X is the amount of money (in dollars) won in a single game. The sample space is $S = \{s \in \mathbb{R} : 0 \leq s \leq 10\}$ and X is a discrete random variable with:

$$X(s) = \begin{cases} -10 & 0 \leq s \leq 3 \\ 0 & 3 < s < 7 \\ 10 & 7 \leq s \leq 10 \end{cases}$$

4.   The random variable X is the lifetime (in hours) of a component in a machine. The component could fail immediately or continue to operate almost indefinitely. The sample space is $S = \{s \in \mathbb{R} : s \geq 0\}$, and X is a continuous random variable defined as:

$$X(s) = s \text{ for all } s \in S$$

5.   The component described in the previous example requires a constant supply of coolant at the rate of 15 cubic centimeters (cc) per hour of operation. The random variable Y is the total amount of coolant required (in cc) during the lifetime of a component. The sample space (which is based on the lifetime of the component) is unchanged, and Y is a continuous random variable defined as:

$$Y(s) = 15s \text{ for all } s \in S$$

6.   The random variable X is the body mass index (BMI) for a randomly selected individual, where BMI is defined as weight (in kilograms) divided by the square of height (in meters). The sample space is $S = \{(w, h) : w > 0, h > 0\}$, where w is an individual's weight (in kilograms) and h is the individual's height (in meters). The random variable X is a continuous random variable defined as:

$$X(w, h) = \frac{w}{h^2} \text{ for all } (w, h) \in S$$

Discrete or continuous?

In Example 4 above, we stated that the lifetime of the component is a continuous random variable, and not a discrete random variable. This is because the lifetime can take any real number if it is measured with sufficient accuracy. For example, a lifetime that is recorded as 3 hours may in fact be 2.98 hours, or 2.9812 hours, or 2.981173 hours *etc*. Similarly, we will typically treat most physical measurements (*eg* the weight of a fish, the circumference of a wheel, the systolic blood pressure of a patient) as continuous random variables.

We'll explore further the relation between discrete and continuous random variables later in this chapter in Section 4.7.

Example 4.1

A game is played with two spinners, each of which is marked with the numbers 0, 1, 2, and 3. A player spins each spinner and wins \$2 if the scores on the two spinners are the same. The player wins nothing if the scores on the two spinners differ by exactly one. The player loses \$1 if the scores on the two spinners differ by more than one.

Describe the random variable that represents the amount won in a single game.

Solution

The sample space is:

$$S = \{(0,0),(0,1),(0,2),(0,3),(1,0),(1,1),(1,2),(1,3)$$
$$(2,0),(2,1),(2,2),(2,3),(3,0),(3,1),(3,2),(3,3)\}$$

The random variable X, which represents the amount won in a single game, is a discrete random variable with:

$$X(0,0) = X(1,1) = X(2,2) = X(3,3) = 2$$
$$X(0,1) = X(1,0) = X(1,2) = X(2,1) = X(2,3) = X(3,2) = 0$$
$$X(0,2) = X(0,3) = X(1,3) = X(2,0) = X(3,0) = X(3,1) = -1$$

◆◆

Example 4.2

The European space agency launches a satellite with two independent communications units. Each unit could fail immediately or continue to operate almost indefinitely. The satellite is deemed to be in working order while at least one of the communications units is operating successfully.

(i)   Describe the random variable X that represents the working lifetime of the satellite if the communications units operate concurrently.

(ii)   Describe the random variable Y that represents the working lifetime of the satellite if the second communication unit is only switched on once the first unit has failed.

Solution

The sample space is:

$$S = \{(t_1,t_2) : t_1 \geq 0, t_2 \geq 0\}$$

where t_1 and t_2 are the working lifetimes of the first and second units respectively.

(i)   If the communications units operate concurrently, the satellite works until the last unit fails. So, we have:

$$X(t_1,t_2) = \max(t_1,t_2) \quad \text{for all } (t_1,t_2) \in S$$

(ii)   If the second communication unit only operates once the first unit has failed, the satellite works for the combined lifetime of the two units. So, we have:

$$Y(t_1,t_2) = t_1 + t_2 \quad \text{for all } (t_1,t_2) \in S$$

◆◆

4.2 *Calculating probabilities*

As we saw in Chapter 1, probabilities are defined on $s \in S$, the outcomes in the sample space. In this section we'll see how to define probabilities for discrete and continuous random variables.

Discrete random variables

The probability that a discrete random variable X takes a particular value x is written $\Pr(X = x)$. It is also commonly written in shorthand as $f_X(x)$ or (if there is no ambiguity about the random variable to which we are referring) $f(x)$. The function $f(x)$ is known as the **probability mass function**, or simply the **probability function** of the random variable X.

From our definition of a discrete random variable, it should be clear that the random variable X takes a particular value x if and only if the outcome belongs to the set:

$$\{s \in S : X(s) = x\}$$

This leads to the following definition:

Probability function

The probability function of a discrete random variable X is:

$$f(x) = \Pr(X = x) = \sum_{s \in S : X(s) = x} \Pr(s)$$

For example, let's again consider the random variable X that represents the number of heads observed when a fair coin is tossed three times. The sample space contains 8 equally probable outcomes. The probability function is:

$$f(0) = \Pr(X = 0) = \Pr(TTT) = 1/8$$

$$f(1) = \Pr(X = 1) = \Pr(HTT) + \Pr(THT) + \Pr(TTH) = 3/8$$

$$f(2) = \Pr(X = 2) = \Pr(HHT) + \Pr(HTH) + \Pr(THH) = 3/8$$

$$f(3) = \Pr(X = 3) = \Pr(HHH) = 1/8$$

$$f(x) = 0 \text{ for all other values of } x$$

The probability function has the following important properties:

Properties of the probability function

(1) $f(x) \geq 0$ for all x

(2) $\sum_x f(x) = 1$

Note that property (2) confirms what we learned in Chapter 1, *ie* that the probabilities of all possible outcomes must sum to one. In our last example, we can see that:

$$\sum_x f(x) = \frac{1}{8} + \frac{3}{8} + \frac{3}{8} + \frac{1}{8} = 1$$

Another function of interest is the **cumulative distribution function**, or simply the **distribution function**. This function is denoted $F_X(x)$ or (if there is no ambiguity about the random variable to which we are referring) $F(x)$. It is defined as follows:

Cumulative distribution function

The cumulative distribution function of a discrete random variable X is:

$$F(x) = \Pr(X \le x)$$

We can calculate the distribution function $F(x)$ that corresponds to the probability mass function $f(x)$ in our last example:

$$F(0) = \Pr(X \le 0) = 1/8$$
$$F(1) = \Pr(X \le 1) = 1/8 + 3/8 = 1/2$$
$$F(2) = \Pr(X \le 2) = 1/8 + 3/8 + 3/8 = 7/8$$
$$F(3) = \Pr(X \le 3) = 1/8 + 3/8 + 3/8 + 1/8 = 1$$

The distribution function can be valued for any value of x. Here is a graph of the distribution function:

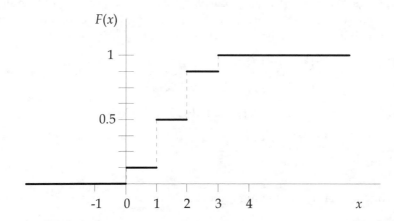

This graph illustrates some important general features of the distribution function:

Features of the distribution function for a discrete random variable

(1) $F(-\infty) = 0$

(2) $F(\infty) = 1$

(3) $F(x)$ is a non-decreasing step function, with steps occurring at every value of x such that $f(x) > 0$

Example 4.3

A New Zealand insurance company has 3,184 automobile insurance policyholders in Wellington. An actuary researches the number of claims filed by each policyholder over the last year. She finds that 1,889 policyholders filed no claims, 933 filed one claim, 341 filed two claims and 21 filed three claims. Identify the probability function of X, the discrete random variable that represents the number of claims filed last year by a randomly selected policyholder.

Solution

We have:

$$f(0) = \Pr(X = 0) = \frac{1,889}{3,184} = 0.5933$$

$$f(1) = \Pr(X = 1) = \frac{933}{3,184} = 0.2930$$

$$f(2) = \Pr(X = 2) = \frac{341}{3,184} = 0.1071$$

$$f(3) = \Pr(X = 3) = \frac{21}{3,184} = 0.0066$$

And of course $f(x) = 0$ for all other values of x.

Finally, we can check that the probabilities add to 1:

$$\sum_x f(x) = 0.5933 + 0.2930 + 0.1071 + 0.0066 = 1$$

♦♦

Example 4.4

An urn contains 4 red balls, 6 blue balls and 10 green balls. Two balls are drawn at random from the urn without replacement.

Identify the probability function of the discrete random variable X that represents the number of red balls drawn.

Solution

We have:

$$f(0) = \Pr(X = 0) = \frac{{}_{16}C_2}{{}_{20}C_2} = 0.6316$$

$$f(1) = \Pr(X = 1) = \frac{\left({}_{16}C_1\right)\left({}_{4}C_1\right)}{{}_{20}C_2} = 0.3368$$

$$f(2) = \Pr(X = 2) = \frac{{}_{4}C_2}{{}_{20}C_2} = 0.0316$$

♦♦

Continuous random variables

A continuous random variable X is defined by a **probability density function**, $f_X(x)$ or $f(x)$.

It's important to note that $f(x)$ is not itself a probability. For a continuous random variable, the probability that any single value is observed is zero, since the number of values which may be assumed by the random variable is infinite.

Instead of calculating probabilities at single points, we calculate probability for a continuous random variable in terms of intervals.

We have:

$$\Pr(a < X < b) = \int_a^b f(x)\,dx$$

So, the probability that the random variable takes a value in the interval $[a,b]$ is the definite integral of the probability density function over this interval. This integral is equal to the area under the graph of $f(x)$.

The probability density function has the following important properties:

Properties of the probability density function

(1) $f(x) \geq 0$ for all x

(2) $\int_{-\infty}^{\infty} f(x)\,dx = 1$

Note: The term "probability density function" is often abbreviated to **pdf**.

For example, suppose that the random variable X is defined by the following probability density function:

$$f(x) = \begin{cases} 0.1 & 10 < x < 20 \\ 0 & \text{otherwise} \end{cases}$$

Then the probability that X takes a value between 12 and 15 is:

$$\Pr(12 < X < 15) = \int_{12}^{15} f(x)\,dx = \int_{12}^{15} 0.1\,dx = \left(0.1x\right)\Big|_{12}^{15} = 0.3$$

The pdf clearly satisfies property (1) above. We can also check that it satisfies property (2):

$$\int_{-\infty}^{\infty} f(x)\,dx = \int_{10}^{20} f(x)\,dx = \int_{10}^{20} 0.1\,dx = \left(0.1x\right)\Big|_{10}^{20} = 1$$

The graph of the pdf in this example is shown below.

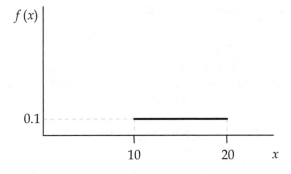

We can also define the **cumulative distribution function** (or **cdf**) of a continuous random variable X.

It is written $F_X(x)$ or $F(x)$, and is defined as follows:

Cumulative distribution function

The cumulative distribution function of a continuous random variable X is:

$$F(x) = \Pr(X \le x) = \int_{-\infty}^{x} f(s)\, ds$$

Note that since the probability that X takes any single value x is zero, we have:

$$\Pr(X \le x) = \Pr(X < x)$$

We can use the cumulative distribution function to calculate the probability that a random variable takes a value in the interval $[a,b]$ as:

$$\Pr(a < X < b) = F(b) - F(a)$$

For example, suppose that the random variable X is again defined by the following probability density function:

$$f(x) = \begin{cases} 0.1 & 10 < x < 20 \\ 0 & \text{otherwise} \end{cases}$$

The cumulative distribution function is:

$$F(x) = \Pr(X \le x) = \int_{-\infty}^{x} f(s)\, ds = \int_{10}^{x} f(s)\, ds = \int_{10}^{x} 0.1\, ds = (0.1s)\Big|_{10}^{x}$$

$$= 0.1(x-10) \quad \text{for } 10 < x < 20$$

and for values outside of this range we have:

$$F(x) = 0 \quad \text{for } x \le 10$$
$$F(x) = 1 \quad \text{for } x \ge 20$$

Hence, the probability that X takes a value between 12 and 15 is:

$$\Pr(12 < X < 15) = F(15) - F(12) = 0.5 - 0.2 = 0.3$$

The graph of the cdf in this example is shown below.

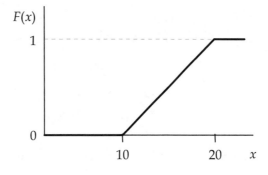

Features of the distribution function for a continuous random variable

(1) $\lim_{x \to -\infty} F(x) = 0$

(2) $\lim_{x \to \infty} F(x) = 1$

(3) $F(x)$ is continuous, non-negative and non-decreasing

How are the probability density function $f(x)$ and the cumulative distribution function $F(x)$ related? Using the Fundamental Theorem of Calculus, we have:

$$\frac{d}{dx} F(x) = \frac{d}{dx} \int_{-\infty}^{x} f(s)\,ds = f(x)$$

In other words, we can obtain the probability density function by differentiating the cumulative distribution function (where this derivative exists).

Relation between the pdf and the cdf for a continuous random variable

$$f(x) = F'(x) \qquad \text{where the derivative exists}$$

Finally, we have seen that the probability that X lies in some interval $[x, x + \Delta x]$ is:

$$\Pr(x < X < x + \Delta x) = \int_{x}^{x + \Delta x} f(s)\,ds$$

Now, if Δx is very small, we have:

$$\Pr(x < X < x + \Delta x) \approx f(x)\Delta x$$

So, although $f(x)$ is not a probability, $f(x)\Delta x$ is approximately equal to $\Pr(x < X < x + \Delta x)$ for small Δx.

Let's work through an example to illustrate the ideas we've just met.

Example 4.5

A continuous random variable X is defined by the following probability density function:

$$f(x) = ke^{-0.2x} \quad \text{for } x > 0$$

(i) Calculate k.

(ii) Identify the cumulative distribution function $F(x)$.

(iii) Calculate $\Pr(2 < X < 10)$.

Solution

(i) From property (2) of the probability density function, we have:

$$\int_{-\infty}^{\infty} f(x)\,dx = 1$$

So, in this case, we have:

$$1 = \int_0^\infty f(x)\,dx = \int_0^\infty ke^{-0.2x}\,dx = \frac{k}{0.2}\left(-e^{-0.2x}\right)\Big|_0^\infty = \frac{k}{0.2}$$

Hence, we have:

$$k = 0.2$$

(ii)   For $x > 0$, the cumulative distribution function is:

$$F(x) = \int_0^x f(s)\,ds = \int_0^x 0.2e^{-0.2s}\,ds = \left(-e^{-0.2s}\right)\Big|_0^x = 1 - e^{-0.2x}$$

The cumulative distribution function is fully defined as:

$$F(x) = \begin{cases} 0 & x \le 0 \\ 1 - e^{-0.2x} & x > 0 \end{cases}$$

(iii)   The probability can be calculated using the cumulative distribution function:

$$\Pr(2 < X < 10) = F(10) - F(2) = \left(1 - e^{-2}\right) - \left(1 - e^{-0.4}\right)$$

$$= e^{-0.4} - e^{-2} = 0.5350$$ ◆◆

Example 4.6

An insurance company's claims (in $millions) are modeled by the continuous random variable X with a probability density function of:

$$f(x) = \frac{2}{(1+x)^3} \quad \text{for } x > 0$$

Calculate the probability that a randomly chosen claim exceeds $1.5million.

Solution

The required probability is:

$$\Pr(X > 1.5) = \int_{1.5}^\infty f(x)\,dx = \int_{1.5}^\infty \frac{2}{(1+x)^3}\,dx$$

$$= \left(-\frac{1}{(1+x)^2}\right)\Big|_{1.5}^\infty = 0 - \left(-\frac{1}{2.5^2}\right)$$

$$= 0.16$$ ◆◆

Functions of random variables

If $Y = g(X)$ is a function of a discrete random variable X, then we can write:

$$\Pr(Y = y) = \Pr(g(X) = y)$$

This means that the cdf of Y can be written:

$$F_Y(y) = \Pr(Y \le y) = \Pr(g(X) \le y)$$

For example, if X is the score observed from rolling a fair die, and $Y = X^2$, then $\Pr(Y \le 20)$ would be:

$$\Pr(Y \le 20) = F_Y(20) = \Pr\left(X^2 \le 20\right) = \Pr(X \le 4.472) = \Pr(X \le 4) = \frac{4}{6}$$

Note that here we have one-to-one (1-1) correspondence between X and Y, there being just one value of X corresponding to a particular value of Y. So, for example, $\Pr(Y = 9) = \Pr(X = 3)$.

Example 4.7

A discrete random variable X can take any integer value between -3 and $+6$ inclusive, with equal probability. If $Y = X^2$, calculate $\Pr(Y \le 20)$.

Solution

We have:

$$\Pr(Y \le 20) = \Pr\left(X^2 \le 20\right) = \Pr(-3 \le X \le 4) = \frac{8}{10} \qquad \blacklozenge \blacklozenge$$

Notice that in this example the relationship between X and Y is not 1-1 because, for example:

$$\Pr(Y = 9) = \Pr(X = -3) + \Pr(X = 3)$$

We can deal with functions of continuous random variables in a similar way, as shown in the next example.

Example 4.8

A continuous random variable X has a probability density function of:

$$f(x) = \begin{cases} 0 & x < -3 \\ \dfrac{1}{9} & -3 \le x \le 6 \\ 0 & x > 6 \end{cases}$$

If $Y = X^2$, calculate $\Pr(Y \le 20)$.

Solution

We need:

$$\Pr(Y \le 20) = \Pr\left(X^2 \le 20\right) = \Pr\left(-\sqrt{20} \le X \le \sqrt{20}\right) = \Pr(-4.472 \le X \le 4.472)$$

$$= \Pr(-3 \le X \le 4.472)$$

as $\Pr(-4.472 \le X \le -3) = 0$

So:

$$\Pr(Y \le 20) = \int_{-3}^{4.472} f(x)\,dx = \frac{x}{9}\Big|_{-3}^{4.472} = \frac{7.472}{9} = 0.83 \qquad \qquad \blacklozenge\blacklozenge$$

Mixed distributions

For completeness, we'll conclude this section by describing **mixed distributions**, which are a hybrid of a discrete distribution and a continuous distribution.

A random variable X has a mixed distribution if it has:

- a discrete distribution component (*ie* it has a positive probability of taking one or more specific values), and

- a continuous component (*ie* it has a positive probability of taking a value in some interval but a zero probability of taking a specific value in that interval).

Let's look at an example.

Example 4.9

A teacher regularly replaces the light bulb in her classroom projector. The lifetime of every working light bulb (in hours) is modeled using a continuous random variable with a constant pdf on the range $[0, 800]$. The teacher replaces the light bulb as soon as it fails, or after it has worked for 600 hours, whichever occurs sooner.

Identify the distribution for the random variable Y, which represents the number of hours for which a randomly chosen light bulb will work.

Solution

The random variable Y has a mixed distribution.

It has a positive probability of taking the value 600. This is the discrete component.

It has a positive probability of taking a value in the range $[0, 600)$. This is the continuous component.

First, let's define the random variable X as the lifetime of the light bulb ignoring the possibility of replacement. The pdf of X is:

$$f_X(x) = c \qquad 0 < x < 800$$

Since the pdf must integrate to 1, we can see that:

$$f_X(x) = \frac{1}{800} \qquad 0 < x < 800$$

Now, what is the probability that $Y = 600$? Well, this is the probability that the lifetime of the light bulb is at least 600 hours, *ie* it is still working after 600 hours and is replaced at that time. Hence:

$$\Pr(Y = 600) = \Pr(X \ge 600) = \int_{600}^{800} f_X(x)\,dx = \int_{600}^{800} \frac{1}{800}\,dx = 0.25$$

Hence, Y has a mixed distribution with a probability function of:

$$f_Y(600) = 0.25$$

and a probability density function of:

$$f_Y(x) = \frac{1}{800} \quad \text{for } 0 < x < 600$$ ◆◆

Let's look at the cumulative distribution function for the random variable Y in Example 4.9. It is equal to:

$$F_Y(y) = \begin{cases} 0 & y \leq 0 \\ \dfrac{y}{800} & 0 < y < 600 \\ 1 & y \geq 600 \end{cases}$$

So, $F_Y(y)$ is continuously increasing on the interval $[0,600)$ and there is a discontinuity at $y = 600$, when the value of $F_Y(y)$ steps from 0.75 to 1.

The cumulative distribution function of Y is shown below:

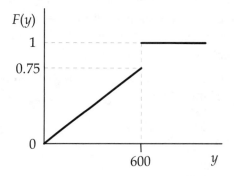

Example 4.10

Insurance losses are modeled using a continuous random variable with a constant pdf on the range $[0, 2000]$. The insurer pays the loss in excess of 250, and subject to an overall maximum of 1,500. Identify the distribution for the random variable Y, which represents the payment by the insurer relating to a randomly chosen loss.

Solution

Let X be the random amount of the loss. The pdf of X is:

$$f_X(x) = \frac{1}{2,000} \quad \text{for } 0 < x < 2,000$$

The random variable Y has a mixed distribution.

For the discrete component, we have:

$$\Pr(Y = 0) = \Pr(X \leq 250) = \frac{250}{2,000} = 0.125$$

and since Y is limited to 1,500 if the loss X exceeds $1,500 + 250 = 1,750$, we also have:

$$\Pr(Y = 1,500) = \Pr(X > 1,750) = 1 - \Pr(X \leq 1,750) = 1 - \frac{1,750}{2,000} = 0.125$$

For the continuous component, we have:

$$f_Y(y) = \frac{1}{2,000} \quad \text{for } 0 < y < 1,500 \qquad \blacklozenge\blacklozenge$$

Independence of random variables

In Chapter 1 we considered what it means for two events to be independent. We studied the concept of independence through the intuitive idea that two events are independent if the probability that the first event occurs is not influenced by the occurrence (or non-occurrence) of the second event, and vice versa.

We also met the formal definition that events A and B are independent if and only if:

$$\Pr(A \cap B) = \Pr(A)\Pr(B)$$

In order to give a formal definition of the independence of two random variables, we must first learn about the features of multivariate distributions, *ie* probability distributions of two or more random variables. We will study this topic in depth in Chapter 8, and at that stage we will also introduce the formal definition of independent random variables. For the time being, however, it is useful to develop an intuitive understanding of what it means for two random variables to be independent.

To do this, let's consider two random variables X and Y. Let event A be some event related to random variable X (*eg* the event that $X = 10$), and let event B be some event related to random variable Y (*eg* the event that $Y > 5$). Then X and Y are **independent random variables** if and only if events A and B are independent.

For example, if random variables X and Y are independent, then:

$$\Pr(X = 4 \cap Y = 2) = \Pr(X = 4)\Pr(Y = 2)$$

$$\Pr(0 < X < 10 \cap Y \geq 25) = \Pr(0 < X < 10)\Pr(Y \geq 25)$$

$$\Pr(X < 4.4 \cap Y \neq 12.5) = \Pr(X < 4.4)\Pr(Y \neq 12.5)$$

Intuitively, the probability of some event related to the random variable X is not influenced by the occurrence (or non-occurrence) of some other event related to the random variable Y.

Independence of two random variables may be assumed implicitly where the random variables are seemingly unconnected (*eg* X is the score observed when a six-sided die is rolled, and Y is the number of heads observed when a fair coin is tossed 10 times). Alternatively, we may state explicitly that two random variables are independent if there is any possible doubt (*eg* if the random variables relate to claims made by policyholders in the same neighborhood).

4.3 Measures of central tendency

In this section we describe some important measures that summarize the *average* value that a random variable may take. These are known formally as **measures of central tendency**.

Mathematical expectation

The **mathematical expectation** of a random variable X, denoted $E[X]$, represents an average of the possible values of X. It is also known as the **mean** or **expected value** or **expectation** of X, and is often denoted by the Greek letter μ (mu).

Mathematical expectation of a random variable

The mathematical expectation of a discrete random variable X is:

$$E[X] = \sum_x x \Pr(X = x) = \sum_x x f(x)$$

The mathematical expectation of a continuous random variable X is:

$$E[X] = \int_x x f(x) dx$$

The expected value of a random variable X is a measure of its average value. However, the expected value does not have to be one of the possible values of the random variable. This is illustrated in Example 4.11.

Example 4.11

A bill is drawn at random from an envelope containing five \$1 bills, two \$5 bills and three \$10 bills. Calculate the expected value of the bill.

Solution

Let X represent the value (in dollars) of the bill drawn at random. Then we have:

$$f(1) = 0.5$$
$$f(5) = 0.2$$
$$f(10) = 0.3$$

and the expected value of X is:

$$E[X] = \sum_x x f(x) = (1)(0.5) + (5)(0.2) + (10)(0.3) = 4.5$$

Note that the random variable cannot take a value of 4.5, the expected value.   ♦♦

Example 4.12

Calculate the expected value of the continuous random variable X with a pdf of:

$$f(x) = \begin{cases} 0.1 & 10 < x < 20 \\ 0 & \text{otherwise} \end{cases}$$

Solution

We have:

$$E[X] = \int_x x f(x) dx = \int_{10}^{20} (x)(0.1) dx = 0.1 \left. \frac{x^2}{2} \right|_{10}^{20}$$

$$= 0.1 \left(\frac{20^2}{2} - \frac{10^2}{2} \right) = 15$$

Note that the expected value is the midpoint of the interval $(10, 20)$. This makes intuitive sense when we remember that the pdf is constant over the interval.   ♦♦

We can also define the expectation of a function of a random variable.

Mathematical expectation of a function of a random variable

The mathematical expectation of a function $g(X)$ of a discrete random variable X is:

$$E[g(X)] = \sum_x g(x)\Pr(X = x) = \sum_x g(x)f(x)$$

The mathematical expectation of a function $g(X)$ of a continuous random variable X is:

$$E[g(X)] = \int_x g(x)f(x)dx$$

For example, if X represents the score observed from rolling a fair die, and $g(x) = x^2$, then:

$$E[X^2] = E[g(X)] = \sum_{x=1}^{6} g(x)f(x) = \sum_{x=1}^{6} \frac{x^2}{6}$$

$$= \frac{1}{6}(1 + 4 + 9 + 16 + 25 + 36) = 15.1667$$

The following theorem explores an important property of expectation.

Theorem 4.1

If X is a random variable and $g(X)$ is a linear function of the form $g(x) = ax + b$ then:

$$E[g(X)] = g(E[X])$$

Proof

For the discrete case, we have:

$$E[g(X)] = E[aX + b] = \sum(ax + b)f(x) = a\sum xf(x) + b\sum f(x)$$

$$= aE[X] + b = g(E[X])$$

For the continuous case we have:

$$E[g(X)] = E[aX + b] = \int(ax + b)f(x)dx = a\int xf(x)dx + b\int f(x)dx$$

$$= aE[X] + b = g(E[X]) \qquad \qquad \square$$

It is important to note that the general result in Theorem 4.1 does not hold for non-linear functions.

To illustrate this, consider the example above, in which X represents the score observed from rolling a fair die, and $g(x) = x^2$. We saw that $E[g(X)] = E[X^2] = 15.1667$. We also have:

$$E[X] = \sum_{x=1}^{6} xf(x) = \frac{1}{6}(1 + 2 + 3 + 4 + 5 + 6) = 3.5$$

and we see that:

$$E[X^2] = E[g(X)] \neq g(E[X]) = (E[X])^2$$

Example 4.13

A game is played with a fair die. A player pays \$20 to play the game. The player rolls the die and receives a sum equal to five times the score on the die. Calculate the expected profit from a single game.

Solution

Let X represent the score on the die, so $E[X] = 3.5$.

The profit (in dollars) can be expressed as:

$$g(x) = 5x - 20$$

Using Theorem 4.1, we have:

$$E[g(X)] = g(E[X]) = 5 \times 3.5 - 20 = -2.5$$

◆ ◆

In addition to the mean, there are two other common measures of central tendency: the mode and the median.

Mode

Another measure of central tendency is the mode of a random variable. It is defined in terms of the most likely outcome.

Mode

The mode of a random variable X is the value (or values) of x at which $f(x)$ achieves its maximum value.

This definition applies equally to discrete random variables (for which $f(x)$ is the probability function) and continuous random variables (for which $f(x)$ is the pdf). Note that — unlike the mean — the mode is always a possible value of the random variable.

For example, in Example 4.4 we saw that the number of red balls drawn from the urn had a probability mass function equal to:

$$f(0) = 0.6316 \qquad f(1) = 0.3368 \qquad f(2) = 0.0316$$

So, the mode of this distribution is 0, the single most likely outcome.

For a continuous random variable, if $f(x)$ achieves its maximum at two, three or more distinct values, the distribution is said to be **bimodal**, **trimodal**, or **multimodal** respectively. These terms are sometimes used — potentially confusingly — to refer to local maximums.

For example, the pdf of the continuous distribution in the graph below could be described as bimodal because it has pronounced peaks at $x = a$ and $x = b$, even though $f(a) \neq f(b)$.

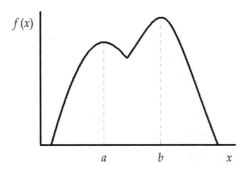

Median

The median is the "middle value" of a distribution, as measured in terms of probability.

Median

The **median** of a random variable is the value x for which:

$$F(x) = \Pr(X \le x) = 0.5$$

For example, if the continuous random variable X has a distribution function equal to:

$$F(x) = 1 - e^{-4x}$$

then the median can be calculated as follows:

$$\Pr(X \le x) = 0.5 \Rightarrow 1 - e^{-4x} = 0.5 \Rightarrow e^{-4x} = 0.5 \Rightarrow x = -\frac{\ln(0.5)}{4} = 0.1733$$

If the pdf of a continuous random variable is symmetrical, then the median is easily identified as the center of symmetry.

The median can always be identified for a continuous distribution. However, the median may not be simple to identify for a discrete distribution for two reasons related to the fact that the distribution function is a step function:

- The distribution function may change from a value of less than 0.5 to a value greater than 0.5 at a step. For example, if $f(x) = 0.2$ for $x = \{1,2,3,4,5\}$, then $F(2) = 0.4$ and $F(3) = 0.6$. There is no value of x such that $F(x) = 0.5$.

- If the distribution function is equal to 0.5 between two steps, the median is not unique. For example, if $f(x) = 0.25$ for $x = \{1,2,3,4\}$, then $F(x) = 0.5$ for all values of x in the interval $[2,3)$.

For these reasons, we'll restrict our consideration of medians to continuous random variables.

Example 4.14

The random variable X has a pdf equal to:

$$f(x) = \frac{3,000}{x^4} \qquad \text{for } x > 10$$

(i)   Calculate the expected value of X.

(ii)   Calculate the mode of X.

(iii)   Calculate the median of X.

Solution

(i)   The expected value is calculated as:

$$E[X] = \int_{10}^{\infty} x\, f(x)\, dx = 3{,}000 \int_{10}^{\infty} x^{-3}\, dx = \left(-1{,}500 x^{-2}\right)\Big|_{10}^{\infty} = 0 - (-15) = 15$$

(ii)   The pdf is a decreasing function of x. So, the pdf achieves in maximum value at $x = 10$. Hence the mode of the distribution is 10.

(iii)   We can calculate the distribution function as:

$$F(x) = \int_{10}^{x} f(s)\, ds = 3{,}000 \int_{10}^{x} s^{-4}\, ds = 3{,}000 \left(-\frac{s^{-3}}{3}\right)\Big|_{10}^{x} = 1{,}000 \left(\frac{1}{1{,}000} - x^{-3}\right) = 1 - \frac{1{,}000}{x^{3}}$$

Setting $F(x)$ equal to 0.5, the median is calculated as:

$$0.5 = 1 - \frac{1{,}000}{x^{3}} \quad \Rightarrow \quad x = 12.5992 \qquad\qquad \blacklozenge\blacklozenge$$

To calculate the expected value of a mixed distribution, we must work with each part of the probability distribution separately.

Example 4.15

Using the information in Example 4.10, calculate the expected value of the insurer's payment, Y.

Solution

The random variable Y has a mixed distribution, with a discrete component:

$$\Pr(Y = 0) = 0.125 \qquad\qquad \Pr(Y = 1{,}500) = 0.125$$

and a continuous component:

$$f_Y(y) = \frac{1}{2{,}000} \quad \text{for } 0 < y < 1{,}500$$

The expected value of Y is:

$$E[Y] = 0 \times \Pr(Y = 0) \;+\; \int_{0}^{1{,}500} y\, \frac{1}{2{,}000}\, dy \;+\; 1{,}500 \times \Pr(Y = 1{,}500)$$

$$= 0 + \left(\frac{y^{2}}{4{,}000}\right)\Big|_{0}^{1{,}500} + 1{,}500 \times 0.125 = 562.5 + 187.5 = 750 \qquad\qquad \blacklozenge\blacklozenge$$

4.4 *Measures of dispersion*

In the last section we studied measures of central tendency, which summarize in different ways the "average" value that a random variable may take. In this section we study **measures of dispersion**, which summarize the dispersion or spread of values around the expected value. The greater the dispersion, the greater the probability that the random variable will take some value far from its expectation.

Variance and standard deviation

The **variance** of a random variable measures the dispersion or spread of values around the expected value. The variance of a random variable X is denoted $\text{var}(X)$.

Variance

The variance of a discrete random variable X is:

$$\text{var}(X) = E\left[(X-\mu)^2\right] = \sum_x (x-\mu)^2 f(x)$$

where $\mu = E[X]$, the expected value of X.

The variance of a continuous random variable X is:

$$\text{var}(X) = E\left[(X-\mu)^2\right] = \int_x (x-\mu)^2 f(x)dx$$

The **standard deviation** of a random variable X is denoted $\text{sd}(X)$. The relationship between variance and standard deviation is as follows:

Standard deviation

The standard deviation of a random variable X with variance $\text{var}(X)$ is:

$$\text{sd}(X) = \sqrt{\text{var}(X)}$$

Standard deviation is often denoted by σ (sigma). To avoid ambiguity about the random variable, we may write σ_X. Similarly, the notation for the variance is: σ^2 or σ_X^2.

The standard deviation is always the positive root of the variance, *ie* $\sigma_X \geq 0$.

An advantage of standard deviation as a measure of dispersion is that it is expressed in the same units as the underlying random variable, often making it easier to interpret than variance.

Example 4.16

Using the information in Example 4.11, calculate the variance and standard deviation of the value of the randomly selected bill.

Solution

Since $\mu = E[X] = 4.5$, we have:

$$\text{var}(X) = \sum_x (x-\mu)^2 f(x) = (1-4.5)^2(0.5) \ + \ (5-4.5)^2(0.2) \ + \ (10-4.5)^2(0.3)$$
$$= 15.25$$

Hence the standard deviation is:

$$\text{sd}(X) = \sqrt{\text{var}(X)} = \sqrt{15.25} = 3.9051 \qquad\qquad \blacklozenge\blacklozenge$$

Example 4.17

Using the information in Example 4.12 calculate the variance and standard deviation of X.

Solution

Since $\mu = E[X] = 15$, we have:

$$\text{var}[X] = \int (x - \mu)^2 f(x)dx = \int_{10}^{20} (x - 15)^2 (0.1)dx$$

$$= 0.1 \frac{(x - 15)^3}{3} \Big|_{10}^{20} = 0.1 \left(\frac{5^3}{3} - \frac{(-5)^3}{3} \right) = 8.3333$$

Hence the standard deviation is:

$$\text{sd}(X) = \sqrt{\text{var}(X)} = \sqrt{8.3333} = 2.8868 \qquad \qquad \blacklozenge \blacklozenge$$

There is another way to calculate the variance of a random variable. This is explored in the following theorem.

Theorem 4.2

If X is a random variable, then:

$$\text{var}(X) = E[X^2] - (E[X])^2$$

Proof

If X is a discrete random variable, then:

$$\text{var}(X) = \sum (x - \mu)^2 f(x) = \sum (x^2 - 2x\mu + \mu^2) f(x)$$

$$= \sum x^2 f(x) - 2\mu \sum x f(x) + \mu^2 \sum f(x)$$

$$= E[X^2] - 2\mu^2 + \mu^2 = E[X^2] - \mu^2$$

We can use a similar approach for continuous random variables.   □

For example, using the information in Example 4.11, we have:

$$E[X] = 4.5$$

$$E[X^2] = \sum_x x^2 f(x) = (1^2)(0.5) \; + \; (5^2)(0.2) \; + \; (10^2)(0.3) = 35.5$$

Hence, we can calculate the variance of X as:

$$\text{var}(X) = E[X^2] - (E[X])^2 = 35.5 - (4.5)^2 = 15.25$$

This agrees with our calculation in Example 4.16.

Let's look at another important theorem for calculating the variance of a linear function of a random variable.

Theorem 4.3

If X is a random variable, and a and b are constants, then:

$$\text{var}(aX+b) = a^2 \,\text{var}(X)$$

Proof

For the discrete case, we have:

$$\text{var}(aX+b) = E\left[(aX+b-E[aX+b])^2\right] = E\left[(aX+b-aE[X]-b)^2\right]$$

$$= E\left[a^2(X-E[X])^2\right] = a^2 E\left[(X-E[X])^2\right]$$

$$= a^2 \,\text{var}(X)$$

We can use a similar approach for continuous random variables.   □

It follows from Theorem 4.3 that:

$$\text{sd}(aX+b) = |a| \cdot \text{sd}(X)$$

Example 4.18

A game is played with a fair die. A player pays \$20 to play the game. The player rolls the die and receives a sum equal to five times the score on the die. Calculate the variance of the profit from a single game.

Solution

Let X represent the score on the die. Then (using the Solution to Example 4.11), we have:

$$E[X] = 3.5$$

$$E\left[X^2\right] = \frac{1}{6} \times \left(1^2 + 2^2 + 3^2 + 4^2 + 5^2 + 6^2\right) = \frac{91}{6} = 15.1667$$

$$\Rightarrow \text{var}(X) = E\left[X^2\right] - (E[X])^2 = 2.9167$$

The profit can be represented by the random variable $Y = 5X - 20$.

Hence, the required variance is:

$$\text{var}(5X-20) = 5^2 \,\text{var}(X) = 25 \times 2.9167 = 72.9167 \qquad \blacklozenge\blacklozenge$$

To calculate the variance of a mixed distribution, we must work with each part of the probability distribution separately.

Example 4.19

Using the information in Example 4.10, calculate the standard deviation of the insurer's payment, Y.

Solution

The random variable Y has a mixed distribution, with a discrete component:

$$\Pr(Y = 0) = 0.125 \qquad\qquad \Pr(Y = 1,500) = 0.125$$

and a continuous component:

$$f_Y(y) = \frac{1}{2,000} \quad \text{for } 0 < y < 1,500$$

From Example 4.15, we have:

$$E[Y] = 750$$

Similarly:

$$E[Y^2] = 0^2 \times \Pr(Y = 0) + \int_0^{1,500} y^2 \frac{1}{2,000} dy + 1,500^2 \times \Pr(Y = 1,500)$$

$$= 0 + \left(\frac{y^3}{6,000} \right)\Bigg|_0^{1,500} + 1,500^2 \times 0.125 = 562,500 + 281,250 = 843,750$$

So, we can calculate the variance of Y as:

$$\text{var}(Y) = E[Y^2] - (E[Y])^2 = 843,750 - (750)^2 = 281,250$$

and the standard deviation of Y is then:

$$\text{sd}(Y) = \sqrt{\text{var}(Y)} = \sqrt{281,250} = 530.3 \qquad\qquad\qquad \blacklozenge\blacklozenge$$

For many students, it takes a while to gain an intuitive understanding of variance and standard deviation. As we've said, these quantities measure the dispersion or spread of values around the expected value: the greater the variance (or standard deviation), the greater the probability that the random variable will take some value far from its expectation.

The following theorem (known as **Chebyshev's inequality**) provides a very powerful general result.

Theorem 4.4

If X is a random variable with mean μ and variance σ^2, then for $k > 0$:

$$\Pr(|X - \mu| \geq k\sigma) \leq \frac{1}{k^2}$$

Proof

For the discrete case, we have:

$$\sigma^2 = \sum_x (x-\mu)^2 f(x)$$

$$= \sum_{x:|x-\mu|\geq k\sigma} (x-\mu)^2 f(x) \; + \sum_{x:|x-\mu|<k\sigma} (x-\mu)^2 f(x)$$

$$\geq \sum_{x:|x-\mu|\geq k\sigma} (k\sigma)^2 f(x) \; + \; 0$$

$$= k^2\sigma^2 \Pr\left(|X-\mu|\geq k\sigma\right)$$

Hence:

$$\Pr\left(|X-\mu|\geq k\sigma\right) \leq \frac{1}{k^2}$$

The proof is similar for the continuous case.   □

Chebyshev's inequality has important implications for our understanding of the variability (measured in terms of the standard deviation) of a random variable.

For example, if $k=2$, we have:

$$\Pr\left(|X-\mu|\geq 2\sigma\right) \leq 0.25$$

or alternatively:

$$\Pr\left(|X-\mu|< 2\sigma\right) \geq 0.75$$

And if $k=3$, we have:

$$\Pr\left(|X-\mu|\geq 3\sigma\right) \leq 0.111$$

or alternatively:

$$\Pr\left(|X-\mu|< 3\sigma\right) \geq 0.889$$

So, for any random variable—discrete or continuous—with any probability distribution, we can say that:

- the probability that the random variable takes a value within 2 standard deviations of the mean is at least 75%

- the probability that the random variable takes a value within 3 standard deviations of the mean is at least 88.9%.

For example, for a random variable X with a mean of $\mu=50$ and a standard deviation of $\sigma=10$:

$$\Pr\left(30 < X < 70\right) \geq 0.75$$

and:

$$\Pr\left(20 < X < 80\right) \geq 0.889$$

Although variance and standard deviation are very much the most common measures of spread, there are other measures. We'll look at two other measures in this section: mean deviation and the interquartile range.

Mean absolute deviation

Mean absolute deviation

The mean absolute deviation of a random variable X is:

$$E\big[|X - \mu|\big] \qquad \text{(where the expectation exists)}$$

In words, the mean absolute deviation of a random variable X is the expected value of the absolute difference between X and the mean of X.

So, for a discrete distribution, we have:

$$E\big[|X - \mu|\big] = \sum_x |x - \mu| \Pr(X = x) = \sum_x |x - \mu| f(x)$$

and for a continuous distribution, we have:

$$E\big[|X - \mu|\big] = \int_x |x - \mu| f(x) dx$$

Example 4.20

Let X be the value of a bill drawn at random from an envelope containing five $1 bills, two $5 bills and three $10 bills. Calculate the mean absolute deviation of X.

Solution

As we saw in Example 4,9, we have:

$$f(1) = 0.5$$
$$f(5) = 0.2$$
$$f(10) = 0.3$$

and the expected value of X is:

$$\mu = E[X] = \sum_x x f(x) = (1)(0.5) + (5)(0.2) + (10)(0.3) = 4.5$$

Hence, the mean absolute deviation of X is:

$$E\big[|X - \mu|\big] = \sum_x |x - \mu| f(x)$$

$$= |1 - 4.5|(0.5) + |5 - 4.5|(0.2) + |10 - 4.5|(0.3)$$

$$= (3.5)(0.5) + (0.5)(0.2) + (5.5)(0.3) = 3.5 \qquad \blacklozenge\blacklozenge$$

Coefficient of variation

Coefficient of variation

The coefficient of variation of a random variable is defined to be:

$$\frac{\text{sd}(X)}{\text{E}(X)}$$

This is a dimensionless quantity that gives an indication of the dispersion of the distribution of the random variable X.

Example 4.21

Using the information in Example 4.11 and Example 4.16, calculate the coefficient of variation of the value of the randomly selected bill.

Solution

Since $\mu = E[X] = 4.5$ and $\text{sd}(X) = 3.9051$, the coefficient of variation is:

$$\frac{\text{sd}(X)}{\text{E}(X)} = \frac{3.9051}{4.5} = 0.868 = 86.8\%$$ ♦♦

Interquartile range

Before we can describe the interquartile range, we need to define a **percentile**.

Percentile

The $(100p)$th percentile of a continuous random variable X is a quantity x_p such that:

$$\Pr\left(X \le x_p\right) = F_X(x_p) = p$$

For example, the 35th percentile of a random variable X is denoted $x_{0.35}$ and:

$$F(x_{0.35}) = 0.35$$

Note that the median of a distribution could be described as the 50th percentile, since it is defined as the value x such that:

$$F(x) = \Pr\left(X \le x\right) = 0.5$$

Accordingly, we will sometimes write the median of a distribution using the symbol $x_{0.5}$.

As we saw in Section 4.3, the median can always be identified for a continuous random variable, but it may not exist or be unique for a discrete random variable. The same is true for percentiles in general, so we will focus on continuous random variables.

The 25th percentile is known as the **lower quartile**, because there is a probability of 25% (*ie* one quarter) that the random variable will be below this value:

$$F(x_{0.25}) = 0.25$$

The 75th percentile is known as the **upper quartile**, because there is a probability of 25% (*ie* one quarter) that the random variable will be above this value:

$$\Pr(X > x_{0.75}) = 1 - F(x_{0.75}) = 1 - 0.75 = 0.25$$

The **interquartile range** is the difference between the 25th percentile and the 75th percentile of a distribution.

Interquartile range

The interquartile range of a random variable X is:

$$x_{0.75} - x_{0.25}$$

So, the interquartile range gives us an idea of the "spread" of a distribution based on the middle 50% of the probability, *ie* excluding the values at the two extremes of the distribution.

Example 4.22

Calculate the interquartile range for a continuous random variable X defined by the following probability density function:

$$f(x) = ke^{-0.2x} \quad \text{for } x \geq 0$$

Solution

From Example 4.5, we know that:

$$F(x) = \begin{cases} 0 & x \leq 0 \\ 1 - e^{-0.2x} & x > 0 \end{cases}$$

Hence, we can calculate the 25th percentile as follows:

$$0.25 = F(x_{0.25}) = 1 - e^{-0.2x_{0.25}} \Rightarrow x_{0.25} = -\frac{\ln(1 - 0.25)}{0.2} = 1.4384$$

Similarly, the 75th percentile is:

$$0.75 = F(x_{0.75}) = 1 - e^{-0.2x_{0.75}} \Rightarrow x_{0.75} = -\frac{\ln(1 - 0.75)}{0.2} = 6.9315$$

Hence the interquartile range is:

$$x_{0.75} - x_{0.25} = 6.9315 - 1.4384 = 5.4931 \qquad \qquad \blacklozenge\blacklozenge$$

4.5 Moments

The **moments** of a random variable are quantities that tell us important information about the characteristics of that random variable. As we'll shortly see, we've already calculated two different types of moments in the preceding part of this section. But let's start with a formal definition.

Moment and central moments

The **k-th moment** of the random variable X is defined as:

$$E\left[X^k\right]$$

The **k-th central moment** of the random variable X is defined as:

$$E\left[(X-\mu)^k\right] \qquad \text{where } \mu = E[X]$$

So, for a random variable X, we can see that the expected value of the distribution, $E[X]$, is the first moment of X, while the variance is the second central moment, since:

$$\text{var}(X) = E\left[(X-\mu)^2\right]$$

The **third central moment** is used to calculate the **skewness** of a distribution. The skewness of a distribution is sometimes denoted α_3 and is defined as:

$$\alpha_3 = \frac{E\left[(X-\mu)^3\right]}{\sigma^3}$$

where σ is the standard deviation of the distribution.

Skewness is a measure of the symmetry (or asymmetry) of a distribution:

*   a symmetric distribution has a skewness of $\alpha_3 = 0$

*   a distribution that is skewed to the left has a skewness of $\alpha_3 < 0$

*   a distribution that is skewed to the right has a skewness of $\alpha_3 > 0$.

The figures below show a distribution that is skewed to the left (with a longer "tail" to the left) and a distribution that is skewed to the right (with a longer "tail" to the right).

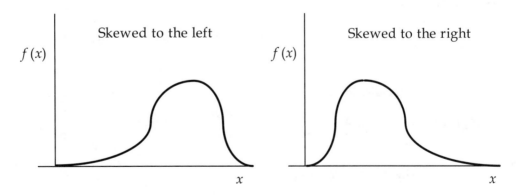

The **fourth central moment** is used to calculate the **kurtosis** of a distribution. The kurtosis of a distribution is sometimes denoted α_4 and is defined as:

$$\alpha_4 = \frac{E\left[(X-\mu)^4\right]}{\sigma^4}$$

Kurtosis is a measure of the "peakedness" of a distribution:

- a distribution that has a pronounced large peak has a high level of kurtosis

- a distribution that has a less pronounced low peak has a low level of kurtosis.

The graph on the following page shows a distribution with a high kurtosis (solid line) and a distribution with a low kurtosis (dotted line).

Note that a high kurtosis indicates that the values of the distribution are concentrated near the mean, while a low kurtosis indicates that the values are more spread out.

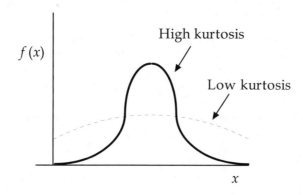

The kurtosis of a distribution is often compared to that of the normal distribution, which we will study in detail in Chapter 7.

Example 4.23

Let X be the value of a bill drawn at random from an envelope containing five \$1 bills, two \$5 bills and three \$10 bills. Calculate the skewness of X.

Solution

From Example 4.11 and Example 4.16, we have $\mu = E[X] = 4.5$ and $\sigma_X = 3.9051$.

The third central moment is:

$$E\left[(X-\mu)^3\right] = \sum_x (x-\mu)^3 f(x) = (1-4.5)^3(0.5) + (5-4.5)^3(0.2) + (10-4.5)^3(0.3)$$
$$= 28.5$$

Hence, the skewness of the distribution is:

$$\alpha_3 = \frac{E\left[(X-\mu)^3\right]}{\sigma^3} = \frac{28.5}{3.9051^3} = 0.4786$$

So, the distribution is slightly skewed to the right. ◆◆

Example 4.24

Calculate the kurtosis for two gamma distributions, the first having parameters $\alpha = 4, \theta = 1$ and the second having parameters $\alpha = 8, \theta = 1$. You are given that, for the gamma distribution,

$E[X^r] = \dfrac{(\alpha+r-1)!\,\theta^r}{(\alpha-1)!}$, and that in all cases $E[(X-\mu)^4] = E[X^4] - 4\mu E[X^3] + 6\mu^2 E[X^2] - 3\mu^4$.

Solution

For the first distribution, we have $\mu = E[X] = \alpha\theta = 4$ and $\sigma^2 = \alpha\theta^2 = 4$.

The fourth central moment is:

$$E\left[(X-\mu)^4\right] = \frac{7!}{3!} - 4\times 4\times\frac{6!}{3!} + 6\times 4^2\times\frac{5!}{3!} - 3\times 4^4 = 72$$

Hence, the kurtosis of the distribution is:

$$\alpha_4 = \frac{E\left[(X-\mu)^4\right]}{\sigma^4} = \frac{72}{4^2} = 4.5$$

For the second distribution, we have $\mu = E[X] = \alpha\theta = 8$ and $\sigma^2 = \alpha\theta^2 = 8$.

The fourth central moment is:

$$E\left[(X-\mu)^4\right] = \frac{11!}{7!} - 4\times 8\times\frac{10!}{7!} + 6\times 8^2\times\frac{9!}{7!} - 3\times 8^4 = 240$$

Hence, the kurtosis of the distribution is:

$$\alpha_4 = \frac{E\left[(X-\mu)^4\right]}{\sigma^4} = \frac{240}{8^2} = 3.75$$

The second distribution has a lower kurtosis. The probability density functions for the two distributions are shown in the following diagram. The second distribution has the lower kurtosis (the flatter curve).

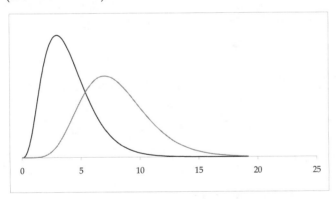

♦♦

4.6 *The moment generating function*

The moment generating function of a random variable has two powerful applications. First, it can provide a neat way to derive the moments of a distribution. Secondly, its property of uniqueness can help us to identify distributions.

Moment generating function

The **moment generating function** of the random variable X is defined as:

$$M_X(t) = E\left[e^{tX}\right]$$

for all values of t for which the expectation exists.

For a discrete random variable, the moment generating function is defined as:

$$M_X(t) = \sum_x e^{tx} f(x)$$

For a continuous random variable, the moment generating function is defined as:

$$M_X(t) = \int_x e^{tx} f(x)\, dx$$

The first important use of the moment generating function is described in the following theorem.

Theorem 4.5

Let X be a random variable with moment generating function $M_X(t)$. Then:

$$M_X^{(k)}(0) = E[X^k]$$

ie the k-th derivative of $M_X(t)$ valued at $t = 0$ is equal to $E[X^k]$, the k-th moment.

Proof

The Taylor series expansion of the exponential function is:

$$e^t = 1 + \frac{t^1}{1!} + \frac{t^2}{2!} + \frac{t^3}{3!} + \cdots = \sum_{k=0}^{\infty} \frac{t^k}{k!} \qquad \text{(which converges for } -\infty < t < \infty\text{)}$$

So, the moment generating function can be expressed as:

$$M_X(t) = E\left[e^{tX}\right] = E\left[1 + \frac{tX}{1!} + \frac{t^2 X^2}{2!} + \frac{t^3 X^3}{3!} + \cdots\right]$$

$$= 1 + \frac{t}{1!} E[X] + \frac{t^2}{2!} E[X^2] + \frac{t^3}{3!} E[X^3] + \cdots = \sum_{k=0}^{\infty} \frac{t^k}{k!} E[X^k]$$

Differentiating k times with respect to t, we have:

$$M_X^{(k)}(t) = E[X^k] + \frac{t}{1!} E[X^{k+1}] + \frac{t^2}{2!} E[X^{k+2}] + \cdots$$

$$\Rightarrow M_X^{(k)}(0) = E[X^k] \qquad \qquad \square$$

This theorem gives us a very useful way to find the moments of a distribution. In particular, we can calculate the mean and variance of a distribution as:

$$E[X] = M_X'(0)$$

$$E[X^2] = M_X''(0)$$

$$\sigma_X^2 = M_X''(0) - \left[M_X'(0)\right]^2$$

 ### Example 4.25

The discrete random variable X has a moment generating function equal to:

$$M_X(t) = \frac{1}{6}\left(e^t + e^{2t} + e^{3t} + e^{4t} + e^{5t} + e^{6t}\right)$$

(i)   Identify the probability function of X.

(ii)   Calculate the mean and variance of X.

Solution

(i)   From the definition of the moment generating function:

$$M_X(t) = \sum_x e^{tx} f(x)$$

We can deduce that the probability function of X is:

$$f(x) = \frac{1}{6} \qquad x = 1, 2, 3, 4, 5, 6$$

Note that X is equivalent to the score obtained by rolling a fair six-sided die.

(ii)   Differentiating, we have:

$$M_X'(t) = \frac{1}{6}\left(e^t + 2e^{2t} + 3e^{3t} + 4e^{4t} + 5e^{5t} + 6e^{6t}\right)$$

Hence:

$$E[X] = M_X'(0) = \frac{21}{6} = 3.5$$

Differentiating again, we have:

$$M_X''(t) = \frac{1}{6}\left(e^t + 4e^{2t} + 9e^{3t} + 16e^{4t} + 25e^{5t} + 36e^{6t}\right)$$

Hence:

$$E[X^2] = M_X''(0) = \frac{91}{6} = 15.1667$$

$$\Rightarrow \text{var}(X) = E[X^2] - \left(E[X]\right)^2 = 2.9167$$

As expected, these calculations agree with the results from Example 4.18.   ◆◆

The next three short theorems explore some basic properties of moment generating functions.

Theorem 4.6

If X is a random variable, and $M_X(t)$ is the moment generating function, then:

$$M_X(0) = 1$$

Proof

For the discrete case, we have:

$$M_X(t) = \sum_x e^{tx} f(x)$$

$$\Rightarrow M_X(0) = \sum_x e^0 f(x) = \sum_x f(x) = 1$$

We can use a similar approach for the continuous case.   □

Theorem 4.7

If X is a random variable, and $Z = a + bX$, then:

$$M_Z(t) = e^{at} M_X(bt)$$

Proof

From the definition of the moment generating function, we have:

$$M_Z(t) = E\left[e^{tZ}\right] = E\left[e^{t(a+bX)}\right] = e^{at} E\left[e^{btX}\right] = e^{at} M_X(bt)$$ □

The next theorem is stated without proof, but we will prove it in Chapter 8 when we have studied joint distributions in more depth.

Theorem 4.8

If X and Y are independent random variables, and $Z = X + Y$, then:

$$M_Z(t) = M_X(t) M_Y(t)$$

From Theorem 4.8 it follows that if $X_1, X_2, \cdots, X_n$ are independent, and $Z = X_1 + X_2 + \cdots + X_n$, then:

$$M_Z(t) = \prod_{i=1}^n M_{X_i}(t)$$

As we'll see in subsequent chapters, this useful result allows us to identify the moment generating function (and hence the moments) of a sum of independent random variables.

Example 4.26

A fair coin is tossed twice. Let X be the total number of heads observed. Identify the moment generating function of X.

Solution

The probability function of X is:

$$f(0) = 1/4$$
$$f(1) = 1/2$$
$$f(2) = 1/4$$

Hence:

$$M_X(t) = \sum_x e^{tx} f(x) = \frac{1}{4} + \frac{e^t}{2} + \frac{e^{2t}}{4} \qquad \blacklozenge \blacklozenge$$

We can also solve this problem using Theorem 4.8.

Let X_1 be the number of heads on the first toss, and X_2 the number of heads on the second toss.

Then the moment generating function of X_1 and X_2 is given by:

$$M_{X_1}(t) = M_{X_2}(t) = \frac{1}{2} + \frac{e^t}{2}$$

Since $X = X_1 + X_2$, and since X_1 and X_2 are independent, we can apply Theorem 4.8:

$$M_Z(t) = M_{X_1}(t) M_{X_2}(t) = \left(\frac{1}{2} + \frac{e^t}{2}\right)\left(\frac{1}{2} + \frac{e^t}{2}\right) = \frac{1}{4} + \frac{e^t}{2} + \frac{e^{2t}}{4} \qquad \blacklozenge \blacklozenge$$

The final theorem in this section provides another extremely important property of moment generating functions.

Theorem 4.9

If X and Y are random variables, with moment generating functions $M_X(t)$ and $M_Y(t)$, then X and Y have the same distribution if and only if $M_X(t)$ is identical to $M_Y(t)$.

The proof of this theorem is beyond the scope of this book, but its implications are very important. The theorem states that the moment generating function completely defines the distribution. So, if we know the probability distribution of a random variable, then we can deduce its moment generating function, and vice versa.

Cumulant generating function

The **cumulant generating function** of a random variable is closely related to the moment generating function. It is defined as follows:

Cumulant generating function

The cumulant generating function of the random variable X with moment generating function $M_X(t)$ is defined as:

$$R_X(t) = \ln M_X(t)$$

In this book we'll use the notation $R(t)$ if there is no ambiguity about the random variable.

The cumulant generating function has some useful properties, which we'll explore in the following theorem.

Theorem 4.10

If X is a random variable with moment generating function $M(t)$ and cumulant generating function $R(t) = \ln M(t)$, then:

(i) $R(0) = 0$

(ii) $R'(0) = E[X]$

(iii) $R''(0) = \text{var}(X)$

Proof

(i)   From Theorem 4.6, we have:

$$M(0) = 1$$

$$\Rightarrow R(0) = \ln M(0) = \ln(1) = 0$$

(ii)   Differentiating, we have:

$$R'(t) = \frac{M'(t)}{M(t)}$$

$$\Rightarrow R'(0) = \frac{M'(0)}{M(0)} = \frac{E[X]}{1} = E[X]$$

(iii)   Differentiating again using the quotient rule, we have:

$$R''(t) = \frac{M(t)M''(t) - \left(M'(t)\right)^2}{M(t)^2}$$

Hence:

$$R''(0) = \frac{M(0)M''(0) - \left(M'(0)\right)^2}{M(0)^2} = M''(0) - \left(M'(0)\right)^2$$

$$= E[X^2] - \left(E[X]\right)^2 = \text{var}(X) \qquad \square$$

It should be clear that we can identify the moment generating function of a random variable from the cumulant generating function and vice versa. In some situations, the moment generating function can be difficult to differentiate, and it may be much easier to use the cumulant generating function to calculate moments. Let's look at an example where this is true.

Example 4.27

The random variable X has a moment generating function equal to:

$$M(t) = e^{\lambda(e^t - 1)}$$

Calculate the mean and variance of X.

Solution

In this situation, it's easier to use the cumulant generating function:

$$R(t) = \ln M(t) = \lambda(e^t - 1)$$

The mean is calculated as follows:

$$R'(t) = \lambda e^t \Rightarrow E[X] = R'(0) = \lambda$$

The variance is calculated as follows:

$$R''(t) = \lambda e^t \Rightarrow \text{var}(X) = R''(0) = \lambda \qquad\qquad \blacklozenge\blacklozenge$$

We'll end this section with an important general result related to the cumulant generating function.

Theorem 4.11

Let X be a random variable with cumulant generating function $R_X(t)$. Then for $k = 2,3$:

$$R_X^{(k)}(0) = E\left[(X - \mu)^k\right]$$

ie the k-th derivative of $R_X(t)$ valued at $t = 0$ is equal to the k-th central moment of X.

4.7 *Approximations of discrete random variables*

Calculating probabilities of discrete random variables can be time consuming when the random variable can take a large number of values. For example, suppose that we wish to calculate the probability that we observe between 80 and 120 heads inclusive when a coin is tossed 200 times. We can calculate this directly as:

$$\Pr(80 \le X \le 120) = f_X(80) + f_X(81) + \cdots + f_X(120) = \sum_{x=80}^{120} f_X(x)$$

where X is the random variable that represents the number of heads observed.

In such cases, it can be more efficient to calculate the probability using an appropriate continuous distribution. (We'll explore what we mean by "appropriate" when we study the most important discrete and continuous distributions in Chapters 5-7 of this book.) The probability will then simply be the definite integral of the probability density function over a chosen interval.

But we need to be careful. When we use a continuous random variable as an approximation to a discrete random variable, we need to make an adjustment to the limits of the definite integral, known as a **continuity correction**. As its name suggests, this adjustment corrects for the fact that a continuous random variable can take any value in a range, while a discrete random variable takes a finite set of values.

In terms of our current example, we may approximate the probability using a continuous random variable Y that can take any value in the range [0,200]. But what does a value of Y of, say, 94.2 or 101.328 mean in relation to the discrete random variable X? One way to think about this is to consider how the values of Y would be rounded to the same accuracy as X (in this case, rounded to integers). For example, any value of Y between 79.5 and 80.5 would be rounded to 80, when expressed as a whole number.

So, if Y is an appropriate continuous distribution, we can use the following approximation for the required probability:

$$\Pr(80 \le X \le 120) \approx \Pr(79.5 < Y < 120.5) = \int_{79.5}^{120.5} f_Y(y)\, dy$$

More generally, if X is a discrete random variable that takes integer values, and Y is an appropriate continuous distribution:

$$\Pr(a \le X \le b) \approx \Pr(a-0.5 < Y < b+0.5) = \int_{a-0.5}^{b+0.5} f_Y(y)\, dy$$

It should be clear that calculating the definite integral can save a considerable amount of effort compared to determining the underlying discrete probability function at a large number of values.

Example 4.28

The discrete random variable X represents the number of times that a score of 6 is observed when a die is rolled 100 times. This random variable can be closely modeled using a continuous distribution Y, with a pdf $f_Y(y)$ defined for $y \in [0,100]$.

Describe in terms of Y an expression to approximate the following probabilities:

(i)   the probability that X is no greater than 24

(ii)   the probability that X is between 15 and 20 inclusive

(iii)   the probability that X is less than 12 or greater than 20

(iv)   the probability that X is equal to 16.

Solution

(i)   The probability that X is no greater than 24 is:

$$\Pr(X \le 24) \approx \Pr(0 < Y < 24.5) = \int_{0}^{24.5} f_Y(y)\, dy$$

(ii)   The probability that X is between 15 and 20 inclusive is:

$$\Pr(15 \le X \le 20) \approx \Pr(14.5 < Y < 20.5) = \int_{14.5}^{20.5} f_Y(y)\, dy$$

(iii)   The probability that X is less than 12 or greater than 20 is:

$$\Pr\big((X<12)\cup(X>20)\big) = 1 - \Pr(12 \le X \le 20)$$

$$\approx 1 - \Pr(11.5 < Y < 20.5) = 1 - \int_{11.5}^{20.5} f_Y(y)\, dy$$

Alternatively:

$$\Pr\big((X<12)\cup(X>20)\big) = \Pr(X<12) + \Pr(X>20)$$

$$\approx \Pr(Y<11.5) + \Pr(Y>20.5) = \int_{0}^{11.5} f_Y(y)\, dy + \int_{20.5}^{100} f_Y(y)\, dy$$

(iv)   The probability that X is equal to 16

$$\Pr(X=16) \approx \Pr(15.5 < Y < 16.5) = \int_{15.5}^{16.5} f_Y(y)\, dy$$

♦ ♦

Chapter 4 Practice Questions

Free online solutions manual

You can download detailed worked solutions to every practice question in this book free of charge from the BPP Professional Education website at **www.bpptraining.com**. You'll also find other useful study resources here.

Question 4.1

An urn contains five red balls and three blue balls. Four balls are chosen without replacement from the urn and their colors are noted.

(i)   Identify the sample space S.

(ii)   Describe the random variable X that represents the number of red balls selected.

(iii)   Describe the random variable Y that represents the difference between the number of red and blue balls selected.

Question 4.2

A sawmill produces wooden planks. Each plank is greater than 70 inches and less than 120 inches long, less than 12 inches wide, and less than 4 inches thick. Identify the sample space that represents that measurements of a plank, and define the random variable X that represents the volume of a plank in cubic inches.

Question 4.3

The random variable X has the following probability distribution:

$$f_X(x) = (ax)^3 \qquad x = 1, 2, 3, 4$$

Calculate a.

Question 4.4   *IOA/FOA*

The discrete variable X takes 4 distinct values with probabilities:

$$\frac{1+3\theta}{4}, \ \frac{1-\theta}{4}, \ \frac{1+2\theta}{4}, \ \frac{1-4\theta}{4}$$

Identify the range of value for θ for which this defines a probability distribution.

Question 4.5

Two fair six-sided dice are rolled. Identify the probability function of X, the product of the two scores observed.

Question 4.6

In modeling the number of claims filed by an individual under an automobile policy during a three-year period, an actuary makes the simplifying assumption that for all integers $n \geq 0$:

$$p_{n+1} = \tfrac{1}{5} p_n$$

where p_n represents the probability that the policyholder files n claims during the period.

Under this assumption, what is the probability that a policyholder files more than one claim during the period?

Question 4.7

Identify the cumulative distribution function of X in Question 4.3.

Question 4.8

A continuous random variable X is defined by the following probability density function:

$$f(x) = 1.4e^{-kx} \quad \text{for } x > 0$$

Calculate k.

Question 4.9

A continuous random variable X is defined by the following probability density function:

$$f(x) = \frac{3,000}{(x+10)^4} \quad \text{for } x > 0$$

Calculate the cumulative distribution function, $F(x)$.

Question 4.10

Using the information in Question 4.9, calculate the probability that X lies in the interval $[4,10]$.

Question 4.11

A group insurance policy covers the medical claims of the employees of a small company. The value, V, of the claims made in one year is described by:

$$V = 100,000\,Y$$

where Y is a random variable with density function:

$$f(y) = \begin{cases} k(1-y)^4 & 0 < y < 1 \\ 0 & \text{otherwise} \end{cases}$$

where k is a constant.

Calculate the conditional probability that $V > 40,000$, given that $V > 10,000$.

Question 4.12

For a manufacturing company, losses from damage to property follow a continuous distribution with a probability density function of:

$$f(x) = 0.02e^{-0.02x} \qquad \text{for } x > 0$$

The manufacturing company has an insurance policy, which reimburses losses in full up to a maximum of 100, for all losses over 10. Identify the distribution of the amount payable from the insurance policy from a single loss.

Question 4.13

An insurance company sells an insurance policy with a deductible of 2. If there is a loss, the probability of a loss of amount X is:

$$\frac{k}{X+1} \qquad \text{for } X = 1, \cdots, 5, \text{ and where } k \text{ is a constant}$$

Calculate the insurance company's expected payment in the event of a loss.

Question 4.14

The number of accidents at a large factory in a particular month has the following distribution:

Number of accidents	0	1	2	3	4	5
Probability	0.12	0.31	0.26	0.16	0.11	0.04

Calculate the expected number of accidents at the factory in a particular month.

Question 4.15   *SOA/CAS*

An insurance company's monthly claims are modeled by a continuous, positive random variable X, whose probability density function is proportional to:

$$(1+x)^{-4} \qquad \text{where } 0 < x < \infty$$

Determine the company's expected monthly claims.

Question 4.16

Using the information in Question 4.12, calculate the median amount payable from the insurance policy from a single loss.

Question 4.17

Using the information in Question 4.14, calculate the standard deviation of the number of accidents in a particular month.

Question 4.18

Using the information in Question 4.15, calculate the variance of the monthly claims.

Question 4.19

If the standard deviation of X is 10, calculate the variance of $Y = 5X + 40$.

Question 4.20

Customer electricity charges C are calculated according to the formula:

$$C = 7.00 + 0.0742N$$

where N is the number of units of electricity used. In a particular area, N is modelled as a random variable with mean 600 and variance 250. Calculate the mean and variance of C.

Question 4.21

Using the information in Question 4.14, calculate the mean absolute deviation of the number of accidents in a particular month.

Question 4.22

Using the information in Question 4.15, calculate the 90th percentile of the monthly claims.

Question 4.23

Using the information in Question 4.9, calculate the interquartile range.

Question 4.24

A discrete random variable X has the following probability function:

$$\Pr(X = 0) = 0.4$$
$$\Pr(X = 1) = 0.6$$

Calculate the coefficient of skewness.

Question 4.25

A continuous random variable X is defined by the following probability density function:

$$f(x) = 0.01 \quad \text{for } 0 < x < 100$$

Calculate the kurtosis of X.

Question 4.26

The moment generating function of X is:

$$M_X(t) = e^{10(e^t - 1)}$$

Calculate $E[X^2]$.

Question 4.27

Suppose that X is a continuous random variable with moment generating function:

$$M_X(t) = \left(1 - 20t + 100t^2\right)^{-1} \quad \text{for } t < 0.10$$

Calculate the variance of X.

Question 4.28 *SOA/CAS*

Let X_1, X_2, X_3 be a random sample from a discrete distribution with probability function:

$$p(x) = \begin{cases} 1/3 & \text{for } x = 0 \\ 2/3 & \text{for } x = 1 \\ 0 & \text{otherwise} \end{cases}$$

Determine the moment generating function, $M(t)$, of $Y = X_1 X_2 X_3$.

Question 4.29 *SOA/CAS*

A company insures homes in three cities, J, K, and L. Since sufficient distance separates the cities, it is reasonable to assume that the losses occurring in these cities are independent.

The moment generating functions for the loss distributions of the cities are:

$$M_J(t) = (1 - 2t)^{-3} \qquad M_K(t) = (1 - 2t)^{-2.5} \qquad M_L(t) = (1 - 2t)^{-4.5}$$

Let X represent the combined losses from the three cities.

Calculate $E[X^3]$.

Question 4.30

The number of claims arising from a portfolio of insurance policies is approximated using a continuous random variable with the following probability density function:

$$f(x) = 0.01 e^{-0.01x} \quad \text{for } x > 0$$

Calculate the approximate probability that there are more than 80 but no more than 150 claims.

5

Common Discrete Distributions

In this chapter we will consider five discrete distributions: binomial, negative binomial, geometric, hypergeometric, and Poisson. Random variables that follow these distributions can take the values $0, 1, 2, \cdots$, so they are ideal for modeling countable events such as:

- the number of earthquakes each year in Alaska

- the number of days between successive claims from a medical insurance policy

- the number of machines in a factory that break down in the first year of operation.

In order to define fully each of these distributions we need to choose one or two **parameters**, which appear as factors in the formula for the probability function. The parameters give us the flexibility to distribute the probability over the possible numerical outcomes in a way that accurately reflects the uncertainty of the situation being modeled. The parameters define a particular distribution within a more general **family** of distributions (*eg* binomial or Poisson).

5.1 The binomial distribution

In order to describe the binomial distribution, we must first define a Bernoulli trial.

A **Bernoulli trial** is the name given to an experiment in which there are exactly two possible outcomes. Examples include:

- tossing a fair coin (the two possible outcomes are "head" and "tail")

- the survival of a 30 year-old policyholder to age 65 (the outcomes are "survives to 65" and "dies before 65")

- the size of a loss under a homeowner's insurance policy (the outcomes are "loss exceeds $10,000" and "loss does not exceed $10,000").

The two outcomes are commonly (and somewhat euphemistically) referred to as "success" and "failure" with associated probabilities p and $q = 1 - p$ respectively.

Note that the outcome of particular interest to us is called "success", even if this event has a negative or unhappy connotation. For example, if we wish to count the number of policyholders who die before age 65, we would classify "dies before age 65" as "success" and we would classify "survives to age 65" as "failure." No wonder some people think that actuaries are morbid!

Let's now consider a series of n Bernoulli trials such that:

- the outcomes of the different trials are independent, and

- the probability of success (p) remains constant from one trial to the next.

If the random variable X represents the number of successes observed from the n Bernoulli trials, then X is said to have a **binomial distribution** with parameters n and p.

What is the probability function of X? We can identify this using the counting techniques that we first met in Chapter 2.

The possible values of X are $0, 1, \cdots, n$. If $X = x$ then the series of n trials has resulted in x successes and $n - x$ failures. Remembering that the number of ways in which these x successes and $n - x$ failures can occur is:

$$_nC_x = \frac{n!}{x!(n-x)!}$$

then the probability function of X is:

$$f(x) = \Pr(X = x) = {_nC_x}\, p^x q^{n-x} = \frac{n!}{x!(n-x)!}\, p^x q^{n-x} \quad \text{for } x = 0, 1, \cdots, n$$

The binomial distribution gets its name from the fact that the probabilities $f(0), f(1), \cdots, f(n)$ are the terms of the sum that results from using the binomial theorem to expand:

$$(p+q)^n = 1^n = 1$$

Note: Recall that $_nC_x$ is also commonly written as $C(n,x)$ or $\binom{n}{x}$.

Example 5.1

Consider a group of $n = 10$ independent life insurance policyholders who are all exactly 28 years old. The probability that any policyholder survives to age 65 is $p = 0.85$. Calculate:

(i)   the probability that exactly 8 of the 10 policyholders will survive to age 65

(ii)   the probability that 8 or more of the 10 policyholders will survive to age 65.

Solution

Let X represent the number of these policyholders that survive to age 65. Then X is a random variable that follows a binomial distribution with parameters $n = 10$ and $p = 0.85$.

(i)   The probability that exactly 8 of the 10 policyholders will survive to age 65 is:

$$f(8) = \Pr(X = 8) = \frac{10!}{8!(10-8)!} \times p^8 \times q^2 = \frac{10!}{8!2!} \times 0.85^8 \times 0.15^2 = 0.2759$$

(i)   The probability that 8 or more of the 10 policyholders survive to age 65 is:

$$f(8) + f(9) + f(10) = \frac{10!}{8!2!} \times 0.85^8 \times 0.15^2 + \frac{10!}{9!1!} \times 0.85^9 \times 0.15^1 + \frac{10!}{10!0!} \times 0.85^{10} \times 0.15^0$$

$$= 0.2759 + 0.3474 + 0.1969 = 0.8202$$

♦♦

The shape of the probability function for the binomial distribution in Example 5.1 can be seen in the following diagram:

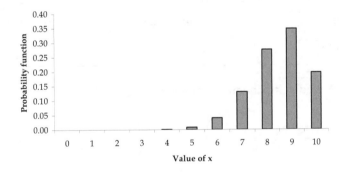

The moment generating function of the binomial distribution is:

$$M_X(t) = E\left[e^{tX}\right] = \sum_{x=0}^{n} e^{tx} \times \frac{n!}{x!(n-x)!} \times p^x \times q^{n-x}$$

$$= \sum_{x=0}^{n} \frac{n!}{x!(n-x)!} \times \left(pe^t\right)^x \times q^{n-x}$$

$$= \left(pe^t + q\right)^n \qquad \text{(by the binomial theorem)}$$

Then using calculus, we have:

$$E[X] = M_X'(0) = np$$

$$E[X^2] = M_X''(0) = npq + n^2 p^2$$

$$\Rightarrow \quad \text{var}(X) = E[X^2] - (E[X])^2 = npq$$

The proofs of these results are included in the end-of-chapter questions.

One important point to note here is that the variance of the binomial distribution is less than the expected value.

Let's return for a minute to Example 5.1.

The expected number of survivors to age 65 is:

$$E[X] = np = 10 \times 0.85 = 8.5$$

The variance of the number of policyholders surviving to age 65 is:

$$\text{var}(X) = npq = 10 \times 0.85 \times 0.15 = 1.275$$

Let's summarize the main results for the binomial distribution.

The binomial distribution

Definition: X is the number of successes in n independent Bernoulli trials, each with $\Pr(\text{Success}) = p$ and $\Pr(\text{Failure}) = q = 1 - p$

Probability function: $f(x) = \Pr(X = x) = \dfrac{n!}{x!(n-x)!} p^x q^{n-x}$ for $x = 0, 1, \cdots, n$

Moments: $E[X] = np$ $\text{var}(X) = npq$

MGF: $M_X(t) = \left(pe^t + q\right)^n$

Additive property: If X_i follows a binomial distribution with parameters n_i and p, and if the various X_i are independent, then $\sum X_i$ follows a binomial distribution with parameters $\sum n_i$ and p

---

The additive property is easily proved using the moment generating function and Theorem 4.8:

$$M_{\sum X_i}(t) = \prod M_{X_i}(t) = \prod \left(pe^t + q\right)^{n_i} = \left(pe^t + q\right)^{\sum n_i}$$

Example 5.2

A student sitting for an exam attempts 28 of the 40 multiple-choice questions. Each question has 5 answer choices, and is worth 1 point. Of the 28 attempted questions, 22 were answered correctly. The student randomly guesses at the other 12 questions. A score of 25 or higher is needed to pass. Determine the probability that this student will pass the exam.

Solution

Each of the $n = 12$ questions guessed constitutes a Bernoulli trial. Since the guessing is random and there are 5 answer choices, the probability of success (*ie* guessing the correct answer) is:

$$p = \frac{1}{5} = 0.2$$

In order to obtain a passing score, the student must have at least $X = 3$ successes. The probability that the student has at least $X = 3$ successes is:

$$\Pr(X \geq 3) = 1 - \Pr(X = 0) - \Pr(X = 1) - \Pr(X = 2)$$

$$= 1 - \frac{12!}{0!12!} \times 0.2^0 \times 0.8^{12} - \frac{12!}{1!11!} \times 0.2^1 \times 0.8^{11} - \frac{12!}{2!10!} \times 0.2^2 \times 0.8^{10}$$

$$= 1 - 0.0687 - 0.2062 - 0.2835$$

$$= 0.4416$$

Hence, the probability that the student passes the exam is 0.4416.   ◆◆

Example 5.3

The number of hurricanes that make landfall on the Eastern United States during a given annual hurricane season is modeled by a binomial distribution with $n = 5$ trials and probability of success $p = 0.35$. The numbers of hurricanes making landfall in different years are independent.

Determine the probability that at least one hurricane makes landfall on the Eastern United States in each of the next 3 seasons.

Solution

Let X be the number of hurricanes that make landfall in a season. Then X follows a binomial distribution with parameters $n = 5$ and $p = 0.35$.

The probability that at least one hurricane makes landfall in a season is thus:

$$\Pr(X \geq 1) = 1 - \Pr(X = 0) = 1 - \frac{5!}{0!5!} \times 0.35^0 \times 0.65^5 = 0.8840$$

Let's now denote the number of hurricanes in year k by X_k. The event of interest is:

$$\{X_1 \geq 1\} \cap \{X_2 \geq 1\} \cap \{X_3 \geq 1\}$$

Since the numbers of hurricanes in different years are assumed to be independent, we have:

$$\Pr\left(\{X_1 \geq 1\} \cap \{X_2 \geq 1\} \cap \{X_3 \geq 1\}\right) = \Pr(X_1 \geq 1) \times \Pr(X_2 \geq 1) \times \Pr(X_3 \geq 1)$$

$$= 0.8840^3$$

$$= 0.6908$$ ◆◆

Example 5.4

A random loss amount Y on a homeowners insurance policy is modeled as a continuous random variable with a constant pdf on the interval $[0, 1000]$. The insurance company imposes a deductible of 200 on each such loss. Let X be the number of losses exceeding the deductible in the next 100 such losses. Calculate the range of values for X that includes all whole numbers that are within two standard deviations of the expected value $E[X]$.

Solution

Each of the $n = 100$ losses is viewed as a Bernoulli trial. Success corresponds to a loss exceeding the deductible. The probability of success is:

$$p = \Pr(Y > 200) = \int_{200}^{1,000} f(y) \, dy = \int_{200}^{1,000} \frac{1}{1,000} \, dy = 0.8$$

If X is the number of losses exceeding the deductible, then we have:

$$E[X]=np=100\times0.8=80$$
$$\mathrm{var}(X)=npq=100\times0.8\times0.2=16$$

So the range $E[X]\pm2\sqrt{\mathrm{var}(X)}$ is from 72 to 88.   ♦♦

5.2 The negative binomial distribution

To describe the negative binomial distribution, we must consider an unlimited series of Bernoulli trials.

We will again assume that:

- the outcomes of the different trials are independent, and

- the probability of success (p) remains constant from one trial to the next.

If the random variable X represents the number of failures observed from the series of Bernoulli trials until r successes have occurred, then X is said to have a **negative binomial distribution** with parameters r and p.

Let's derive the formula for the probability function.

The event $X=x$ occurs if we observe x failures and r successes in the first $(r+x)$ trials. More particularly, the final success must occur in the $(r+x)$th trial, and so there must be exactly x failures and $(r-1)$ successes in the first $(r+x-1)$ trials.

The probability function of X is thus:

$$f(x)=\Pr(X=x)={}_{r+x-1}C_x\,p^rq^x=\frac{(r+x-1)!}{x!(r-1)!}\,p^rq^x\qquad\text{for } x=0,1,2,\cdots$$

Notice that—in contrast to the binomial distribution—the possible values of X are unbounded under the negative binomial distribution.

Example 5.5

Suppose that the annual number of claims against a single auto insurance policy is modeled by a negative binomial distribution with $r=5$ and $p=0.9$. Calculate:

(i)   the probability that no claims are filed against the policy during the next year

(ii)   the probability that 3 or more claims are filed in the next year.

Solution

Let X be the number of claims during the next year.

(i)   The probability that no claims are filed against the policy during the next year is:

$$\Pr(X=0)=\frac{(r-1)!}{0!(r-1)!}p^r=0.9^5=0.59049$$

(ii)   The probability of 3 or more claims being filed in the next year is:

$$\Pr(X \geq 3) = 1 - \Pr(X = 0) - \Pr(X = 1) - \Pr(X = 2)$$

$$= 1 - p^r - \frac{r!}{1!(r-1)!}p^r q - \frac{(r+1)!}{2!(r-1)!}p^r q^2$$

$$= 1 - 0.9^5 - \frac{5!}{1!4!} \times 0.9^5 \times 0.1 - \frac{6!}{2!4!} \times 0.9^5 \times 0.1^2$$

$$= 1 - 0.5905 - 0.2952 - 0.0886 = 0.0257 \qquad\qquad \blacklozenge\blacklozenge$$

The shape of the probability function for the negative binomial distribution in Example 5.5 can be seen in the following diagram:

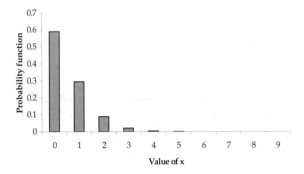

This distribution gets its name from the fact that the probabilities are terms in a binomial series with a negative exponent. From calculus we know a formula for the binomial series:

$$(1+x)^k = 1 + \frac{k}{1}x + \frac{k(k-1)}{2!}x^2 + \frac{k(k-1)(k-2)}{3!}x^3 + \cdots \qquad \text{when } |x| < 1$$

This series stops after the term in x^k if k is a positive whole number. Otherwise it is an infinite series.

By setting $x = -q$ and $k = -r$, we can use this series to expand $p^{-r} = (1-q)^{-r}$ as follows:

$$(1-q)^{-r} = 1 + \frac{-r}{1}(-q) + \frac{-r(-r-1)}{2!}(-q)^2 + \frac{-r(-r-1)(-r-2)}{3!}(-q)^3 + \cdots$$

$$= 1 + \frac{r}{1}q + \frac{r(r+1)}{2!}q^2 + \frac{r(r+1)(r+2)}{3!}q^3 + \cdots$$

$$= \sum_{k=0}^{\infty} \frac{r(r+1)\cdots(r+k-1)}{k!}q^k$$

Let's now multiply both sides of this series by p^r so that the left hand side becomes 1. The terms on the right hand side are the values of the negative binomial probability function (which must of course sum to 1).

This same power series expansion can help us develop a formula for the moment generating function:

$$M_X(t) = E\left[e^{tX}\right] = \sum_{x=0}^{\infty} e^{tx} \frac{r(r+1)\cdots(r+x-1)}{x!} q^x p^r$$

$$= p^r \sum_{x=0}^{\infty} \frac{r(r+1)\cdots(r+x-1)}{x!} \left(e^t q\right)^x$$

$$= p^r \left(1 - qe^t\right)^{-r} = \left(\frac{1 - qe^t}{p}\right)^{-r}$$

Once again, we can use calculus to derive the mean and variance:

$$E[X] = \frac{rq}{p} \qquad\qquad \text{var}(X) = \frac{rq}{p^2}$$

The proofs of these results are included in the end-of-chapter questions.

Let's consider Example 5.5 again, where X (the annual number of claims against an auto insurance policy) follows a negative binomial distribution with $r = 5$ and $p = 0.9$. The expected number of claims and variance in the number of claims are:

$$E[X] = \frac{rq}{p} = \frac{5 \times 0.1}{0.9} = 0.5556 \qquad\qquad \text{var}(X) = \frac{rq}{p^2} = \frac{5 \times 0.1}{0.9^2} = 0.6173$$

Note that the variance exceeds the expected value. (In contrast, the variance of a binomial distribution is less than the expected value.) Thus, the negative binomial distribution is often used in actuarial practice to model the number of claims against a single policy or group of policies over a specified time period when the variance in this number tends to be larger than the expected number of claims.

The negative binomial distribution

Definition: X is the number of failures before r successes in a series of independent Bernoulli trials, each with $\Pr(\text{Success}) = p$ and $\Pr(\text{Failure}) = q = 1 - p$

Probability function: $f(x) = \Pr(X = x) = \dfrac{(r+x-1)!}{x!(r-1)!} p^r q^x$ for $x = 0, 1, 2, \cdots$ and $r > 0$

Moments: $E[X] = \dfrac{rq}{p} \qquad \text{var}(X) = \dfrac{rq}{p^2}$

MGF: $M_X(t) = \left(\dfrac{1 - qe^t}{p}\right)^{-r}$

Additive property: If X_i follows a negative binomial distribution with parameters r_i and p, and if the various X_i are independent, then $\sum X_i$ follows a negative binomial distribution with parameters $\sum r_i$ and p

The additive property is again easily established using the moment generating function:

$$M_{\sum X_i}(t) = \prod M_{X_i}(t) = \prod \left(\frac{1-qe^t}{p}\right)^{-r_i} = \left(\frac{1-qe^t}{p}\right)^{-\sum r_i}$$

Note that we can rewrite the probability function more generally as:

$$f(x) = \Pr(X=x) = \begin{cases} p^r & \text{for } x=0 \\ \dfrac{(r)(r+1)\cdots(r+x-1)}{(1)(2)\cdots(x)}\, p^r q^x & \text{for } x=1,2,\cdots \end{cases}$$

With this generalization in mind, the formulas above still define a discrete probability distribution even when r is not a whole number. However, X cannot then be interpreted as the number of failures before r successes in a series of Bernoulli trials.

Example 5.6

The annual number of losses against an insurance policy is to be modeled by a negative binomial distribution with mean 0.2 and variance 0.4. Determine the values of the parameters p and r.

Solution

We must solve two simultaneous equations involving the two parameters:

$$0.2 = E[X] = \frac{rq}{p} \qquad\qquad 0.4 = \text{var}(X) = \frac{rq}{p^2}$$

If we divide the first equation by the second, we see that:

$$p = \frac{E[X]}{\text{var}(X)} = \frac{0.2}{0.4} = 0.5 \quad\Rightarrow\quad q = 1-p = 0.5 \quad\Rightarrow\quad r = 0.2 \qquad\qquad \blacklozenge\blacklozenge$$

Example 5.7

For the policy in Example 5.6, determine the probability that the number of claims in the next year is at least 1 and at most 3.

Solution

Using the parameters $p = 0.5$ and $r = 0.2$, we have:

$$\Pr(X=0) = p^r$$
$$\Pr(X=x) = \frac{(0.2)(1.2)\cdots(0.2+x-1)}{(1)(2)\cdots(x)}\, 0.5^{x+0.2} \qquad \text{for } x=1,2,\cdots$$

So, the probability that the number of claims in the next year is at least 1 and at most 3 is:

$$\Pr(X=1) + \Pr(X=2) + \Pr(X=3) = \frac{0.2}{1}\, 0.5^{1.2} + \frac{(0.2)(1.2)}{(1)(2)}\, 0.5^{2.2} + \frac{(0.2)(1.2)(2.2)}{(1)(2)(3)}\, 0.5^{3.2}$$

$$= 0.0871 + 0.0261 + 0.0096$$

$$= 0.1228 \qquad\qquad \blacklozenge\blacklozenge$$

Example 5.8

For the policy in Example 5.6, determine the probability that the total number of claims over the next two years is at least 1. Assume that the numbers of claims in different years are independent.

Solution

Let X_i denote the number of claims in year i. We must therefore calculate:

$$\Pr(X_1 + X_2 \geq 1)$$

This may look complicated at first, but bear in mind that these two random variables have possible values 0, 1, 2, 3 and so on.

As a result we have:

$$\Pr(X_1 + X_2 \geq 1) = 1 - \Pr(X_1 + X_2 = 0) = 1 - \Pr(\{X_1 = 0\} \cap \{X_2 = 0\})$$

$$= 1 - \Pr(X_1 = 0)\Pr(X_2 = 0)$$

$$= 1 - \left(0.5^{0.2}\right)\left(0.5^{0.2}\right) = 0.2421$$

Alternatively, we could use the additive property to conclude that the distribution of $X^* = X_1 + X_2$ follows a negative binomial distribution with $r = r_1 + r_2 = 0.4$ and $p = 0.5$.

Then:

$$\Pr(X^* \geq 1) = 1 - \Pr(X^* = 0) = 1 - 0.5^{0.4} = 0.2421 \qquad \blacklozenge\blacklozenge$$

5.3 *The geometric distribution*

The geometric distribution is also related to an unlimited series of independent Bernoulli trials, for which the probability of success (p) remains constant from one trial to the next.

If the random variable X represents the number of failures observed from the series of Bernoulli trials until the *first* success occurs, then X is said to have a **geometric distribution** with parameter p.

It should be straightforward to see that the geometric distribution is a special type of negative binomial distribution, with $r = 1$.

The probability function is simple to derive. The event $X = x$ occurs if we observe x failures before the first success. Hence:

$$f(x) = \Pr(X = x) = q^x p \qquad \text{for } x = 0, 1, 2, \cdots$$

The geometric distribution derives its name from the fact that the probabilities $f(0), f(1), f(2)$ and so on are the terms of a geometric series.

We can use this fact to derive a neat result for the distribution function:

$$F(x) = \Pr(X \leq x) = p + qp + q^2 p + \cdots + q^x p = p\left[1 + q + q^2 + \cdots + q^x\right]$$

$$= \frac{p\left(1 - q^{x+1}\right)}{1 - q} = 1 - q^{x+1}$$

Intuitively, the probability $\Pr(X \le x)$ must be equal to one minus the probability of $(x+1)$ consecutive failures.

For convenience, let's summarize the main results for the geometric distribution (*ie* for the negative binomial distribution with $r = 1$), and then work through some numerical examples.

The geometric distribution

Definition: X is the number of failures before the first success in a series of independent Bernoulli trials, each with $\Pr(\text{Success}) = p$

Probability function: $f(x) = \Pr(X = x) = q^x p \qquad \text{for } x = 0, 1, 2, \cdots$

Distribution function: $F(x) = \Pr(X \le x) = 1 - q^{x+1}$

Moments: $E[X] = \dfrac{q}{p} \qquad \text{var}(X) = \dfrac{q}{p^2}$

MGF: $M_X(t) = \left(\dfrac{1 - qe^t}{p} \right)^{-1}$

Additive property: A sum of n independent geometric distributions with parameter p follows a negative binomial distribution with parameters $r = n$ and p

---

The shape of the probability function for the geometric distribution with parameter $p = 0.4$ can be seen in the following diagram:

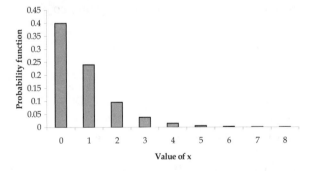

Example 5.9

Earthquakes occur regularly in a certain region of Japan. Earthquakes measuring 7 or more on the Richter scale are classed as "severe." The probability that a severe earthquake occurs in the region in any year is 0.037. Let X be the number of consecutive years with no severe earthquakes until the next year with a severe earthquake. Determine $E[X]$.

Solution

Using the geometric distribution with $p = 0.037$ and $q = 1 - p = 0.963$, we have:

$$E[X] = \frac{q}{p} = \frac{0.963}{0.037} = 26.03 \qquad\qquad \blacklozenge\blacklozenge$$

Example 5.10

When a certain machine is operating at the start of a day, there is always a 0.025 probability that it will break down at the end of that day. If such a machine is currently operating at the start of a day, determine the probability that it will operate with no breakdowns for at least 10 days and at most 20 days.

Solution

Each day is considered to be a Bernoulli trial. Since we wish to count the number of days until the first breakdown occurs, we'll define (somewhat confusingly!) "failure" to be the event that the machine continues to operate, and "success" as the event that the machine breaks down.

Let X be the number of failures (*ie* the number of days on which the machine operates) before the first success (*ie* breakdown). The random variable X follows a geometric distribution with parameter $p=0.025$.

We are asked to calculate $\Pr(10 \le X \le 20)$. This calculation is made much easier by the simple form of the distribution function. We have:

$$\Pr(10 \le X \le 20) = \Pr(X \le 20) - \Pr(X \le 9) = \left(1 - q^{21}\right) - \left(1 - q^{10}\right)$$

$$= \left(1 - 0.975^{21}\right) - \left(1 - 0.975^{10}\right)$$

$$= 0.4124 - 0.2237 = 0.1887$$

♦♦

Example 5.11

Consider the machine in Example 5.10. Determine a general formula for the probability that the machine will not break down in the first $n+m$ days, given that it has not broken down in the first n days.

Solution

We have:

$$\Pr(X \ge n+m \mid X \ge n) = \frac{\Pr(X \ge n+m)}{\Pr(X \ge n)} = \frac{1 - \Pr(X \le n+m-1)}{1 - \Pr(X \le n-1)} = \frac{q^{n+m}}{q^n} = q^m$$

♦♦

Example 5.11 illustrates the so-called **memory-less property** of the geometric distribution.

Let X follow a geometric distribution with parameter p. If we are given the additional information that $X \ge n$, then the additional number of failures until the first success (namely $X-n$) has the same distribution as X.

To see this, let's compute the conditional distribution function for the additional number of failures:

$$\Pr\left(X-n \le m \mid X \ge n\right) = \Pr\left(X \le n+m \mid X \ge n\right)$$

$$= \frac{\Pr\left(n \le X \le n+m\right)}{\Pr\left(X \ge n\right)} = \frac{\Pr\left(X \le n+m\right) - \Pr\left(X \le n-1\right)}{1 - \Pr\left(X \le n-1\right)}$$

$$= \frac{\left(1-q^{n+m+1}\right) - \left(1-q^{n}\right)}{1 - \left(1-q^{n}\right)} = \frac{q^{n} - q^{n+m+1}}{q^{n}}$$

$$= 1 - q^{m+1} = \Pr\left(X \le m\right)$$

Notation conventions

You should be aware that the definition of the negative binomial distribution (and hence the geometric distribution) varies between textbooks.

Some authors define the negative binomial distribution variable (we'll denote this X' to differentiate it from our earlier definition) to be the *total number of Bernoulli trials* before r successes are observed. In this case, the probability function of X' is:

$$\Pr\left(X' = x\right) = {}_{x-1}C_{r-1}\, p^{r}q^{x-r} = \frac{(x-1)!}{(x-r)!(r-1)!}\, p^{r}q^{x-r} \qquad \text{for } x = r, r+1, r+2, \cdots$$

The relationship between X and X' is simply:

$$X' = r + X$$

Hence, we can quickly derive the expected value and variance as follows:

$$E[X'] = E[r+X] = r + E[X] = r + \frac{rq}{p} = \frac{r}{p}$$

$$\text{var}(X') = \text{var}(r+X) = \text{var}(X) = \frac{rq}{p^2}$$

Similarly, the geometric distribution variable (we'll again denote this X' to differentiate it from our earlier definition) can be defined as the *total number of Bernoulli trials* before the first success is observed. Then (setting $r=1$ in the formulas above) we have:

$$\Pr\left(X' = x\right) = q^{x-1}p \qquad \text{for } x = 1, 2, 3, \cdots$$

$$E[X'] = \frac{1}{p}$$

$$\text{var}(X') = \frac{q}{p^2}$$

5.4 *The hypergeometric distribution*

The hypergeometric distribution is derived from random sampling without replacement from a finite population. Let's explain this with an example.

Suppose that we test the quality of a batch of 1,000 fuses, of which D are defective and $(1,000-D)$ are non-defective. A random sample of 10 of these fuses is selected (without replacement) and each fuse is tested to see whether it is defective or non-defective. The selected fuses are randomly numbered 1 through 10 and are tested in this order. Let X be the number of defective fuses in the sample.

Let's ask ourselves an important question: if we consider each fuse tested as constituting a trial, and if we view success as meaning that the fuse was defective, then can we assume that X follows a binomial distribution?

The probability that the first fuse is defective is:

$$p_1 = \frac{D}{1,000}$$

However, when the next fuse is tested, the probability of being defective has shifted slightly, since it is drawn from a population of 999 fuses and there may be one less defective fuse than there was originally.

If the first fuse was non-defective, the probability that the second fuse is defective is:

$$p_2 = \frac{D}{999}$$

If the first fuse was defective, the probability that the second fuse is defective is:

$$p_2 = \frac{D-1}{999}$$

So, the outcomes of different trials are dependent. The probability of success does not remain constant over the series of 10 trials, so a binomial distribution is not appropriate.

So what distribution is appropriate? The answer is the **hypergeometric distribution**.

This distribution is based on random sampling without replacement from a population of m objects that can be separated into two distinct categories: Type 1 and Type 2. (In the example above, we could define a defective fuse as Type 1, and a non-defective fuse as Type 2.)

Further, let's assume that there are m_1 objects of Type 1, and m_2 objects of Type 2, hence:

$$m = m_1 + m_2$$

Let X be the number of Type 1 objects in a sample of n objects selected without replacement from the population (where $n<m$). Then the random variable X follows a hypergeometric distribution.

First, note that X can take any integer value in the range from 0 to $\min\{m_1,n\}$, since X is limited not only by the sample size (n) but also by the total number of Type 1 objects (m_1).

The event $X = x$ occurs if the sample of n objects contains x Type 1 objects and $n-x$ Type 2 objects.

The number of ways in which n objects can be selected from m objects is:

$$_mC_n$$

The number of ways in which the x Type 1 objects can be selected from the m_1 Type 1 objects is:

$$_{m_1}C_x$$

Finally, the number of ways in which the $n-x$ Type 2 objects can be selected from the m_2 Type 2 objects is:

$$_{m_2}C_{n-x}$$

Assuming that each sample is equally likely, the probability function is therefore:

$$\Pr(X = x) = \frac{(_{m_1}C_x)(_{m_2}C_{n-x})}{_mC_n} \qquad \text{where } 0 \leq x \leq \min\{m_1, n\}$$

Example 5.12

There are 50 defective fuses in a batch of 1,000 fuses. If 10 fuses are randomly selected for testing, what is the probability that exactly 2 of the 10 fuses tested are defective?

Solution

Let X be the random number of defective fuses in this sample. If we define a defective fuse to be Type 1 and a non-defective fuse to be Type 2, then X follows a hypergeometric distribution with parameters:

$$m = 1,000 \qquad m_1 = 50 \qquad m_2 = 950 \qquad n = 10$$

The probability that exactly 2 of the 10 fuses tested are defective is:

$$\Pr(X = 2) = \frac{(_{50}C_2)(_{950}C_8)}{_{1,000}C_{10}} = \frac{\left(\dfrac{50 \times 49}{2!}\right)\left(\dfrac{950 \times 949 \times \cdots \times 943}{8!}\right)}{\left(\dfrac{1,000 \times 999 \times \cdots \times 991}{10!}\right)} = 0.0743$$

$\blacklozenge\blacklozenge$

The shape of the probability function for the hypergeometric distribution in Example 5.12 can be seen in the following diagram:

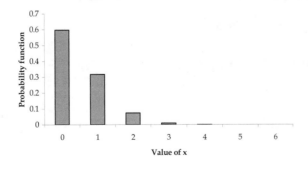

The expected value and variance formulas are difficult to derive so we will simply state them:

$$E[X] = \frac{nm_1}{m}$$

$$var(X) = n\left(\frac{m_1}{m}\right)\left(\frac{m_2}{m}\right)\left(\frac{m-n}{m-1}\right)$$

Example 5.13

Using the information in Example 5.12, calculate the expected value and variance of the number of defective fuses in the test sample.

Solution

Using the parameters in the solution to Example 5.12, we have:

$$E[X] = \frac{nm_1}{m} = \frac{(10)(50)}{1,000} = 0.5$$

$$var(X) = n\left(\frac{m_1}{m}\right)\left(\frac{m_2}{m}\right)\left(\frac{m-n}{m-1}\right) = 10\left(\frac{50}{1,000}\right)\left(\frac{950}{1,000}\right)\left(\frac{1,000-10}{1,000-1}\right) = 0.4707 \qquad \blacklozenge\blacklozenge$$

It's useful to note that the formulas for the mean and variance of the hypergeometric distribution are closely related to those for the binomial distribution.

If we think of a Type 1 object as a "success", and let $p = m_1/m$ denote the proportion of Type 1 objects in the population, then we have:

$$E[X] = np$$

$$var(X) = npq\left(\frac{m-n}{m-1}\right)$$

Notice that the final factor in the variance formula is approximately equal to 1 when the sample size n is small relative to the population size m. When this is true, the probability function, mean and variance of the hypergeometric distribution are approximately equal to those of the binomial distribution. This is because the small size of the sample has little effect on the overall proportion of Type 1 and Type 2 objects in the population.

So, when the sample size n is small relative to the population size m, we can approximate the hypergeometric distribution by using the binomial distribution instead. To test this, let's rework Examples 5.12 and 5.13 using the binomial distribution approximation, with:

$$p = \frac{m_1}{m} = \frac{50}{1,000} = 0.05$$

The probability that exactly 2 of the 10 fuses tested are defective is:

$$Pr(X = 2) \approx {}_{10}C_2 \times 0.05^2 \times 0.95^8 = 0.0746$$

The expected number of defective fuses in the sample is:

$$E[X] = np = 10 \times 0.05 = 0.5$$

The variance of the number of defective fuses in the sample is:

$$var(X) \approx npq = 10 \times 0.05 \times 0.95 = 0.475$$

As you can see, the binomial distribution provides a good approximation to the hypergeometric distribution in this case – this is because the sample size (10) is small relative to the population size (1,000).

This approximation is useful, because many of the important calculations are much simpler under the binomial distribution.

For example, suppose that we choose a sample of $n = 50$ objects from a population of $m = 10,000$ objects. If we wish to calculate the probability function under the hypergeometric distribution, we'll need to calculate the term $_{10,000}C_{50}$, which is more than my calculator can cope with! (It returns an error message.) On the other hand, the binomial distribution requires a term in the form $_{50}C_k$, which my calculator is happy to provide.

Let's see how to use this approximation in another numerical example.

Example 5.14

In a population of 100,000 voters, exactly 42% support proposed anti-speeding legislation and 58% oppose it. If the opinions of 25 voters are sampled, determine the probability that exactly 10 of these voters support the proposed legislation.

Solution

Let X be the random number of voters in this sample who support the legislation. If we define a voter who supports the legislation to be Type 1 and a voter who opposes it to be Type 2, then X follows a hypergeometric with parameters:

$$m = 100,000 \qquad m_1 = 42,000 \qquad m_2 = 58,000 \qquad n = 25$$

The probability that exactly 10 of the 25 voters surveyed support the proposed legislation is:

$$\Pr(X = 10) = \frac{\left(_{42,000}C_{10}\right)\left(_{58,000}C_{15}\right)}{_{100,000}C_{25}}$$

which is difficult and very time-consuming to calculate.

So, let's approximate the probability using the binomial distribution instead, with:

$$p = \frac{m_1}{m} = 0.42 \qquad \text{and} \qquad q = 1 - p = 0.58$$

The probability that exactly 10 of the 25 voters surveyed support the proposed legislation is then:

$$\Pr(X = 10) \approx {}_{25}C_{10} \times 0.42^{10} \times 0.58^{15} = 0.1579 \qquad\qquad \blacklozenge\,\blacklozenge$$

Note: As an exercise, you may like to verify that the correct answer (using the hypergeometric distribution) is 0.1579.

Let's end this section with a summary of the main features of the hypergeometric distribution.

The hypergeometric distribution

Definition: X is the number of Type 1 objects in a sample of n objects randomly selected without replacement from a population of m objects, of which m_1 are Type 1 and m_2 are Type 2 (where $m = m_1 + m_2$)

Probability function: $f(x) = \Pr(X = x) = \dfrac{(_{m_1}C_x)(_{m_2}C_{n-x})}{_mC_n}$ where $0 \le x \le \min\{m_1, n\}$

Moments: $E[X] = \dfrac{nm_1}{m}$

                       $\mathrm{var}(X) = n\left(\dfrac{m_1}{m}\right)\left(\dfrac{m_2}{m}\right)\left(\dfrac{m-n}{m-1}\right)$

Approximation: When the sample size n is small relative to the population size m, we can approximate the hypergeometric distribution by using the binomial distribution with parameters $p = m_1/m$ and n

---

5.5 The Poisson distribution

The Poisson distribution is frequently used to model the random number of occurrences of some "rare" event over a given time period. For example, it might be used to model the annual number of accidents on a particular road, or the number of hurricanes in Florida in September.

The Poisson distribution can take any non-negative integer value, *ie* $0, 1, 2, \cdots$. The probability function is defined by a single parameter λ (lambda) such that:

$$\Pr(X = x) = \frac{e^{-\lambda}\lambda^x}{x!} \qquad \text{for } x = 0, 1, 2, \cdots \text{ and } \lambda > 0$$

Let's take a moment to explore the origin of this formula, since doing so should improve our understanding of this important distribution.

Recall that X represents the number of occurrences of some "rare" event over a given time period. The parameter λ is the rate at which the events take place per unit of time. The approximate probability that one of these rare events takes place in a short time period of duration Δt is:

$$\lambda \cdot \Delta t$$

The probability function of the Poisson distribution arises as the limiting case of the binomial distribution. If we divide a unit time period $[0,1]$ into n equal parts where n is a large positive integer, so that each of these subintervals has length:

$$\Delta t = 1/n$$

The approximate probability of an event occurring in any one of the subintervals is:

$$\lambda \cdot \Delta t = \lambda/n$$

Since the interval is very short we will assume that the probability of two or more events occurring in any subinterval is zero. So, in each subinterval we have either one event occurring or no event occurring.

Now let's consider each of the n short subintervals as a Bernoulli trial where "success" means that exactly one event occurs in the subinterval. Then there are n trials, each with associated probabilities of success and failure of:

$$p = \frac{\lambda}{n} \qquad q = 1 - p = \frac{n - \lambda}{n}$$

Let X denote the number of successes in the n trials (*ie* the number of events that occur in $[0,1]$). We can calculate the approximate probability of x events occurring in the unit time period (*ie* x successes in n trials) using the binomial distribution as:

$$\Pr(X = x) \approx \frac{n!}{x!(n-x)!} p^x q^{n-x}$$

This approximation should get better as n increases, since as the subintervals become smaller the probability of two or more events occurring will approach zero.

We can rewrite the probability function as follows:

$$\Pr(X = x) \approx \frac{n!}{x!(n-x)!} p^x q^{n-x}$$

$$= \frac{n(n-1)\cdots(n-x+1)}{x!} \left(\frac{\lambda}{n}\right)^x \left(\frac{n-\lambda}{n}\right)^{n-x}$$

$$= \frac{n(n-1)\cdots(n-x+1)}{(n-\lambda)^x} \left(1 - \frac{\lambda}{n}\right)^n \frac{\lambda^x}{x!}$$

We now take the limit of this expression as n tends to infinity. The first term in this expression approaches 1 as n increases, since x and λ are fixed, and there are x factors in both the numerator and the denominator. From calculus, the limit of the second term is:

$$\lim_{n \to \infty} \left(1 - \frac{\lambda}{n}\right)^n = e^{-\lambda}$$

Hence, we have the probability function of the Poisson distribution with parameter λ:

$$\Pr(X = x) = \lim_{n \to \infty} \left[\frac{n(n-1)\cdots(n-x+1)}{(n-\lambda)^x} \left(1 - \frac{\lambda}{n}\right)^n \frac{\lambda^x}{x!} \right] = \frac{e^{-\lambda} \lambda^x}{x!}$$

There is a quick way to see that this formula makes sense, and this may also help you to remember it. Recall the Taylor series for the exponential function:

$$e^{\lambda} = 1 + \frac{\lambda^1}{1!} + \frac{\lambda^2}{2!} + \cdots$$

Dividing all terms by e^{λ}, we have:

$$1 = e^{-\lambda} + \frac{e^{-\lambda} \lambda}{1!} + \frac{e^{-\lambda} \lambda^2}{2!} + \cdots$$

The terms on the right hand side are the Poisson probabilities.

Let's look at a numerical example.

Example 5.15

Claims occur against a certain insurance policy at the rate of 0.3 per year. Using a Poisson distribution, calculate the probability that two or more claims occur in the next year.

Solution

Let X be the number of claims in the next year.

Using a Poisson distribution with parameter $\lambda = 0.3$, we have:

$$\Pr(X \geq 2) = 1 - \Pr(X = 0) - \Pr(X = 1)$$

$$= 1 - e^{-\lambda} - \frac{e^{-\lambda} \lambda}{1!}$$

$$= 1 - e^{-0.3} - \frac{e^{-0.3} \times 0.3}{1!}$$

$$= 0.0369 \hspace{4cm} \blacklozenge \blacklozenge$$

The shape of the probability function for the Poisson distribution in Example 5.15 can be seen in the following diagram:

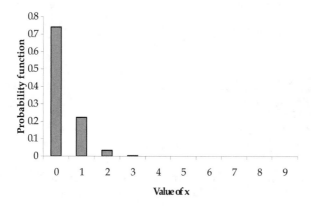

The moment generating function for the Poisson distribution is derived as follows:

$$M_X(t) = E\left[e^{tX}\right] = \sum_{x=0}^{\infty} e^{tx} e^{-\lambda} \frac{\lambda^x}{x!} = e^{-\lambda} \sum_{x=0}^{\infty} \frac{\left(\lambda e^t\right)^x}{x!} = e^{-\lambda} e^{\lambda e^t} = e^{\lambda(e^t - 1)}$$

The moments of the Poisson distribution are most easily derived using the cumulant generating function:

$$R_X(t) = \ln M_X(t) = \lambda(e^t - 1)$$

We have:

$$E[X] = R'_X(0) = \lambda$$

$$\operatorname{var}(X) = R''_X(0) = \lambda$$

The Poisson distribution

Definition: X is the number of occurrences of some "rare" event in a unit time period where λ is the rate of occurrence per unit time period

Probability function: $f(x) = \Pr(X = x) = \dfrac{e^{-\lambda}\lambda^x}{x!}$ for $x = 0, 1, 2, \cdots$ and $\lambda > 0$

Moments: $E[X] = \lambda$ $\mathrm{var}(X) = \lambda$

MGF: $M_X(t) = e^{\lambda(e^t - 1)}$

Additive property: If X_i follows a Poisson distribution with parameters λ_i, and if the various X_i are independent, then $\sum X_i$ follows a Poisson distribution with parameter $\sum \lambda_i$

The additive property is proved using the moment generating function.

$$M_{\sum X_i}(t) = \prod M_{X_i}(t) = \prod e^{\lambda_i(e^t - 1)} = e^{\left(\sum \lambda_i\right)\left(e^t - 1\right)}$$

The additive property is explored in the following example.

Example 5.16

Claims occur against a certain insurance policy at the rate of 0.3 per year. The numbers of claims in different years are independent. What is the probability of exactly 2 claims in the next 5 years?

Solution

Let X_i be the number of claims in year i, where $i = 1, 2, \cdots, 5$. Since X_i follows a Poisson distribution with parameter $\lambda_i = 0.3$, then by the additive property $X = \sum X_i$ follows a Poisson distribution with parameter $\sum \lambda_i = 1.5$. Hence:

$$\Pr(X = 2) = \frac{e^{-1.5}1.5^2}{2!} = 0.2510 \qquad\qquad \blacklozenge\blacklozenge$$

Example 5.17

Logan Airport in Boston, Massachusetts is often forced to close in the winter due to heavy snowstorms. The number of such closures each year is modeled by a Poisson distribution with a mean of 3.2. Determine the probability that the airport is closed twice in a particular year, given that it was closed at least once.

Solution

Let X be the number of closures in a particular year. We require the conditional probability:

$$\Pr(X = 2 \mid X \geq 1) = \frac{\Pr(X = 2 \cap X \geq 1)}{\Pr(X \geq 1)} = \frac{\Pr(X = 2)}{1 - \Pr(X = 0)}$$

For a Poisson distribution with parameter $\lambda = 3.2$, we have:

$$\Pr(X = 0) = e^{-3.2} = 0.0408$$

$$\Pr(X = 2) = \frac{e^{-3.2}(3.2)^2}{2!} = 0.2087$$

Hence the required probability is:

$$\Pr(X = 2 \mid X \geq 1) = \frac{\Pr(X = 2)}{1 - \Pr(X = 0)} = \frac{0.2087}{1 - 0.0408} = 0.2176 \qquad \blacklozenge\blacklozenge$$

Example 5.18

An auto insurance policy is written on a family with 3 drivers (mother, father, and teenage son), for whom the annual Poisson claims rates are 0.15, 0.2, and 0.85 respectively. The annual numbers of claims associated with different drivers are assumed to be independent. Determine the smallest whole number m such that there is at least a 95% chance that the total number of annual claims against the policy is no greater than m.

Solution

Let X be the number of annual claims. By the additive property, X follows a Poisson distribution with parameter $\lambda = 0.15 + 0.2 + 0.85 = 1.2$.

The probability function is given by:

$$\Pr(X = x) = \frac{e^{-1.2}1.2^x}{x!} \qquad \text{for } x = 0, 1, 2, \cdots$$

We have:

x	0	1	2	3
$\Pr(X = x)$	0.3012	0.3614	0.2169	0.0867
$\Pr(X \leq x)$	0.3012	0.6626	0.8795	0.9662

So, the smallest whole number such that $\Pr(X \leq m) \geq 0.95$ is $m = 3$. $\blacklozenge\blacklozenge$

Chapter 5 Practice Questions

Free online solutions manual

You can download detailed worked solutions to every practice question in this book free of charge from the BPP Professional Education website at **www.bpptraining.com**. Select support for the SOA/CAS exams and click on the Probability (P) home page. You'll also find other useful study resources here.

Question 5.1

The probability that a visit to a primary care physician's office results in a referral to a specialist is 0.28. Calculate the probability that exactly 4 of the next 10 visits result in a referral to a specialist.

Question 5.2   *IOA/FOA*

The probability of suffering a side effect from a certain flu vaccine is 0.005. If 1,000 people are inoculated, calculate the probability that at most 1 person suffers a side effect.

Question 5.3

The number of injuries at a college football game has the following distribution:

Number of injuries	0	1	2	3	4	5
Probability	0.14	0.33	0.23	0.17	0.09	0.04

The coach must file a report whenever there is more than one injury in a game. Calculate the expected number of reports and the standard deviation of the number of reports from 20 games.

Question 5.4

X follows a binomial distribution with parameters n and p. Using the moment generating function or otherwise, show that:

(i) $E[X] = np$

(ii) $\text{var}(X) = npq$

Question 5.5

An insurance company sells product liability insurance to 10 firms that manufacture electronic goods. Each policy stipulates a fixed claim amount of $10 million in the event of a valid claim. Each company may submit no more than one claim on its policy. The probability of any company submitting a claim on its policy is 0.125. The probability a claim from any one company is considered independent of a claim from any other.

At the outset of the insurance policies, the insurance company sets aside a reserve equal to the expected total payment plus two standard deviations. Calculate the amount of the reserve.

Question 5.6

A company prices its hurricane insurance using the following assumptions:

(i)   In any calendar year, there can be at most one hurricane.

(ii)   In any calendar year, the probability of a hurricane is 0.05.

(iii) The numbers of hurricanes in different years are independent.

Calculate the probability that there are fewer than 3 hurricanes in a 20-year period.

Question 5.7

A tour operator has a bus that can accommodate 20 tourists. The operator knows that tourists may not show up, so he sells 21 tickets. The probability that a tourist will not show up is 0.02, independent of all other tourists.

Each ticket costs 50, and is non-refundable if a tourist fails to show up. If a tourist shows up and a seat is not available, the operator has to pay 100 (ticket cost plus 50 penalty) to the tourist.

What is the expected revenue of the tour operator?

Question 5.8

The annual number of claims against an insurance policy is modeled using a negative binomial distribution with $r = 8$ and $p = 0.7$.

Calculate the probability that no more than two claims are filed against the policy during the next year

Question 5.9

The annual number of claims against a certain group insurance policy is modeled using a negative binomial distribution with mean 3 and variance 7.5.

Calculate the probability that exactly three claims occur over the next year.

Question 5.10

X follows a negative binomial distribution with parameters r and p. Using the moment generating function or otherwise, show that:

(i) $E[X] = \dfrac{rq}{p}$

(ii) $\mathrm{var}(X) = \dfrac{rq}{p^2}$

Question 5.11

A forestry company insures its machinery against accidental damage. The probability that one or more accidents will occur during any given month is 0.30. The numbers of accidents in different months are independent.

Calculate the probability that there will be at least three months in which no accidents occur before the third month in which at least one accident occurs.

Question 5.12

An experiment consists of five fair coins being tossed simultaneously. Repeated trials of the experiment are conducted until all five coins are heads. The outcome N is the number of trials required until all five coins are heads.

Calculate $\Pr(N \geq 20)$.

Question 5.13

Using the information in Question 5.3, calculate the expected number of football games to be played before the first game in which there are at least 4 injuries.

Question 5.14

Out of 20 trucks, 6 have engine problems. If 4 trucks are randomly selected for testing, calculate the probability that exactly 2 will have engine problems.

Question 5.15

An experiment consists of drawing 5 cards without replacement from a standard deck of 52 playing cards. Let X be the number of hearts among the 5 cards drawn. Calculate:

(i) $E[X]$

(ii) $\text{var}(X)$

(iii) $\Pr(X = 0)$

Question 5.16

The annual number of accidents that occur at a certain road junction is modeled using a Poisson distribution with mean 5.

Calculate the probability of exactly 3 accidents at the road junction in the next year.

Question 5.17

The number of hurricanes in Florida each year is modeled by a Poisson distribution with a mean of 2.8.

Determine the probability that there are at least 3 hurricanes in a particular year, given that there is at least 1 hurricane.

Question 5.18   *SOA/CAS*

An actuary has discovered that policyholders are three times as likely to file two claims as to file four claims.

If the number of claims filed has a Poisson distribution, what is the variance of the number of claims filed?

Question 5.19

A baseball team has scheduled its opening game for April 1. If it rains on April 1, the game is postponed and will be played on the next day that it does not rain.

The team purchases insurance against rain. The policy will pay 1,000 for each day, up to 2 days, that the opening game is postponed.

The insurance company determines that the number of consecutive days of rain beginning on April 1 is a Poisson random variable with mean 0.6.

What is the standard deviation of the amount the insurance company will have to pay?

Question 5.20

A random sample of size 4 is selected from the Poisson distribution with parameter λ. If $\overline{X}$ denotes the sample mean (*ie* the arithmetic average of the sample values), determine an expression for $\Pr(\overline{X} < 0.5)$ in terms of λ.

6

Common Continuous
Distributions

Overview

In this chapter we continue our study of important distributions by considering three families of continuous distributions: uniform, exponential, and gamma. Random variables that follow these distributions can take any value in an interval, often $[0, \infty)$.

In theoretical and practical actuarial applications these distributions are often used to model:

- the random amount of an insurance loss

- the random future lifetime of a person (*ie* until death) or a machine (*ie* until failure)

- the random time between particular unpredictable events, *eg* typhoons.

In addition, there are several other families of continuous distributions that can be used for these purposes, as well as the three just mentioned. We will give some examples of these towards the end of this chapter.

As for discrete distributions, we will need to choose a number of parameters in order to define fully each of these distributions. These parameters appear as factors in the formula for the probability density function, and consequently in all moment formulas of the distribution. The parameters give us the flexibility to distribute the probability over the possible numerical outcomes in a way that accurately reflects the uncertainty of the situation being modeled.

6.1 The uniform distribution

A random variable X follows the **uniform distribution** if it has a constant probability density function (pdf) on the interval $[a,b]$.

Since the area under the pdf must equal 1, we have:

$$f(x) = \frac{1}{b-a} \qquad \text{for } a \le x \le b$$

Notice that if $I = [c,d]$ is a subinterval of $[a,b]$, then the probability that the value of X falls within the interval I is proportional to its length:

$$\Pr(c \le X \le d) = \int_c^d f(x)\,dx = \frac{d-c}{b-a} = \frac{\text{length of } [c,d]}{\text{length of } [a,b]}$$

For example, if X is uniformly distributed on the interval $[0,1000]$, then the pdf of X is:

$$f(x) = \frac{1}{1,000-0} = 0.001 \qquad \text{for } 0 \le x \le 1,000$$

and the probability that X lies between 360 and 640 is:

$$\Pr(360 \le X \le 640) = \frac{640-360}{1,000-0} = 0.28$$

(Recall that when a random variable is continuous, the probability that it falls in an interval is the same whether the interval contains both of the endpoints, one endpoint, or neither endpoint. On the other hand, this distinction is important for discrete variables.)

Let's now derive the formula for the cumulative distribution function (cdf):

$$F(x) = \Pr(X \le x) = \int_a^x f(u)\,du = \int_a^x \frac{1}{b-a}\,du = \frac{x-a}{b-a} \qquad \text{for } a \le x \le b$$

We can see that this is a linear function. Of course, the cdf is equal to 0 when $X \le a$, and it is equal to 1 when $X \ge b$, since all of the probability is concentrated within the interval $[a,b]$.

Due to its very elementary pdf formula, moments of all orders are easily calculated for the uniform distribution:

$$E\left[X^k\right] = \int_a^b x^k f(x)\,dx = \int_a^b \frac{x^k}{b-a}\,dx = \left(\frac{x^{k+1}}{(k+1)(b-a)}\right)\Bigg|_a^b = \frac{b^{k+1}-a^{k+1}}{(k+1)(b-a)}$$

From this formula it follows that the expected value is the midpoint of $[a,b]$:

$$E[X] = \frac{b^2-a^2}{2(b-a)} = \frac{b+a}{2}$$

and the variance is:

$$\text{var}(X) = E\left[X^2\right] - (E[X])^2 = \frac{b^3-a^3}{3(b-a)} - \left(\frac{b+a}{2}\right)^2$$

$$= \frac{(b-a)^2}{12}$$

For example, if X is uniformly distributed on the interval $[0,1000]$, then we have:

$$E[X] = \frac{1,000 + 0}{2} = 500$$

$$\text{var}(X) = \frac{(1,000 - 0)^2}{12} = 83,333.33$$

Due to the constant pdf it is easy to see that the median is also the mid-point of the interval.

The uniform distribution

PDF: $f(x) = \dfrac{1}{b-a}$ for $a \leq x \leq b$, zero otherwise

CDF: $F(x) = \dfrac{x-a}{b-a}$ for $a \leq x \leq b$

Moments: $E[X] = \dfrac{b+a}{2}$

$$\text{var}(X) = \frac{(b-a)^2}{12}$$

Median: $m = \dfrac{b+a}{2}$

MGF: $M_X(t) = \dfrac{e^{bt} - e^{at}}{t(b-a)}$

Example 6.1

The random variable X is uniformly distributed on the interval $[20,160]$. Calculate the interquartile range of X.

Solution

The cumulative distribution function of X is:

$$F(x) = \frac{x-20}{160-20} \qquad \text{for } 20 \leq x \leq 160$$

The lower quartile, $x_{0.25}$, is calculated as:

$$0.25 = F(x_{0.25}) = \frac{x_{0.25} - 20}{160 - 20} \quad \Rightarrow \quad x_{0.25} = 55$$

The upper quartile, $x_{0.75}$, is calculated as:

$$0.75 = F(x_{0.75}) = \frac{x_{0.75} - 20}{160 - 20} \quad \Rightarrow \quad x_{0.75} = 125$$

Hence the interquartile range is:

$$x_{0.75} - x_{0.25} = 125 - 55 = 70$$

◆◆

Example 6.2

The amount charged for a visit to a dental clinic is uniformly distributed from 0 to 1,000. Given that the amount charged for a visit exceeds 500, compute the probability that it exceeds 750.

Solution

Let X be the amount charged. We require the conditional probability:

$$\Pr\left(X > 750 \mid X > 500\right) = \frac{\Pr\left(X > 750\right)}{\Pr\left(X > 500\right)}$$

Remember that the probability that X falls in an interval is proportional to its length. Hence:

$$\Pr\left(X > 750 \mid X > 500\right) = \frac{\Pr\left(X > 750\right)}{\Pr\left(X > 500\right)} = \frac{250/1,000}{500/1,000} = 0.5 \qquad \blacklozenge\blacklozenge$$

Example 6.3

The amount charged for a visit to a dental clinic is uniformly distributed from 0 to 1,000. Assume that the charges for different visits are independent.

An individual makes three visits to the clinic. Determine the range that is two standard deviations either side of the expected total charge for the three visits.

Solution

Let X_i be the amount charged on the i-th visit ($i = 1, 2, 3$).

For a single visit we have:

$$E[X_i] = \frac{1,000}{2} = 500$$

$$\text{var}(X_i) = \frac{1,000^2}{12} = 83,333.33$$

Let X be the total amount charged, *ie* $X = X_1 + X_2 + X_3$.

Then, by independence, we have:

$$E[X] = E[X_1 + X_2 + X_3] = E[X_1] + E[X_2] + E[X_3] = 3 \times 500 = 1,500$$

$$\text{var}(X) = \text{var}[X_1 + X_2 + X_3] = \text{var}[X_1] + \text{var}[X_2] + \text{var}[X_3] = 3 \times 83,333.33 = 250,000$$

Hence the standard deviation of X is:

$$\sigma_X = \sqrt{\text{var}(X)} = 500$$

and the range that is two standard deviations either side of the expected total charge is:

$$\left[E[X] - 2\sigma_X, E[X] + 2\sigma_X\right] = [500, 2500] \qquad \blacklozenge\blacklozenge$$

6.2   *The exponential distribution*

A random variable X follows the **exponential distribution** with parameter $\theta > 0$ if it has a probability density function equal to:

$$f(x) = \frac{1}{\theta}\, e^{-x/\theta} \qquad \text{for } x > 0$$

The pdf of an exponential distribution with $\theta = 20$ is shown in Figure 6.1 below.

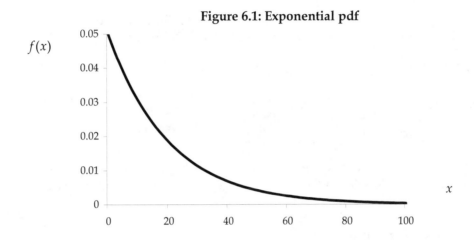

Figure 6.1: Exponential pdf

The cdf of the exponential distribution is:

$$F(x) = \Pr\left(X \le x\right) = \int_0^x \frac{1}{\theta} e^{-u/\theta}\, du = 1 - e^{-x/\theta} \qquad \text{for } x > 0$$

The moments can be easily derived using the moment generating function:

$$M(t) = E\left[e^{tX}\right] = \frac{1}{1-\theta t} \qquad \text{for } t < 1/\theta$$

The expected value is:

$$E[X] = M_X'(0) = \theta$$

and the variance is calculated as:

$$E\left[X^2\right] = M_X''(0) = 2\theta^2 \quad \Rightarrow \quad \text{var}(X) = E\left[X^2\right] - \left(E[X]\right)^2 = \theta^2$$

 Example 6.4

The mean lifetime of a light bulb is 1,000 hours. The lifetime is assumed to follow an exponential distribution. Determine the probability that a bulb will function for at least 500 hours.

Solution

Let X be the lifetime of a bulb. Since the mean is 1,000, we have $E[X] = \theta = 1,000$. Hence the probability that a bulb will function for at least 500 hours is:

$$\Pr\left(X > 500\right) = 1 - F\left(500\right) = 1 - \left(1 - e^{-500/1,000}\right) = e^{-0.5} = 0.60653 \qquad \blacklozenge\blacklozenge$$

The exponential distribution has a **memoryless property**. For any x_0 we have:

$$\Pr(X > x_0 + x \mid X > x_0) = \frac{\Pr(X > x_0 + x)}{\Pr(X > x_0)} = \frac{1 - F(x_0 + x)}{1 - F(x_0)}$$

$$= \frac{e^{-(x_0 + x)/\theta}}{e^{-x_0/\theta}} = e^{-x/\theta}$$

$$= \Pr(X > x)$$

Example 6.5

Using the information in Example 6.4, calculate the probability that a bulb will function for a further 500 hours, given that it has already functioned for 1,000 hours.

Solution

Using the memoryless property, we have:

$$\Pr(X > 1,500 \mid X > 1,000) = \Pr(X > 500) = 1 - \left(1 - e^{-500/1,000}\right) = e^{-0.5} = 0.60653$$

Note: A bulb that is 1,000 hours old has the same chance of surviving a further 500 hours of use as a brand new bulb. The bulb has "forgotten" its age (hence the term "memoryless"). ♦♦

The exponential distribution

PDF: $\qquad\qquad\qquad f(x) = \dfrac{1}{\theta} e^{-x/\theta} \qquad$ for $x > 0$, $\theta > 0$

CDF: $\qquad\qquad\qquad F(x) = 1 - e^{-x/\theta}$

Moments: $\qquad\qquad E[X] = \theta \qquad\qquad \text{var}(X) = \theta^2$

Median: $\qquad\qquad\quad m = \theta \ln(2)$

MGF: $\qquad\qquad\qquad M(t) = \dfrac{1}{1 - \theta t} \qquad$ for $t < 1/\theta$

Memoryless property: $\Pr(X > x_0 + x \mid X > x_0) = \Pr(X > x)$

Note: Some textbooks use slightly different notation for the exponential distribution, with the pdf defined as:

$$f(x) = \beta e^{-\beta x} \qquad \text{for } x > 0$$

The connection between the two notational schemes is $\beta = 1/\theta$. Hence:

$$E[X] = \frac{1}{\beta} \qquad\qquad \text{var}(X) = \frac{1}{\beta^2}$$

Example 6.6

The pdf for a random loss amount is given by:

$$f(x) = ce^{-0.004x} \quad \text{for } x > 0$$

Determine the expected loss amount.

Solution

The pdf is from the exponential family.

Using our standard notation, we have:

$$f(x) = \frac{e^{-x/\theta}}{\theta} = ce^{-0.004x}$$

$$\Rightarrow c = \frac{1}{\theta} = 0.004 \quad \Rightarrow \quad E[X] = \theta = \frac{1}{0.004} = 250$$

Using the alternative notation, we have:

$$f(x) = \beta e^{-\beta x} = ce^{-0.004x}$$

$$\Rightarrow c = \beta = 0.004 \quad \Rightarrow \quad E[X] = \frac{1}{\beta} = 250 \qquad \blacklozenge\blacklozenge$$

Example 6.7

The lifetime of an electrical component follows an exponential distribution. The median lifetime of a component is 1,000 hours. Calculate the probability that a component operates for more than 2,000 hours.

Solution

The first step is to use the median formula to determine the value of the parameter:

$$1,000 = m = \theta \ln(2)$$

$$\Rightarrow \theta = \frac{1,000}{\ln(2)}$$

The required probability is:

$$\Pr(X > 2,000) = 1 - F(2,000)$$

$$= 1 - \left(1 - e^{-2,000/\theta}\right) = 1 - \left(1 - e^{-2\ln(2)}\right)$$

$$= e^{-2\ln(2)} = e^{\ln(0.25)} = 0.25 \qquad \blacklozenge\blacklozenge$$

Example 6.8

The random variable X is exponentially distributed with mean θ. Determine the third central moment of X.

Solution

The third moment is calculated using the moment generating function as:

$$M(t) = \frac{1}{1-\theta t} \;\Rightarrow\; M'''(t) = \frac{3!\theta^3}{(1-\theta t)^4} \;\Rightarrow\; E\left[X^3\right] = M'''(0) = 6\theta^3$$

Hence we have:

$$E\left[(X-\theta)^3\right] = E\left[X^3 - 3\theta X^2 + 3\theta^2 X - \theta^3\right] = E\left[X^3\right] - 3\theta E\left[X^2\right] + 3\theta^2 E[X] - \theta^3$$

$$= 6\theta^3 - 3\theta\left(2\theta^2\right) + 3\theta^2(\theta) - \theta^3$$

$$= 2\theta^3 \qquad\qquad \blacklozenge\blacklozenge$$

Finally, there is an important link between the exponential distribution and the Poisson distribution (which we studied in Chapter 5). We will not consider this topic in depth here. However, we will state the fundamental properties and their consequences.

Let's start by defining a **Poisson process**. A Poisson process is a model for the occurrence of "rare" events over an extended period of time. The fundamental assumptions are as follows:

- The number of events occurring in any time period of duration t follows a Poisson distribution with parameter λt.

- The numbers of events that occur in disjoint time periods are independent.

Let T_k be the random time at which the k-th event occurs. A **waiting time** is defined as the random time between consecutive events. The waiting time W_k is the waiting time between the $(k-1)$-th event and the k-th event, *ie*:

$$W_k = T_k - T_{k-1}$$

Then it follows from the basic assumptions of the Poisson process that each waiting time W_i follows an exponential distribution with mean $\theta = 1/\lambda$.

To see why this is true, let $N(t)$ be the number of events by time t. We know that $N(t)$ follows a Poisson distribution with parameter λt. Then the probability that the waiting time until the first event exceeds some value w is:

$$\Pr\left(W_1 > w\right) = \Pr\left(N(w) = 0\right) = e^{-\lambda w}$$

Hence, we have:

$$F_{W_1}(w) = \Pr\left(W_1 \le w\right) = 1 - \Pr\left(W_1 > w\right) = 1 - e^{-\lambda w}$$

$$\Rightarrow f_{W_1}(w) = F'_{W_1}(w) = \lambda e^{-\lambda w}$$

This is an exponential pdf where $\theta = 1/\lambda$.

6.3   *The gamma distribution*

The **gamma distribution** has two parameters, α and θ, which are both positive. The probability density function is defined as:

$$f(x) = \frac{x^{\alpha-1} e^{-x/\theta}}{\theta^{\alpha} \Gamma(\alpha)} \qquad \text{for } x > 0, \; \alpha > 0, \; \theta > 0$$

The gamma function $\Gamma(\alpha)$ in the denominator of this expression deserves some explanation.

Setting $\theta = 1$, we have:

$$f(x) = \frac{x^{\alpha-1} e^{-x}}{\Gamma(\alpha)}$$

Since this pdf must integrate to 1, we have:

$$\Gamma(\alpha) = \int_0^{\infty} x^{\alpha-1} e^{-x} \, dx$$

Setting $\alpha = 1$, we have:

$$\Gamma(1) = \int_0^{\infty} e^{-x} \, dx = 1$$

It is easy to derive the following recursive relation with integration by parts:

$$\Gamma(\alpha) = (\alpha-1)\Gamma(\alpha-1)$$

From these two facts, it then follows that for any positive integer n:

$$\Gamma(n) = (n-1)!$$

On the other hand, an expression such as $\Gamma(5.01)$ defies exact calculation, and must be approximated numerically.

The shape of the pdf depends on the chosen value of α. In Figure 6.2 below, the black line represents the gamma pdf with parameters $\alpha = 4, \theta = 1$. The gray line represents the gamma pdf with parameters $\alpha = 1, \theta = 1$.

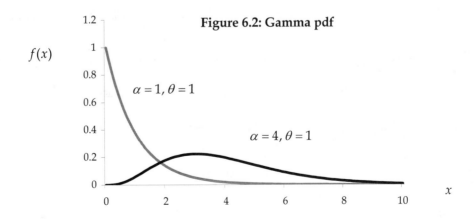

The parameter α determines the shape of the pdf, while the parameter θ determines it scale.

It is only possible to obtain a compact formula for the cdf of the gamma distribution in the case that α is a positive integer. When this is true, we have:

$$F_X(x) = 1 - e^{-x/\theta}\left(1 + \frac{x/\theta}{1!} + \frac{(x/\theta)^2}{2!} + \cdots + \frac{(x/\theta)^{\alpha-1}}{(\alpha-1)!}\right)$$

Since the cdf has a factor that is a product of an exponential and a polynomial, percentiles cannot be easily calculated, even in the case that α is a positive integer.

The moment generating function is:

$$M_X(t) = \frac{1}{(1-\theta t)^\alpha}$$

Hence we can derive the mean:

$$E[X] = M_X'(0) = \alpha\theta$$

and variance:

$$E\left[X^2\right] = \alpha(\alpha+1)\theta^2 \quad \Rightarrow \quad \text{var}(X) = \alpha\theta^2$$

The gamma distribution

PDF:
$$f(x) = \frac{x^{\alpha-1}e^{-x/\theta}}{\theta^\alpha\,\Gamma(\alpha)} \quad \text{for } x > 0,\ \alpha > 0,\ \theta > 0$$

CDF:
$$F(x) = 1 - e^{-x/\theta}\left(1 + \frac{x/\theta}{1!} + \frac{(x/\theta)^2}{2!} + \cdots + \frac{(x/\theta)^{\alpha-1}}{(\alpha-1)!}\right) \quad \text{for } x > 0,\ \alpha \in \mathbb{Z}^+$$

Moments:
$$E[X] = \alpha\theta \qquad \text{var}(X) = \alpha\theta^2$$

MGF:
$$M(t) = \frac{1}{(1-\theta t)^\alpha}$$

Additive property: If $\{X_i\}$ is a family of independent, gamma distributed variables with parameters α_i and θ, then $\sum X_i$ is gamma distributed with parameters $\sum \alpha_i$ and θ.

The additive property can be shown using the moment generating function:

$$M_{\sum X_i}(t) = \prod M_{X_i}(t) = \prod (1-\theta t)^{-\alpha_i} = (1-\theta t)^{-\sum \alpha_i}$$

Hence, $\sum X_i$ follows a gamma distribution with parameters $\sum \alpha_i$ and θ.

Example 6.9

Determine the formula for the pdf of a gamma variable with mean 10 and variance 50.

Solution

First, we need to determine the value of the parameters α and θ.

$$E[X] = \alpha\theta = 10$$

$$\text{var}(X) = \alpha\theta^2 = 50$$

$$\Rightarrow \quad \theta = \frac{\text{var}(X)}{E[X]} = 5 \quad \Rightarrow \quad \alpha = 2$$

The pdf is:

$$f(x) = \frac{x^{2-1}e^{-x/5}}{5^2\Gamma(2)} = \frac{xe^{-x/5}}{25} \quad \text{for } x > 0 \qquad\qquad \blacklozenge\blacklozenge$$

Example 6.10

A random variable has a pdf of the form:

$$f(x) = cx^3 e^{-0.1x} \quad \text{for } x > 0$$

Determine the value of c.

Solution

The pdf must belong to the gamma family of distributions, since it is a multiple of an exponential and a power of x. To find the parameters, we need to compare the given pdf with the general formula:

$$x^3 = x^{\alpha-1} \quad \Rightarrow \quad \alpha = 4$$

$$e^{-0.1x} = e^{-x/\theta} \quad \Rightarrow \quad \theta = 10$$

As a result, we have:

$$c = \frac{1}{\theta^\alpha \Gamma(\alpha)} = \frac{1}{10^4 \Gamma(4)} = \frac{1}{10^4\, 3!} = \frac{1}{60,000} \qquad\qquad \blacklozenge\blacklozenge$$

The exponential distribution and gamma distribution are closely related. In fact, the exponential distribution is a special case of the gamma distribution with $\alpha = 1$. With this in mind, you might like to look over the summary of the gamma distribution, setting $\alpha = 1$ in each case.

We can also use the additive property of the gamma distribution to state a similar result for the exponential distribution.

If $X_1, X_2, \cdots, X_k$ are independent, exponentially distributed variables each with parameter θ, then $\sum X_i$ follows a gamma distribution with parameters $\alpha = k$ and θ.

As we saw with the exponential distribution, there is a link between the gamma distribution and the Poisson process. Gamma distributions occur naturally as the distribution of the times at which events occur in a Poisson process with rate λ, such as the number of claims against a policy or portfolio of policies. The time of the k-th event follows a gamma distribution with $\alpha = k$ and $\theta = 1/\lambda$.

Example 6.11

An actuary models the occurrence of claims from a portfolio of insurance policies. The time until the occurrence of the second claim is modeled by a gamma distribution with mean 10 and variance 50. Given that this time exceeds 10, determine the probability that it exceeds 20.

Solution

From Example 6.9, the parameter values are $\alpha = 2$ and $\theta = 5$. The required probability is:

$$\Pr(X > 20 | X > 10) = \frac{\Pr(X > 20)}{\Pr(X > 10)} = \frac{1 - F(20)}{1 - F(10)}$$

The cdf is given by:

$$F(x) = 1 - e^{-x/5}\left(1 + \frac{x}{5}\right) \Rightarrow F(10) = 0.5940, \ F(20) = 0.9084$$

Hence the probability is:

$$\Pr(X > 20 | X > 10) = \frac{1 - 0.9084}{1 - 0.5940} = 0.2256$$

◆◆

Example 6.12

At a certain industrial facility there have been 12 accidents in the last 15 months of operation. It is decided to model the time between accidents by an exponential distribution with mean 15/12 months. The times between accidents are assumed to be independent. Determine the probability that two or more accidents occur in the next month.

Solution

Let W_i denote the time between accidents. It is assumed to follow an exponential distribution with mean $\theta = 15/12 = 1.25$ months. The time of the second accident is:

$$T_2 = W_1 + W_2$$

By the additive property, T_2 follows a gamma distribution with parameters $\alpha = 2$ and $\theta = 1.25$.

The crucial idea here is that the occurrence of 2 or more accidents in the next month is equivalent to $T_2 \leq 1$. The probability of this event can be computed from the cdf of T_2:

$$F_{T_2}(t) = 1 - e^{-t/\theta}\left(1 + \frac{t}{\theta}\right)$$

$$\Rightarrow \Pr(T_2 \leq 1) = 1 - e^{-1/1.25}\left(1 + \frac{1}{1.25}\right) = 0.1912$$

◆◆

6.4   *Examples using other continuous distributions*

There are many other families of continuous distributions that can be used for the purposes set out at the start of this chapter. Provided we are given appropriate information about the distribution, such as its pdf or cdf, then we can calculate probabilities and moments as required from first principles.

Example 6.13

A random insurance loss X has pdf:

$$f(x) = \frac{2(10)^{10}}{(100,000+x)^3} \quad \text{where } x > 0$$

Calculate the probability that the loss exceeds 50,000.

Solution

The probability that the loss exceeds 50,000 is:

$$\Pr(X > 50,000) = 2(10)^{10} \int_{50,000}^{\infty} (100,000+x)^{-3}\, dx$$

$$= -(10)^{10}(100,000+x)^{-2}\Big|_{50,000}^{\infty} = (10)^{10}\left[\frac{1}{(150,000)^2} - 0\right] = \frac{4}{9} \qquad \blacklozenge\blacklozenge$$

Example 6.14

A random insurance loss X has cdf:

$$F(x) = 1 - \left(\frac{300,000}{x+300,000}\right)^{2.5} \qquad \text{where } x > 0$$

Calculate the expected loss amount.

Solution

First we need the pdf. This is:

$$f(x) = \frac{d}{dx}F(x) = -(300,000)^{2.5}\frac{d}{dx}(x+300,000)^{-2.5} = 2.5(300,000)^{2.5}(x+300,000)^{-3.5}$$

The expected loss amount is:

$$E[X] = \int_0^{\infty} x\, f(x)\, dx = 2.5(300,000)^{2.5}\int_0^{\infty} x(x+300,000)^{-3.5}\, dx$$

$$= (300,000)^{2.5}\left[-x(x+300,000)^{-2.5}\Big|_0^{\infty} + \int_0^{\infty}(x+300,000)^{-2.5}\, dx\right] = 200,000$$

(integrating by parts). $\qquad\qquad\blacklozenge\blacklozenge$

Example 6.15

Calculate the median of the distribution given in Example 6.14.

Solution

Using the given cdf, the median value of X is $x_{0.5}$, where:

$$F(x_{0.5}) = 0.5$$

$$\Rightarrow \left(\frac{300,000}{x_{0.5} + 300,000} \right)^{2.5} = 0.5$$

$$\Rightarrow \frac{300,000}{x_{0.5} + 300,000} = (0.5)^{0.4}$$

$$\Rightarrow x_{0.5} = 300,000 \left[(0.5)^{-0.4} - 1 \right] = 95,852$$

◆◆

Example 6.16

Calculate the standard deviation of the distribution given in Example 6.14.

Solution

We need σ_X where:

$$\sigma_X^2 = \text{var}[X] = E\left[X^2\right] - \left(E[X]\right)^2$$

From Example 6.14 we know that $E[X] = 200,000$ and we know $f(x)$, and so we can calculate:

$$E\left[X^2\right] = \int_0^\infty x^2 \, f(x) \, dx = 2.5(300,000)^{2.5} \int_0^\infty x^2 \, (x + 300,000)^{-3.5} \, dx$$

Integrating by parts (twice) we find that:

$$E\left[X^2\right] = \frac{2}{(1.5)(0.5)}(300,00)^2$$

and so:

$$\sigma_X = \left(\frac{2}{(1.5)(0.5)}(300,00)^2 - (200,000)^2 \right)^{0.5} = 447,214$$

◆◆

Example 6.17

The pdf for a random loss amount is proportional to:

$$xe^{-0.0016x^2} \qquad \text{for } x > 0$$

Calculate the probability that the loss exceeds 25.

Solution

We know that:

$$f(x) = kxe^{-0.0016x^2} \qquad \text{for } x > 0$$

where k is some constant. To find k we use:

$$\int_0^\infty f(x)\,dx = 1 \Rightarrow k\int_0^\infty xe^{-0.0016x^2}\,dx = 1$$

Now:

$$\int_a^b u'(x)e^{u(x)}\,dx = e^{u(x)}\Big|_a^b$$

so:

$$1 = \frac{k}{-0.0032}\int_0^\infty (-0.0032)xe^{-0.0016x^2}\,dx = -\frac{ke^{-0.0016x^2}}{0.0032}\Bigg|_0^\infty = \frac{k}{0.0032} \Rightarrow k = 0.0032$$

The we need:

$$\Pr(X > 25) = \int_{25}^\infty 0.0032e^{-0.0016x^2}\,dx = -e^{-0.0016x^2}\Big|_0^\infty = e^{-1} = 0.3679 \qquad \blacklozenge\blacklozenge$$

Example 6.18

The random variable X has pdf:

$$f(x) = 12x(1-x)^2 \qquad \text{where } 0 \le x \le 1$$

Calculate the expected value of X.

Solution

We need:

$$E[X] = 12\int_0^1 x^2(1-x)^2\,dx$$

$$= 12\int_0^1 \left(x^2 - 2x^3 + x^4\right)dx = 12\left(\frac{x^3}{3} - \frac{2x^4}{4} + \frac{x^5}{5}\right)\Bigg|_0^1 = 12\left(\frac{1}{3} - \frac{1}{2} + \frac{1}{5}\right) = 0.4 \qquad \blacklozenge\blacklozenge$$

Example 6.19

The random fraction of healthy employees in a large group of employees follows a distribution with a pdf of $f(x) = cx^9$ for $0 \le x \le 1$. Determine the expected fraction of healthy employees.

Solution

First we need to find c from:

$$1 = \int_0^1 f(x)\,dx = c\int_0^1 x^9\,dx = c\left.\frac{x^{10}}{10}\right|_0^1 = \frac{c}{10} \Rightarrow c = 10$$

Then we need:

$$E[X] = \int_0^1 x\,f(x)\,dx = 10\int_0^1 x^{10}\,dx = 10\left.\frac{x^{11}}{11}\right|_0^1 = \frac{10}{11}$$

♦♦

Chapter 6 Practice Questions

Free online solutions manual

You can download detailed worked solutions to every practice question in this book free of charge from the BPP Professional Education website at **www.bpptraining.com**. Select support for the SOA/CAS exams and click on the Probability (P) home page. You'll also find other useful study resources here.

Question 6.1

In a small metropolitan area, annual losses due to storm, fire, and theft are assumed to be independent uniformly distributed random variables on the respective intervals $[0,2]$, $[0,3]$, and $[0,4]$. Determine the probability that the maximum of these losses exceeds 2.5.

Question 6.2

A sawmill produces planks for decking. The length of each plank (in millimeters) is distributed uniformly on the range $[a,b]$. If the expected length is 1,879, and the variance of the length is 507, calculate the values of a and b.

Question 6.3

Determine the 90th percentile of a distribution that has the following pdf:

$$f(x) = \frac{375}{(x+5)^4} \qquad \text{for } x > 0$$

Question 6.4   SOA/CAS

A loss for an individual policyholder, X, follows a distribution whose density function is given by:

$$f(x) = \frac{3 \times 2,000^3}{(x+2,000)^4} \qquad \text{for } x > 0$$

Calculate the expected loss for the policyholder.

Question 6.5   SOA/CAS

An insurance company insures a large number of homes. The insured value, X, of a randomly selected home is assumed to follow a distribution function with density function:

$$f(x) = \begin{cases} 3x^{-4} & \text{for } x > 1 \\ 0 & \text{otherwise} \end{cases}$$

Given that a randomly selected home is insured for at least 1.5, what is the probability that it is insured for less than 2?

Question 6.6

The lifetime (in years) of a solar power cell has a pdf of the form:

$$f(x) = \frac{c}{x^4} \quad \text{where } x > 3$$

Determine the expected lifetime.

Question 6.7 IOA/FOA

Claim sizes are modeled by an exponential distribution with mean 50. Calculate the probability that an individual claim exceeds 200 given that it exceeds 50.

Question 6.8 SOA/CAS

The number of days that elapse between the beginning of a calendar year and the moment a high-risk driver is involved in an accident is exponentially distributed. An insurance company expects that 30% of high-risk drivers will be involved in an accident during the first 50 days of a calendar year.

What portion of high-risk drivers is expected to be involved in an accident during the first 80 days of a calendar year?

Question 6.9

When a machine breaks down there are labor costs and additional costs for replacement parts.

Labor costs 75 per hour. Labor time per breakdown is assumed to be exponentially distributed with a mean time of 2 hours.

The cost of replacement parts per breakdown is modeled by a gamma distribution with mean 100 and variance 5,000.

These two cost components are assumed to be independent. The total cost per breakdown is the sum of these two components.

For a given breakdown, determine the probability that the required labor exceeds three hours or the cost of parts exceeds 150.

Question 6.10 SOA/CAS

You are given the following information about N, the annual number of claims for a randomly selected insured:

$$\Pr(N = 0) = \tfrac{1}{2}$$

$$\Pr(N = 1) = \tfrac{1}{3}$$

$$\Pr(N > 1) = \tfrac{1}{6}$$

Let S denote the total annual claim amount for an insured. When $N = 1$, S is exponentially distributed with mean 5. When $N > 1$, S is exponentially distributed with mean 8.

Determine $\Pr(4 < S < 8)$.

Question 6.11   *IOA/FOA*

The number of accidents in a factory is represented by a Poisson distribution averaging 2 accidents per 5 days. Calculate the probability that the time from one accident to the next exceeds 3 days.

Question 6.12

The random variable X is defined by the pdf:

$$f(x) = cx^5 e^{-0.01x} \qquad \text{for } x > 0$$

Calculate the mean of X.

Question 6.13

The time until the arrival of the third claim in a claims process is modeled by a gamma distribution with mean 15 and variance 75.

Given that this time exceeds 15, determine the probability that it exceeds 30.

Question 6.14   *IOA/FOA*

The moment generating function of X is:

$$M_X(t) = \frac{1}{(1-3t)^2}$$

Calculate the variance of X.

Question 6.15

If X follows a gamma distribution with parameters α and θ, show that the skewness of X is:

$$2/\sqrt{\alpha}$$

Hint: Use the cumulant generating function.

Question 6.16

X is the lifetime, in years, of a telecommunications satellite. X has pdf:

$$f(x) = \frac{2^{1.25}}{0.8x^{2.25}} \qquad \text{where } x > 1.25$$

Calculate the probability that the lifetime of the satellite exceeds 10 years.

Question 6.17

The k-th moment of the distribution of the random variable X is given by:

$$E\left[X^k\right] = 10^k \Gamma(1+4k)$$

Calculate the mean and variance of X.

Question 6.18

The random variable X is defined by the pdf:

$$f(x) = cx^2 e^{-4x^3} \qquad \text{for } x > 0$$

Calculate $\Pr(X > 0.5)$.

Question 6.19

The random proportion of accidents at a certain intersection that are fatal each year, X, is assumed to follow a distribution with pdf:

$$f(x) = 7(1-x)^6 \qquad \text{for } 0 \le x \le 1$$

Determine the median of X.

Question 6.20

The fraction X of defective fuses in a large batch of fuses has pdf:

$$f(x) = c(1-x)^8 \qquad \text{for } 0 \le x \le 1$$

If there are 10,000 fuses in the batch, calculate the expected number of these fuses that will be defective.

7

The Normal Distribution

Overview

The fact that we devote a full chapter of this book to the normal distribution should tell you something about the importance of this continuous distribution. It is significant on two levels:

- Many random variables observed in practice (*eg* students' test scores, the weight of adults, the size of measurement errors) closely follow the normal distribution.

- The Central Limit Theorem (which we discuss in Section 7.3) is a very powerful result that allows us to use the normal distribution in a wide range of circumstances as an approximation to other distributions.

7.1   *The normal distribution*

The **normal distribution** is a continuous distribution with two parameters: μ and σ. The probability density function is equal to:

$$f(x) = \frac{1}{\sigma\sqrt{2\pi}} \exp\left[-\frac{(x-\mu)^2}{2\sigma^2}\right] \qquad \text{for } -\infty < x < \infty$$

This seemingly complex formula produces a symmetric pdf with a distinctive shape sometimes referred to as a *bell-curve*. Figure 7.1 shows the normal pdf with $\mu = 10, \sigma = 2$.

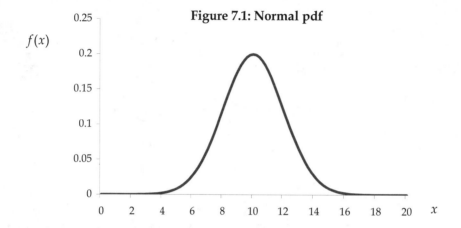

Figure 7.1: Normal pdf

The parameter μ is the mean of the distribution, and it determines the location (or center) of the pdf. The parameter μ can take any real number.

The parameter σ is the standard deviation of the distribution, and it can take any positive real number. This parameter determines the shape of the pdf. A normal distribution with a greater standard deviation (and hence a greater variance) has a flatter curve, because there is a greater chance of observing values far away from the mean. In contrast, a normal distribution with a lower standard deviation (and hence a lower variance) has a more pointed curve, because there is a lower chance of observing values far away from the mean.

This is illustrated in Figure 7.2 below, in which we show the pdf of a normal distribution with $\mu = 10$, $\sigma = 1.5$ (the black line) and the flatter pdf of a normal distribution with $\mu = 10$, $\sigma = 3$ (the gray line).

Figure 7.2: Normal pdfs with different standard deviations

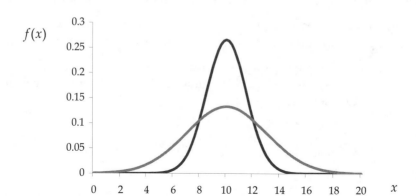

The cdf of the normal distribution is:

$$F(x) = \Pr(X \le x) = \int_{-\infty}^{x} f(s)\,ds = \int_{-\infty}^{x} \frac{1}{\sigma\sqrt{2\pi}}\ \exp\left[-\frac{(s-\mu)^2}{2\sigma^2}\right]ds \qquad \text{for}\ -\infty < x < \infty$$

This is simple enough to write, but it cannot be solved algebraically, and numerical techniques must be used to evaluate the distribution function. In practice, the process is simplified by the use of statistical tables and modern calculators.

Most statistical tables include a table of values of the cdf of a **standard normal distribution**, that is a normal distribution with parameters $\mu = 0$, $\sigma = 1$.

The pdf of the standard normal distribution is written $\phi(x)$, and is equal to:

$$\phi(x) = \frac{1}{\sqrt{2\pi}}\ \exp\left(-\frac{x^2}{2}\right) \qquad \text{for}\ -\infty < x < \infty$$

The cdf of the standard normal distribution is written $\Phi(x)$, and is equal to:

$$\Phi(x) = \int_{-\infty}^{x} \phi(s)\,ds = \int_{-\infty}^{x} \frac{1}{\sqrt{2\pi}}\ \exp\left(-\frac{s^2}{2}\right)ds \qquad \text{for}\ -\infty < x < \infty$$

The following table shows the value of $\Phi(x)$ for a range of values of x, from 0 to 4. The column title shows the integer part of x, and the row title shows the non-integer part of x.

Table 7.1 Standard normal distribution cdf

	0	1	2	3
0	0.5000	0.8413	0.9772	0.9987
0.1	0.5398	0.8643	0.9821	0.9990
0.2	0.5793	0.8849	0.9861	0.9993
0.3	0.6179	0.9032	0.9893	0.9995
0.4	0.6554	0.9192	0.9918	0.9997
0.5	0.6915	0.9332	0.9938	0.9998
0.6	0.7257	0.9452	0.9953	0.9998
0.7	0.7580	0.9554	0.9965	0.9999
0.8	0.7881	0.9641	0.9974	0.9999
0.9	0.8159	0.9713	0.9981	1.0000

For example, if X follows a normal distribution with parameters $\mu = 0$, $\sigma = 1$, we have:

$$\Pr(X \le 1.2) = \Phi(1.2) = 0.8849$$

This value is found from the table using the column titled 1 and the row titled 0.2.

Similarly, we have:

$$\Pr(X \le 2.8) = \Phi(2.8) = 0.9974$$

Note: Recall that $\Pr(X \le x) = \Pr(X < x)$ for a continuous random variable X, so we also have $\Pr(X < 1.2) = 0.8849$ and $\Pr(X < 2.8) = 0.9974$.

The symmetrical nature of the pdf allows us to calculate $\Phi(x)$ for $x < 0$ as follows:

$$\Pr(X \le x) = 1 - \Pr(X > x) = 1 - \Pr(X \ge x) = 1 - \Pr(X \le -x)$$

$$\Rightarrow \Phi(x) = 1 - \Phi(-x)$$

For example:

$$\Pr(X \le -0.7) = \Phi(-0.7) = 1 - \Phi(0.7) = 1 - 0.7580 = 0.2420$$

Example 7.1

The random variable X follows the standard normal distribution. Calculate the following:

(i) $\Pr(X > 1.1)$

(ii) $\Pr(X < -2.4)$

(iii) $\Pr(0.3 < X < 0.7)$

(iv) $\Pr(-1 < X < 1)$

Solution

(i) $\Pr(X > 1.1) = 1 - \Pr(X < 1.1) = 1 - \Phi(1.1) = 1 - 0.8643 = 0.1357$

(ii) $\Pr(X < -2.4) = \Phi(-2.4) = 1 - \Phi(2.4) = 1 - 0.9918 = 0.0082$

(iii) $\Pr(0.3 < X < 0.7) = \Phi(0.7) - \Phi(0.3) = 0.7580 - 0.6179 = 0.1401$

(iv) $\Pr(-1 < X < 1) = \Phi(1) - \Phi(-1) = \Phi(1) - [1 - \Phi(1)] = 2\Phi(1) - 1 = 2 \times 0.8413 - 1 = 0.6826$ ♦♦

We can use Table 7.1 to see how the probability falls within 1, 2, 3, and 4 standard deviations of the mean of a standard normal distribution. As we can see from Figure 7.3 below, the probability that X takes a value within one standard deviation of the mean, *ie* in the interval $(-1,1)$, is around 68%. And there is a 95% chance that X takes a value within two standard deviations of the mean, *ie* in the interval $(-2,2)$.

Figure 7.3: Standard normal probabilities

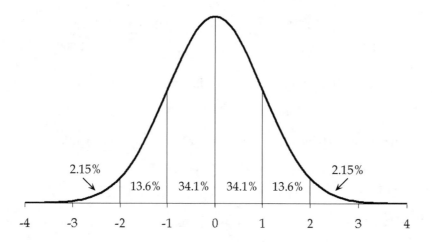

We've looked at the values of the cdf for the standard normal distribution, but what use is this if the random variable of interest has a normal distribution with parameters of, say, $\mu = 20, \sigma = 15$? This is a critically important question that we will cover in much more detail in Section 7.2. For now though, let's work through the remainder of the basic properties of the normal distribution.

As we've already noted, the parameters μ and σ are the mean and standard deviation of the distribution respectively, *ie*:

$$E[X] = \mu$$

$$\text{var}(X) = \sigma^2$$

These results can also be proved easily from the moment generating function of the normal distribution:

$$M_X(t) = \exp\left(\mu t + \frac{\sigma^2 t^2}{2} \right)$$

These proofs are included in the questions at the end of this chapter.

The moment generating function of the standard normal distribution is therefore:

$$M(t) = \exp\left(\frac{t^2}{2} \right)$$

From the symmetric bell-shaped curve of the pdf, it is also simple to identify that the median and the mode of the normal distribution are both equal to μ.

Finally, in order to specify a normal distribution fully, we need to specify the values of the parameters μ and σ, and there is useful notation for doing so. In this book, we will write:

$$X \sim N\left(\mu, \sigma^2 \right)$$

to mean that the random variable X is normally distributed with mean μ and variance σ^2.

The normal distribution

PDF:	$f(x) = \dfrac{1}{\sigma\sqrt{2\pi}} \exp\left[-\dfrac{(x-\mu)^2}{2\sigma^2} \right] \qquad$ for $-\infty < x < \infty$
CDF:	Must be calculated numerically or from statistical tables
Moments:	$E[X] = \mu$ $\text{var}(X) = \sigma^2$
Median, mode:	Median = Mode = μ
MGF:	$M_X(t) = \exp\left(\mu t + \dfrac{\sigma^2 t^2}{2} \right)$

7.2　*Properties of the normal distribution*

In Chapter 4, we looked in general at how to calculate probabilities and moments of functions of random variables. In this section we'll explore some very powerful properties of the normal distribution by considering various functions of normally distributed random variables, which we will present through a series of theorems. We'll focus not only on the proof of each result, but also the important practical implications.

Theorem 7.1

If $X \sim N\left(\mu, \sigma^2\right)$ and $Z = \dfrac{X - \mu}{\sigma}$, then $Z \sim N(0,1)$.

Proof

We are asked to prove that Z follows a standard normal distribution. We can do so by considering the cdf of Z.

$$F_Z(z) = \Pr(Z \le z) = \Pr\left(\frac{X - \mu}{\sigma} \le z\right) = \Pr(X \le z\sigma + \mu)$$

Hence:

$$F_Z(z) = \int\limits_{-\infty}^{z\sigma + \mu} f_X(x)\, dx = \int\limits_{-\infty}^{z\sigma + \mu} \frac{1}{\sigma\sqrt{2\pi}}\, \exp\left[-\frac{(x - \mu)^2}{2\sigma^2}\right] dx$$

Substituting $s = \dfrac{x - \mu}{\sigma}$, the upper limit on the integral changes to $\dfrac{(z\sigma + \mu) - \mu}{\sigma} = z$ and we have:

$$\frac{ds}{dx} = \frac{1}{\sigma} \quad \Rightarrow \quad ds = \frac{1}{\sigma} dx$$

Hence, we have:

$$F_Z(z) = \int\limits_{-\infty}^{z} \frac{1}{\sqrt{2\pi}}\, \exp\left(-\frac{s^2}{2}\right) ds$$

which is the cdf of the standard normal distribution, $N(0,1)$.　　　　　□

What makes this property so important is that it allows us to use the standard normal distribution tables to calculate probabilities for **any** normal distribution.

For example, suppose that $X \sim N(10,16)$, *ie* it is normally distributed with $\mu = 10, \sigma = 4$. Then by Theorem 7.1:

$$Z = \frac{X - \mu}{\sigma} = \frac{X - 10}{4} \sim N(0,1)$$

So, we can calculate the probability that $X < 12$ as:

$$\Pr(X < 12) = \Pr\left(\frac{X - \mu}{\sigma} < \frac{12 - \mu}{\sigma}\right) = \Pr\left(\frac{X - 10}{4} < \frac{12 - 10}{4}\right) = \Pr\left(Z < \frac{12 - 10}{4}\right)$$

$$= \Phi\left(\frac{12 - 10}{4}\right) = \Phi(0.5) = 0.6915$$

Example 7.2

For a group of college students, the score achieved on an algebra exam is distributed normally with a mean of 65 and a standard deviation of 8. Calculate the probability that a randomly selected member of the group scored more than 77.

Solution

Let X be the score achieved by the student.

The required probability is:

$$\Pr(X > 77) = 1 - \Pr(X < 77)$$

$$= 1 - \Pr\left(\frac{X-65}{8} < \frac{77-65}{8}\right) = 1 - \Phi\left(\frac{77-65}{8}\right)$$

$$= 1 - \Phi(1.5) = 1 - 0.9332 = 0.0668 \qquad \blacklozenge\blacklozenge$$

Example 7.3

An insurance loss follows a normal distribution with mean 1,000 and variance 40,000. Calculate the probability that the loss is below 700 or above 1,500.

Solution

Let X be the amount of the loss.

Then X follows a normal distribution with parameters $\mu = 1,000$ and $\sigma = \sqrt{40,000} = 200$.

The required probability is:

$$\Pr(X < 700 \cup X > 1,500) = 1 - \Pr(700 < X < 1,500)$$

We have:

$$\Pr(700 < X < 1,500) = \Pr(X < 1,500) - \Pr(X < 700)$$

$$= \Pr\left(\frac{X-1,000}{200} < \frac{1,500-1,000}{200}\right) - \Pr\left(\frac{X-1,000}{200} < \frac{700-1,000}{200}\right)$$

$$= \Phi\left(\frac{1,500-1,000}{200}\right) - \Phi\left(\frac{700-1,000}{200}\right)$$

$$= \Phi(2.5) - \Phi(-1.5) = \Phi(2.5) - \left[1 - \Phi(1.5)\right]$$

$$= 0.9938 - (1 - 0.9332) = 0.9938 - 0.0668$$

$$= 0.9270$$

Hence, the required probability is:

$$\Pr(X < 700 \cup X > 1,500) = 1 - \Pr(700 < X < 1,500)$$

$$= 1 - 0.9270 = 0.0730 \qquad \blacklozenge\blacklozenge$$

Example 7.4

Individual insurance claim amounts are modeled by the random variable $Y = e^X$, where X is normally distributed with mean 6 and variance 4. Calculate the probability that a claim exceeds $5,000.

Solution

Noting that the relationship between X and Y is 1-1, we have:

$$\Pr(Y > 5{,}000) = \Pr\left(e^X > 5{,}000\right) = \Pr(X > \ln 5{,}000) = \Pr\left(Z > \frac{\ln 5{,}000 - 6}{2}\right) = \Pr(Z > 1.2586)$$

$$= 1 - \Phi(1.2586) = 1 - 0.8956 = 0.1044$$

(using interpolation between the values of $\Phi(1.2)$ and $\Phi(1.3)$ shown in Table 7.1).   ◆◆

Theorem 7.2

The independent random variables $X_1, \cdots, X_n$ follow normal distributions with $X_i \sim N\left(\mu_i, \sigma_i^2\right)$. Let $Y = X_1 + \cdots + X_n$. Then:

$$Y \sim N\left(\sum_{i=1}^{n} \mu_i, \sum_{i=1}^{n} \sigma_i^2\right)$$

Proof

Using the moment generating function of the normal distribution, we have:

$$M_Y(t) = \prod_{i=1}^{n} M_{X_i}(t) = \prod_{i=1}^{n} \exp\left(\mu_i t + \frac{1}{2}\sigma_i^2 t^2\right) = \exp\left(\sum_{i=1}^{n} \mu_i t + \frac{1}{2}\sum_{i=1}^{n}\sigma_i^2 t^2\right)$$

which we recognize as the MGF of a normal distribution with mean μ and variance σ^2 where:

$$\mu = \sum_{i=1}^{n} \mu_i \qquad \text{and} \qquad \sigma^2 = \sum_{i=1}^{n} \sigma_i^2 \qquad\qquad\qquad \square$$

This theorem also has important practical implications. It states that if we add independent normal distributions together, the result is also a normal distribution.

For example, if $X_1 \sim N(30, 100)$ and $X_2 \sim N(40, 150)$ are independent, and if $Y = X_1 + X_2$ then $Y \sim N(70, 250)$.

Example 7.5

The lifetime of an electrical component (in hours) is modeled by a normal distribution with mean 200 and variance 500. The lifetimes of the components are considered to be independent. Calculate the probability that the total lifetime of 5 randomly selected components exceeds 1,020 hours.

Solution

Let X_i be the lifetime of the i-th component. Let $Y = X_1 + \cdots + X_5$.

Then by Theorem 7.2, Y follows a normal distribution with:

$$\mu = E[Y] = 5 \times 200 = 1{,}000$$
$$\sigma^2 = \text{var}(Y) = 5 \times 500 = 2{,}500$$
$$\Rightarrow \sigma = \sqrt{2{,}500} = 50$$

Hence, the required probability is:

$$\Pr(Y > 1{,}020) = 1 - \Pr(Y < 1{,}020) = 1 - \Pr\left(\frac{Y - 1{,}000}{50} < \frac{1{,}020 - 1{,}000}{50}\right)$$

$$= 1 - \Phi\left(\frac{1{,}020 - 1{,}000}{50}\right) = 1 - \Phi(0.4)$$

$$= 1 - 0.6554 = 0.3446 \qquad \blacklozenge \blacklozenge$$

Theorem 7.3

If $X \sim N\left(\mu, \sigma^2\right)$ and $Y = aX + b$, then $Y \sim N\left(a\mu + b, a^2\sigma^2\right)$.

Proof

The proof follows a similar approach to that of Theorem 7.1, except that this time we will use a substitution of $s = ax + b$:

$$F_Y(y) = \Pr(Y \le y) = \Pr(aX + b \le y) = \Pr\left(X \le \frac{y - b}{a}\right)$$

$$= \int_{-\infty}^{(y-b)/a} \frac{1}{\sigma\sqrt{2\pi}} \exp\left[-\frac{(x - \mu)^2}{2\sigma^2}\right] dx$$

$$= \int_{-\infty}^{y} \frac{1}{a\sigma\sqrt{2\pi}} \exp\left[-\frac{(s - (a\mu + b))^2}{2a^2\sigma^2}\right] ds$$

which is the cdf of the normal distribution, $N\left(a\mu + b, a^2\sigma^2\right)$. $\qquad \square$

For example, if $X \sim N(10, 120)$ and $Y = 5X + 15$ then by Theorem 7.3 (with $a = 5, b = 15$), Y follows a normal distribution with:

$$\mu_Y = a\mu_X + b = 5\mu_X + 15 = 65$$
$$\sigma_Y^2 = a^2\sigma_X^2 = 5^2 \times 120 = 3{,}000$$

We can combine Theorem 7.2 and Theorem 7.3 to give a general result for linear combinations of normal distributions. This is stated in Theorem 7.4.

Theorem 7.4

The independent random variables $X_1, \cdots, X_n$ follow normal distributions with $X_i \sim N\left(\mu_i, \sigma_i^2\right)$. Let $Y = a_1 X_1 + \cdots + a_n X_n$. Then:

$$Y \sim N\left(\sum_{i=1}^{n} a_i \mu_i \, , \, \sum_{i=1}^{n} a_i^2 \sigma_i^2\right)$$

This result is easily proved using Theorems 7.2 and 7.3.

We can use Theorem 7.4 to determine the distribution of the *difference* between two independent random variables, which both follow a normal distribution.

Let $X_1 \sim N\left(\mu_1, \sigma_1^2\right)$ and $X_2 \sim N\left(\mu_2, \sigma_2^2\right)$, and let $Y = X_1 - X_2$ be the difference between these random variables. Then by Theorem 7.4 (with $a_1 = 1$ and $a_2 = -1$), we have:

$$Y \sim N\left(a_1 \mu_1 + a_2 \mu_2 \, , \, a_1^2 \sigma_1^2 + a_2^2 \sigma_2^2\right) = N\left(\mu_1 - \mu_2, \sigma_1^2 + \sigma_2^2\right)$$

For example, if $X_1 \sim N(30, 100)$ and $X_2 \sim N(40, 150)$ are independent, and if $Y = X_1 - X_2$ then $Y \sim N(-10, 250)$.

Example 7.6

Insurance losses on a tenants' package are assumed to be distributed normally with mean 600 and standard deviation 80. With every claim, the insurance company incurs variable expenses equal to 3% of the amount of each loss and a fixed cost of 50 per claim. Calculate the probability that the total cost of a claim (*ie* the loss and associated costs) exceeds 610.

Solution

Let X represent the amount of the loss. Let Y represent the total cost of a claim, including costs.

Then $X \sim N\left(600, (80)^2\right)$ and $Y = 1.03X + 50$. By Theorem 7.3 (with $a = 1.03, b = 50$):

$$Y \sim N\left(a\mu + b, a^2\sigma^2\right) = N\left(1.03 \times 600 + 50, 1.03^2 \times 80^2\right) = N\left(668, (82.4)^2\right)$$

The probability that the total cost of a claim exceeds 610 is:

$$\Pr\left(Y > 610\right) = 1 - \Pr\left(Y < 610\right) = 1 - \Pr\left(\frac{Y - 668}{82.4} < \frac{610 - 668}{82.4}\right) = 1 - \Phi\left(\frac{610 - 668}{82.4}\right)$$

$$= 1 - \Phi\left(-0.704\right) = \Phi(0.704) \approx 0.7592$$

Note: The value of $\Phi(0.704)$ was found using linear interpolation between $\Phi(0.7)$ and $\Phi(0.8)$:

$$\Phi(0.704) \approx \Phi(0.7) + \frac{0.704 - 0.7}{0.8 - 0.7} \times \left[\Phi(0.8) - \Phi(0.7)\right] = 0.7592 \qquad \blacklozenge\blacklozenge$$

Example 7.7

Two independent insurance losses, X and Y, are normally distributed. Loss X has mean 1,000 and variance 9,225. Loss Y has mean 950 and variance 6,400. Calculate the probability that X exceeds Y.

Solution

Let $W = X - Y$. The required probability is:

$$\Pr(X > Y) = \Pr(X - Y > 0) = \Pr(W > 0)$$

By Theorem 7.4, W is normally distributed with:

$$\mu_W = \mu_X - \mu_Y = 1,000 - 950 = 50$$

$$\sigma_W^2 = \sigma_X^2 + \sigma_Y^2 = 9,225 + 6,400 = 15,625$$

$$\Rightarrow \sigma_W = \sqrt{15,625} = 125$$

The required probability is therefore:

$$\Pr(W > 0) = \Pr\left(\frac{W - 50}{125} > \frac{0 - 50}{125}\right) = 1 - \Pr\left(\frac{W - 50}{125} < \frac{0 - 50}{125}\right)$$

$$= 1 - \Phi\left(\frac{0 - 50}{125}\right) = 1 - \Phi(-0.40)$$

$$= \Phi(0.40) = 0.6554 \qquad\qquad \blacklozenge\blacklozenge$$

Theorem 7.5

If $X \sim N(\mu, \sigma^2)$ and $Y = e^X$, then:

$$E[Y] = \exp\left(\mu + \frac{\sigma^2}{2}\right)$$

and:

$$\mathrm{var}[Y] = \exp(2\mu + 2\sigma^2) - \exp(2\mu + \sigma^2)$$

Proof

We find that we can use the moment generating function of X for this. The expected value of Y is:

$$E[Y] = E\left[e^X\right]$$

But now recall from Chapter 4 that the moment generating function of X is:

$$M_X(t) = E\left[e^{tX}\right]$$

$$= \exp\left(\mu t + \frac{\sigma^2 t^2}{2}\right)$$

for the given normal distribution. Hence we can see that:

$$E[Y] = M_X(1) = \exp\left(\mu + \frac{\sigma^2}{2}\right)$$

Similarly, for the variance we need:

$$\text{var}[Y] = E\left[e^{2X}\right] - \left(E\left[e^{X}\right]\right)^2$$

$$= M_X(2) - \left(M_X(1)\right)^2$$

$$= \exp\left(2\mu + 2\sigma^2\right) - \exp\left(2\mu + \sigma^2\right) \qquad \square$$

Example 7.8

If $Y = e^X$, and X is normally distributed with mean 0.5 and variance 0.25, calculate the mean and variance of Y.

Solution

We have $\mu = 0.5$ and $\sigma^2 = 0.25$, and so using Theorem 7.5 we have:

$$E[Y] = \exp\left(0.5 + \frac{0.25}{2}\right) = e^{0.625} = 1.868$$

$$\text{var}[Y] = \exp\left(2 \times 0.5 + 2 \times 0.25\right) = e^{1.5} - e^{1.25} = 0.9913 \qquad \blacklozenge\blacklozenge$$

Example 7.9

Let X represent the rate of growth of a disease through a population. X is assumed to follow a normal distribution with mean 0.05 and standard deviation 0.01. The number of individuals affected by the disease in one year's time is modeled as:

$$Y = 50,000e^X$$

Calculate the expected number of individuals affected by the disease in one year's time.

Solution

The expected number of individuals affected by the disease in one year's time is:

$$E[Y] = 50,000 \exp\left(\mu + \frac{1}{2}\sigma^2\right) = 50,000 \exp\left(0.05 + \frac{0.01^2}{2}\right) = 52,566 \qquad \blacklozenge\blacklozenge$$

7.3   *The Central Limit Theorem*

The **Central Limit Theorem** is perhaps the most important theorem in all of probability and statistics. The result demonstrates the true significance of the normal distribution.

Theorem 7.5   (The Central Limit Theorem)

Suppose that $X_1, \cdots, X_n$ are independent and identically distributed random variables with mean μ and variance σ^2.

Then for large n (typically $n \geq 30$):

$$\sum_{i=1}^{n} X_i \text{ is approximately distributed } N\left(n\mu, n\sigma^2\right)$$

The proof of this theorem is lengthy and beyond the scope of this introductory textbook (it relies on finding the limiting form of the moment generating function, as n increases to infinity), but let's take a moment to understand the implications.

The Central Limit Theorem states that the sum of a large number of *any* independent and identically distributed random variables approximately follows a normal distribution.

The underlying random variables $X_1, \cdots, X_n$ can follow any family of distributions. They could follow a discrete distribution, such as the binomial or geometric or Poisson. Or they could follow a continuous distribution, such as the exponential or gamma. But whatever the underlying distribution, the sum of a sufficiently large number of these random variables approximately follows a normal distribution.

So, even if $X_1, \cdots, X_n$ are not normally distributed, we can use the normal distribution to calculate probabilities relating to the sum of these random variables, as in the following example.

Example 7.10

The random variables $X_1, \cdots, X_{48}$ are independent and uniformly distributed on the interval $[0, 10]$. Calculate the probability that the sum of these random variables exceeds 300.

Solution

From Chapter 6, for a uniform distribution we have:

$$\mu = E[X_i] = \frac{a+b}{2} = 5 \qquad\qquad \sigma^2 = \text{var}(X_i) = \frac{(b-a)^2}{12} = \frac{10^2}{12}$$

Hence:

$$E\left[\sum X_i\right] = 48 \times 5 = 240 \qquad\qquad \text{var}\left(\sum X_i\right) = 48 \times \frac{10^2}{12} = 400$$

and using the Central Limit Theorem:

$$\Pr\left(\sum X_i > 300\right) = 1 - \Pr\left(\sum X_i < 300\right) = 1 - \Pr\left(\frac{\sum X_i - 240}{\sqrt{400}} < \frac{300 - 240}{\sqrt{400}}\right)$$

$$\approx 1 - \Phi(3) = 1 - 0.9987 = 0.0013 \qquad\qquad\qquad \blacklozenge\blacklozenge$$

The Central Limit Theorem is sometimes stated in a different but equivalent way.

If we define $\bar{X}$ to be the arithmetic mean of the random variables, *ie*:

$$\bar{X} = \frac{1}{n}\left(X_1 + \cdots + X_n\right)$$

then the Central Limit Theorem states that:

$\bar{X}$ is approximately distributed $N\left(\mu, \frac{1}{n}\sigma^2\right)$

This result follows easily from the Central Limit Theorem, because:

$$E\left[\bar{X}\right] = \frac{1}{n}E\left[\sum X_i\right] = \frac{1}{n} \times n\mu = \mu$$

$$\text{var}\left(\bar{X}\right) = \left(\frac{1}{n}\right)^2 \text{var}\left(\sum X_i\right) = \left(\frac{1}{n}\right)^2 \times n\sigma^2 = \frac{1}{n}\sigma^2$$

The random variable $\bar{X}$ is known as the **sample mean**, since it is the arithmetic mean of a sample of n values of a random variable.

Note that the variance of $\bar{X}$ decreases as the sample size n increases. This means that as the sample size n increases, the sample mean gets closer to the mean of the underlying random variable. So, when we do not know the true value of the mean of the underlying random variable, we can estimate it by calculating the mean of the observed values.

Example 7.11

The random variables $X_1, \cdots, X_{50}$ are independent and identically distributed with a mean of 20 and a variance of 25. Identify the distribution of the sample mean, $\bar{X}$.

Solution

By the Central Limit Theorem, $\bar{X}$ approximately follows a normal distribution with:

$$E\left[\bar{X}\right] = \mu = 20$$

$$\text{var}\left(\bar{X}\right) = \frac{1}{n}\sigma^2 = \frac{1}{50} \times 25 = 0.5$$

Notice how the variance has reduced dramatically from 25 for a single observation, down to 0.5 for the sample mean. In other words, the sample mean is much more likely to be close to 20 than a single observation.   ♦♦

We can also calculate probabilities related to the sample mean, such as:

$$\Pr\left(a < \bar{X} < b\right) = \Pr\left(\frac{a-\mu}{\sigma/\sqrt{n}} < \frac{\bar{X}-\mu}{\sigma/\sqrt{n}} < \frac{b-\mu}{\sigma/\sqrt{n}}\right)$$

$$\approx \Phi\left(\frac{b-\mu}{\sigma/\sqrt{n}}\right) - \Phi\left(\frac{a-\mu}{\sigma/\sqrt{n}}\right)$$

Using the normal distribution to approximate a discrete distribution

The binomial and Poisson distributions share the common problem of increasingly complex calculation.

If X has a binomial distribution with $n = 100$ trials, then the probability function is given by:

$$\Pr(X = x) = \frac{100!}{x!(100-x)!} p^x (1-p)^{100-x} \quad \text{for } x = 0, 1, \cdots, 100$$

The enormously large factorial expressions and the infinitesimal power terms can make it difficult to calculate a value of this expression.

Similarly, if X follows a Poisson distribution with mean $\lambda = 100$, then the probability function is given by:

$$\Pr(X = x) = e^{-100} \frac{100^x}{x!} \quad \text{for } x = 0, 1, 2, \cdots$$

The computational difficulties should again be obvious.

Even if we are able to calculate each of these terms, it will still be time-consuming to calculate the probability that X lies in some wide interval $[a, b]$ for two positive integers a and b, since:

$$\Pr(a \le X \le b) = \Pr(X = a) + \Pr(X = a+1) + \cdots + \Pr(X = b)$$

So if it is difficult and/or time-consuming to calculate such values, can we make a reasonable approximation? The Central Limit Theorem comes to the rescue.

The binomial variable above can be viewed as a sum of 100 independent, identically distributed Bernoulli variables, which take a value of 1 with probability p and a value of 0 with probability $1 - p$. Similarly, the Poisson variable can be viewed as a sum of 100 independent, identically distributed Poisson variables each with parameter $\lambda = 1$. In both cases, we can invoke the Central Limit Theorem to approximate the probability functions.

However, one slight complication arises from the use of a continuous distribution (which can take any value) to model a discrete distribution (which can take only integer values). This problem is solved by using a continuity correction, which we described in Chapter 4.

In general terms, if X is a discrete random variable that takes integer values, and Y is an appropriate continuous distribution, then we can approximate probabilities of X as:

$$\Pr(a \le X \le b) \approx \Pr(a - 0.5 < Y < b + 0.5) = \int_{a-0.5}^{b+0.5} f_Y(y)\, dy$$

Now, if Y follows a normal distribution with mean μ and variance σ^2, this simplifies to:

$$\Pr(a \le X \le b) \approx \Pr(a - 0.5 < Y < b + 0.5)$$

$$= \Pr\left(\frac{a - 0.5 - \mu}{\sigma} < \frac{Y - \mu}{\sigma} < \frac{b + 0.5 - \mu}{\sigma}\right)$$

$$= \Phi\left(\frac{b + 0.5 - \mu}{\sigma}\right) - \Phi\left(\frac{a - 0.5 - \mu}{\sigma}\right)$$

For example, if X has a binomial distribution with n trials, and probability p of success in any trial, then:

$$\mu = E[X] = np$$
$$\sigma^2 = \text{var}(X) = npq$$

We can model the distribution of X using a normal distribution Y with the same parameters, *ie*:

$$Y \sim N(np, npq)$$

and we can calculate probabilities using the continuity correction as follows:

$$\Pr(x_1 \leq X \leq x_2) \approx \Pr(x_1 - 0.5 < Y < x_2 + 0.5)$$

$$= \Pr\left(\frac{x_1 - 0.5 - np}{\sqrt{npq}} < \frac{Y - np}{\sqrt{npq}} < \frac{x_2 + 0.5 - np}{\sqrt{npq}} \right)$$

$$= \Phi\left(\frac{x_2 + 0.5 - np}{\sqrt{npq}} \right) - \Phi\left(\frac{x_1 - 0.5 - np}{\sqrt{npq}} \right)$$

Similarly, if X follows a Poisson distribution with mean λ, then:

$$\mu = E[X] = \lambda$$

$$\sigma^2 = \text{var}(X) = \lambda$$

and we can model the distribution of X using a normal distribution Y with the same parameters, *ie*:

$$Y \sim N(\lambda, \lambda)$$

We can then calculate probabilities using the continuity correction as follows:

$$\Pr(x_1 \leq X \leq x_2) \approx \Pr(x_1 - 0.5 < Y < x_2 + 0.5)$$

$$= \Pr\left(\frac{x_1 - 0.5 - \lambda}{\sqrt{\lambda}} < \frac{Y - \lambda}{\sqrt{\lambda}} < \frac{x_2 + 0.5 - \lambda}{\sqrt{\lambda}} \right)$$

$$= \Phi\left(\frac{x_2 + 0.5 - \lambda}{\sqrt{\lambda}} \right) - \Phi\left(\frac{x_1 - 0.5 - \lambda}{\sqrt{\lambda}} \right)$$

Example 7.12

A fair coin is flipped 100 times. Using the Central Limit Theorem, calculate the approximate probability that the number of heads is at least 48 and at most 52.

Solution

The number of heads in 100 flips, X, follows a binomial distribution with $n = 100$ and $p = 0.5$.

The expected value and variance of X are:

$$E[X] = np = 50$$
$$\text{var}(X) = npq = 25$$

By the Central Limit Theorem, the distribution of X can be approximated using a normally distributed random variable Y such that:

$$Y \sim N(50, 25)$$

The required probability can be calculated using the continuity correction as follows:

$$\Pr(48 \leq X \leq 52) \approx \Pr(47.5 < Y < 52.5)$$

$$= \Pr\left(\frac{47.5 - 50}{\sqrt{25}} < \frac{Y - 50}{\sqrt{25}} < \frac{52.5 - 50}{\sqrt{25}}\right)$$

$$= \Pr\left(-0.5 < \frac{Y - 50}{\sqrt{25}} < 0.5\right)$$

$$= \Phi(0.5) - \Phi(-0.5)$$

$$= \Phi(0.5) - \left[1 - \Phi(0.5)\right]$$

$$= 2 \times \Phi(0.5) - 1$$

$$= 2 \times 0.6915 - 1$$

$$= 0.3830 \qquad \qquad \blacklozenge\blacklozenge$$

Example 7.13

The number of automobile accidents each year in a particular suburb of Chicago is modeled using a Poisson distribution with mean 225. Using the Central Limit Theorem, calculate the approximate probability that the number of motor accidents in a given year exceeds 247.

Solution

Let X be the number of motor accidents each year. Then X follows a Poisson distribution with parameter $\lambda = 225$, and we can model the distribution of X using a normal distribution Y with the same mean and variance, *ie*:

$$Y \sim N(225, 225)$$

The required probability is:

$$\Pr(X > 247) \approx \Pr(Y > 247.5) = 1 - \Pr(Y < 247.5)$$

$$= 1 - \Pr\left(\frac{Y - 225}{\sqrt{225}} < \frac{247.5 - 225}{\sqrt{225}}\right)$$

$$= 1 - \Phi\left(\frac{247.5 - 225}{\sqrt{225}}\right)$$

$$= 1 - \Phi(1.5)$$

$$= 1 - 0.9332$$

$$= 0.0668 \qquad \qquad \blacklozenge\blacklozenge$$

Chapter 7 Practice Questions

Question 7.1

If X follows a standard normal distribution, calculate (using Table 7.1 in Section 7.1):

(i) $\Pr(X > 3.1)$

(ii) $\Pr(X < -1.4)$

(iii) $\Pr(0.4 < X < 2.2)$

(iv) $\Pr(-1.7 < X < -0.2)$

Question 7.2

Let $X \sim N(\mu, \sigma^2)$. Using the moment generating or otherwise, show that:

(i) $E[X] = \mu$

(ii) $\text{var}(X) = \sigma^2$

Question 7.3

The random variable X has the following moment generating function:

$$M_X(t) = e^{8(t^2 - 1.5t)}$$

Identify the distribution of X.

Question 7.4

If $X \sim N(15, 100)$, then calculate:

(i) $\Pr(X > 18)$

(ii) $\Pr(3 < X < 27)$

(iii) $\Pr(-4 < X < 4)$

Question 7.5   IOA/FOA

A random sample of size 6 is selected from a normal distribution with mean 10 and variance 2. Calculate the probability that 2 of the sample values are less than 9, and the remaining 4 sample values are greater than 9.

Question 7.6   IOA/FOA

The sizes of claims under a certain type of policy are distributed normally with a mean of $1,800 and a standard deviation of $400. Calculate the probability that the sizes of two randomly selected claims differ by more than $500.

Question 7.7   SOA/CAS

A company manufactures a brand of light bulb with a lifetime in months that is normally distributed with mean 3 and variance 1. A consumer buys a number of these bulbs with the intention of replacing them successively as they burn out. The light bulbs have independent lifetimes. What is the smallest number of bulbs to be purchased so that the succession of light bulbs will produce light for at least 40 months with probability at least 0.9772?

Question 7.8   SOA/CAS

Two instruments are used to measure the height h of a tower. The error made by the less accurate instrument is normally distributed with mean 0 and standard deviation $0.0056h$. The error made by the more accurate instrument is normally distributed with mean 0 and standard deviation $0.0044h$. Assuming the two measurements are independent random variables, what is the probability that their average value is within $0.005h$ of the height of the tower?

Question 7.9   IOA/FOA

For a certain class of insurance business, extensive data show that the distribution of claims amounts has mean $237 and standard deviation $202. If a total of 200 claims are lodged, calculate the probability that the total amount of these claims exceeds $50,000.

Question 7.10

For a certain class of insurance business, claims amounts have mean $574 and standard deviation $186. If a total of 80 claims are lodged, calculate the probability that the average amount of these claims is below $565.

Question 7.11   SOA/CAS

The total claim amount for a health insurance policy follows a distribution with density function:

$$f(x) = \frac{1}{1,000} e^{-x/1,000} \quad \text{for } x > 0$$

The premium for the policy is set at 100 over the expected total claim amount. If 100 policies are sold, what is the approximate probability that the insurance company will have claims exceeding the premium?

Question 7.12

For the 100 policies in Question 7.11, the premium is determined in a different fashion. The premium for the group is set so that there is only a 10% chance that the group premium will be insufficient to meet claims for the 100 policies. The individual premium is obtained by dividing the premium for the group equally among the 100 policies. Calculate the premium for an individual policy.

Note: $\Phi(1.282) = 0.9$

Question 7.13

In an analysis of healthcare data, ages have been rounded to the nearest multiple of 5 years. The difference between the true age and the rounded age is assumed to be uniformly distributed on the interval $[-2.5, 2.5]$. The healthcare data are based on a random sample of 48 people. What is the approximate probability that the mean of the rounded ages is within 0.25 years of the mean of the true ages?

Question 7.14

The probability that an inquiry leads to a sale is 0.7, independently for each inquiry. Over a period of time 200 such inquiries are received. By making a suitable approximation, estimate the probability that N, the number of sales from inquiries, satisfies:

$$124 < N \leq 153$$

Question 7.15

The number of claims which arise in a year under each individual auto policy has a Poisson distribution with mean 0.3. Consider a group of 1,000 independent auto policies. Calculate the probability that at least 340 claims in total arise under this group of policies in a year.

Question 7.16

If $X \sim N(0.5, 0.16)$ and $Y = e^X$, calculate $E[Y]$.

Question 7.17

If $Y = e^X$, and X follows a normal distribution with parameters $\mu = 2.5$ and $\sigma = 1.6$, calculate $\text{var}(Y)$.

Question 7.18

Let X represent the rate of growth due to interest of money in a savings account. X is assumed to follow a normal distribution with mean 0.06 and standard deviation 0.015. The value of the savings account in one year's time is modeled as:

$$Y = 10,000e^X$$

Calculate the expected value of the savings account in one year's time.

Question 7.19

A man buys an investment bond for $1,000 on April 1. The value of the bond in one year's time is:

$$1,000e^\Delta$$

where:

$$\Delta \sim N(0.1, 0.16)$$

Calculate the probability that the man will lose more than $500 on his investment.

Question 7.20

If $Y = e^{0.5X}$, and X is normally distributed with mean 10 and standard deviation 4, calculate the probability that Y exceeds its mean.

8

Multivariate Distributions

Overview

In this chapter we'll extend much of the theory we have covered so far to the concept of distributions of more than one random variable. In many cases, we may be interested in measuring two or more random variables at the same time, *eg*:

- the age of a machine that manufactures electrical components, and the failure rate (*ie* the number of faulty components as a % of all components produced) of that machine

- the timing and severity of insurance losses

- the diastolic blood pressure, systolic blood pressure, and resting pulse rate of a group of patients recovering from surgery.

We'll focus our attention entirely on bivariate distributions (*ie* distributions of exactly two random variables) and study basic properties such as probability functions, moments, and conditional distributions. The same basic theory can easily be extended to multivariate distributions with three or more variables.

8.1 Joint discrete distributions

We'll start by considering the simplest case involving two discrete random variables, X and Y.

The probability that $X = x$ and $Y = y$, ie $\Pr(X = x, Y = y)$ is denoted:

$$f_{X,Y}(x,y)$$

This is known as the **joint probability function** of X and Y. The joint distribution of X and Y is a probability model for pairs of outcomes.

The joint probability function measures the probability of a single pair of outcomes. It can also be used to calculate the probability of a specified collection of outcomes, which we call event E:

$$\Pr(E) = \sum_{(x,y) \in E} f_{X,Y}(x,y)$$

For example, suppose that X is the number of tornadoes in country P in any one year and let Y be the number of tornadoes in country Q during the same year. The joint probability function of X and Y is shown in the table below.

Table 8.1

Joint probability function		Annual number of tornadoes in country Q			
		0	**1**	**2**	**3**
Annual	**0**	0.12	0.06	0.05	0.02
number of tornadoes	**1**	0.13	0.15	0.12	0.03
in country P	**2**	0.05	0.15	0.10	0.02

The probability that both countries experience exactly one tornado in a given year is:

$$\Pr(X = 1, Y = 1) = f_{X,Y}(1,1) = 0.15$$

The probability that both countries experience at least one tornado in a year (event E) is:

$$\Pr(E) = \sum_{(x,y) \in E} f_{X,Y}(x,y)$$

$$= f_{X,Y}(1,1) + f_{X,Y}(1,2) + f_{X,Y}(1,3) + f_{X,Y}(2,1) + f_{X,Y}(2,2) + f_{X,Y}(2,3)$$

$$= 0.15 + 0.12 + 0.03 + 0.15 + 0.10 + 0.02$$

$$= 0.57$$

Finally, the probability that country Q experiences more tornadoes than country P is given by:

$$\Pr(X < Y) = f_{X,Y}(0,1) + f_{X,Y}(0,2) + f_{X,Y}(0,3) + f_{X,Y}(1,2) + f_{X,Y}(1,3) + f_{X,Y}(2,3)$$

$$= 0.06 + 0.05 + 0.02 + 0.12 + 0.03 + 0.02$$

$$= 0.30$$

The joint probability function has the following important properties:

Properties of the joint probability function

(1) $f_{X,Y}(x,y) \geq 0$ for all (x,y)

(2) $\displaystyle\sum_{\text{all } (x,y)} f_{X,Y}(x,y) = 1$

Example 8.1

Using the information in Table 8.1, calculate the following:

(i)   the probability that neither country experiences a tornado in a given year

(ii)   the probability that the two countries experience a total of two tornadoes in a given year.

Solution

(i)   The probability that neither country experiences a tornado in a given year is:
$$\Pr(X=0, Y=0) = f_{X,Y}(0,0) = 0.12$$

(ii)   The probability that the two countries experience a total of two tornadoes in a given year is:
$$\Pr(X+Y=2) = f_{X,Y}(2,0) + f_{X,Y}(1,1) + f_{X,Y}(0,2)$$
$$= 0.05 + 0.15 + 0.05 = 0.25 \qquad \blacklozenge\blacklozenge$$

What if we are interested in only one of these random variables? We can calculate the probability that $X = x$ by summing the joint probabilities in the appropriate row of the table, and we can calculate the probability that $Y = y$ by summing the joint probabilities in the appropriate column of the table.

For example:
$$\Pr(X=0) = f_{X,Y}(0,0) + f_{X,Y}(0,1) + f_{X,Y}(0,2) + f_{X,Y}(0,3)$$
$$= 0.12 + 0.06 + 0.05 + 0.02 = 0.25$$

Table 8.2 below shows the row and column totals derived from Table 8.1.

Table 8.2

	Y=0	Y=1	Y=2	Y=3	Total
X=0	0.12	0.06	0.05	0.02	0.25
X=1	0.13	0.15	0.12	0.03	0.43
X=2	0.05	0.15	0.10	0.02	0.32
Total	0.30	0.36	0.27	0.07	1.00

In general, the probability that $X = x$ is:

$$\Pr(X = x) = f_X(x) = \sum_{\text{all } y} f_{X,Y}(x,y)$$

and the probability that $Y = y$ is:

$$\Pr(Y = y) = f_Y(y) = \sum_{\text{all } x} f_{X,Y}(x,y)$$

The functions $f_X(x)$ and $f_Y(y)$ are called the **marginal probability functions** of X and Y respectively. They are the models for the probability function of a single discrete random variable, which we covered in Chapter 4.

In the tornado example, the marginal probability function of X is identified by the individual row totals, and the marginal probability function of Y by the individual column totals. For example, we have $f_X(2) = 0.32$ and $f_Y(1) = 0.36$.

Recall from Chapter 3 the definition of conditional probability:

$$\Pr(A|B) = \frac{\Pr(A \cap B)}{\Pr(B)} \qquad \text{where } \Pr(B) > 0$$

For a joint probability distribution, we can also define the **conditional probability function** of either X or Y, given the value of the other random variable.

The conditional probability function of X given that $Y = y$ is:

$$f_X(x|Y = y) = \frac{f_{X,Y}(x,y)}{f_Y(y)} \qquad \text{where } f_Y(y) > 0$$

and the conditional probability function of Y given that $X = x$ is:

$$f_Y(y|X = x) = \frac{f_{X,Y}(x,y)}{f_X(x)} \qquad \text{where } f_X(x) > 0$$

In the tornado example, suppose that we know that exactly 1 tornado occurred in country Q in a given year (*ie* $Y = 1$). Then the distribution of X, the number of tornadoes in country P during the same year, is:

$$f_X(0|Y = 1) = \frac{f_{X,Y}(0,1)}{f_Y(1)} = \frac{0.06}{0.36} = 0.1667$$

$$f_X(1|Y = 1) = \frac{f_{X,Y}(1,1)}{f_Y(1)} = \frac{0.15}{0.36} = 0.4167$$

$$f_X(2|Y = 1) = \frac{f_{X,Y}(2,1)}{f_Y(1)} = \frac{0.15}{0.36} = 0.4167$$

 Example 8.2

Using the information in Table 8.1, calculate the following:

(i)   the probability that country Q experiences at least two tornadoes in a given year

(ii)   the probability that country P experiences no tornadoes, given that country Q experiences no tornadoes in that year

(iii)   the probability that country Q experiences at least two tornadoes, given that country P experiences exactly one tornado.

Solution

(i)   The probability that country Q experiences at least two tornadoes in a given year is:

$$f_Y(2) + f_Y(3) = 0.27 + 0.07 = 0.34$$

(ii)   The probability that country P experiences no tornadoes, given that country Q experiences no tornadoes in that year is:

$$f_X\left(0|Y=0\right) = \frac{f_{X,Y}(0,0)}{f_Y(0)} = \frac{0.12}{0.30} = 0.40$$

(iii)   The probability that country Q experiences at least two tornadoes, given that country P experiences exactly one tornado is:

$$f_Y\left(2|X=1\right) + f_Y\left(3|X=1\right) = \frac{f_{X,Y}(1,2)}{f_X(1)} + \frac{f_{X,Y}(1,3)}{f_X(1)} = \frac{0.12}{0.43} + \frac{0.03}{0.43} = 0.3488 \qquad \blacklozenge\blacklozenge$$

We can also use the concepts introduced in this section to restate the definition of independence of random variables, which we met in Chapter 4.

Independent random variables

The random variables X and Y are **independent** if and only if

$$f_{X,Y}\left(x,y\right) = f_X\left(x\right)f_Y\left(y\right) \qquad \text{for all } x,y$$

As a consequence of this definition, if X and Y are independent, then:

$$f_X\left(x|Y=y\right) = f_X\left(x\right)$$

and:

$$f_Y\left(y|X=x\right) = f_Y\left(y\right)$$

In the tornado example, we can see that X and Y are not independent (*ie* they are **dependent**) since:

$$f_X(0)f_Y(1) = 0.25 \times 0.36 = 0.09$$

$$f_{X,Y}(0,1) = 0.06$$

$$\Rightarrow f_{X,Y}\left(x,y\right) \neq f_X\left(x\right)f_Y\left(y\right) \qquad \text{for } x=0, y=1$$

8.2 *Joint continuous distributions*

Let's now consider the joint distribution of two continuous random variables, X and Y.

The joint distribution of X and Y is a probability model for pairs of outcomes, and it is defined in terms of the **joint cumulative distribution function**:

$$F\left(x,y\right) = \Pr\left(X \leq x \text{ and } Y \leq y\right)$$

The **joint probability density function** is denoted:

$$f_{X,Y}\left(x,y\right)$$

Remember that the pdf is not itself a probability. In order to calculate the probability of some event E, we must integrate the pdf over the set of outcomes in E. For a joint continuous distribution, this results in the following double integral:

$$\Pr(E) = \iint_E f_{X,Y}(x,y)\,dy\,dx$$

The joint probability density function has the following important properties, which are analogous to those of the joint probability function in the discrete case:

Properties of the joint probability density function

(1) $f_{X,Y}(x,y) \geq 0$ for all (x,y)

(2) $\int_{-\infty}^{\infty} \int_{-\infty}^{\infty} f_{X,Y}(x,y)\,dy\,dx = 1$

Recall from Chapter 4 that the probability that a single continuous random variable falls in an interval (a,b) is calculated by integrating the pdf over the interval, *ie*:

$$\Pr(a < X < b) = \int_a^b f_X(x)\,dx$$

We can think of this probability in a graphical sense as the **area** above the interval (a,b) and below the graph of the density function $f_X(x)$.

There is an analogous result for a joint continuous distribution:

$$\Pr(a < X < b, c < Y < d) = \int_a^b \int_c^d f_{X,Y}(x,y)\,dy\,dx$$

Again, there is a graphical interpretation for this probability. It is the **volume** above the area in the $X \times Y$ plane (such that $a < X < b$ and $c < Y < d$) and below the surface $z = f_{X,Y}(x,y)$.

Example 8.3

For a certain insurance policy X is a loss amount claimed by an insured and Y is the amount of the loss that is allowed by the claim adjuster. The joint density of X and Y is modeled by:

$$f(x,y) = \begin{cases} \dfrac{8xy}{100^4} & 0 < y \leq x < 100 \\ 0 & \text{otherwise} \end{cases}$$

Calculate the probability that the amount allowed by the claim adjuster is 25 or more below the amount claimed.

Solution

We require $\Pr(Y \leq X - 25)$.

We'll start by identifying the region in the $X \times Y$ plane where the pdf is positive ($100 > x > y > 0$) and such that $y \leq x - 25$. This area is shaded in the diagram on the following page.

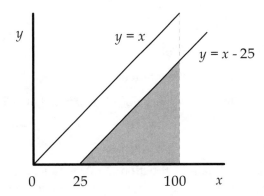

We can compute $\Pr(Y \leq X - 25)$ by calculating the double integral of the joint density function over this area:

$$\Pr(Y \leq X - 25) = \int_{x=25}^{100} \int_{y=0}^{y=x-25} f_{X,Y}(x,y)\,dy\,dx$$

$$= \int_{x=25}^{100} \int_{y=0}^{y=x-25} \frac{8xy}{100^4}\,dy\,dx = \frac{1}{100^4} \int_{x=25}^{100} \left(4xy^2 \Big|_{y=0}^{x-25} \right) dx$$

$$= \frac{4}{100^4} \int_{25}^{100} x(x-25)^2\,dx = \frac{4}{100^4} \int_{25}^{100} x^3 - 50x^2 + 625x\,dx$$

$$= \frac{4}{100^4} \times \left(\frac{x^4}{4} - \frac{50x^3}{3} + \frac{625x^2}{2} \right) \Bigg|_{25}^{100}$$

$$= 0.4583 - 0.0013 = 0.4570$$

Note: In problems of this type, the most difficult step is often to identify the intervals over which to integrate the pdf. A simple graph can often be very useful.   ◆◆

We can also calculate marginal and conditional probability density functions for joint continuous distributions.

The **marginal probability density functions** of X and Y are:

$$f_X(x) = \int_{y=-\infty}^{\infty} f_{X,Y}(x,y)\,dy$$

$$f_Y(y) = \int_{x=-\infty}^{\infty} f_{X,Y}(x,y)\,dx$$

The resulting functions $f_X(x)$ and $f_Y(y)$ are the models for the probability function of a single continuous random variable, which we covered in Chapter 4.

The **conditional probability density function** of X given that $Y = y$ is:

$$f_X(x|Y=y) = \frac{f_{X,Y}(x,y)}{f_Y(y)}$$

and the conditional probability density function of Y given that $X = x$ is:

$$f_Y(y|X=x) = \frac{f_{X,Y}(x,y)}{f_X(x)}$$

Example 8.4

Using the information in Example 8.3, calculate:

(i)   the marginal probability density function of X

(ii)   the conditional probability density function of Y given that $X = 50$.

Solution

(i)   To compute the marginal density function of X, we must integrate out the Y variable from the joint density function, remembering that the joint density is positive only when $0 < y \le x$.

For $0 < x < 100$, we have:

$$f_X(x) = \int_{-\infty}^{\infty} f_{X,Y}(x,y)\, dy = \int_{y=0}^{x} \frac{8xy}{100^4}\, dy = \left. \frac{4xy^2}{100^4} \right|_{y=0}^{x}$$

$$= \frac{4x^3}{100^4} \qquad \text{for } 0 < x < 100$$

(ii)   It's now quite simple to compute the conditional density of Y given $X = 50$, but we must be careful where the formula is defined: the joint density function is positive when $0 < y \le x < 100$. Since we are given that $X = 50$, the conditional density function of Y is positive only when $0 < y < 50$, and is equal to:

$$f_Y(y|X=50) = \frac{f_{X,Y}(50,y)}{f_X(50)} = \left(\frac{8 \times 50 \times y}{100^4} \right) \Big/ \left(\frac{4 \times 50^3}{100^4} \right)$$

$$= \frac{2y}{50^2} \qquad \text{for } 0 < y < 50 \qquad\qquad \blacklozenge\ \blacklozenge$$

8.3 *Moments*

We can also calculate moments of joint distributions. To simplify the formulas, let's start by defining the expected value of a function $g(x,y)$ of random variables X and Y.

For a joint discrete distribution:

$$E\big[g(X,Y)\big] = \sum_{\text{all } x,y} g(x,y) f_{X,Y}(x,y)$$

and for a joint continuous distribution:

$$E\big[g(X,Y)\big] = \int_{-\infty}^{\infty} \int_{-\infty}^{\infty} g(x,y) f_{X,Y}(x,y)\, dy\, dx$$

Hence, if we define $g(x) = x$, then for a joint discrete distribution we have:

$$\mu_X = E[X] = \sum_{\text{all } x,y} x\, f_{X,Y}(x,y)$$

and for a joint continuous distribution we have:

$$\mu_X = E[X] = \int_{-\infty}^{\infty} \int_{-\infty}^{\infty} x\, f_{X,Y}(x,y)\, dy\, dx$$

We can also calculate the variance of X by setting $g(x) = (x - \mu_X)^2$. For example, for a joint discrete distribution we have:

$$\sigma_X^2 = \text{var}(X) = \sum_{\text{all } x,y} (x - \mu_X)^2 f_{X,Y}(x,y)$$

Example 8.5

Surgeons at a Toronto hospital perform 0, 1, or 2 high-risk operations each year on conjoined twins. Let X denote the number of such operations carried out in a year, and let Y denote the number of operations that are classified as successful. Calculate the variance of Y based on the following probabilities:

$$\Pr(X = 0, Y = 0) = 0.3 \quad \Pr(X = 1, Y = 0) = 0.15 \quad \Pr(X = 1, Y = 1) = 0.25$$
$$\Pr(X = 2, Y = 0) = 0.05 \quad \Pr(X = 2, Y = 1) = 0.1 \quad \Pr(X = 2, Y = 2) = 0.15$$

Solution

The expected value of Y is:

$$\mu_Y = E[Y] = \sum_{\text{all } x,y} y f_{X,Y}(x,y)$$
$$= 0 \times (0.3 + 0.15 + 0.05) + 1 \times (0.25 + 0.1) + 2 \times 0.15 = 0.65$$

The variance of Y is:

$$\sigma_Y^2 = \text{var}(Y) = \sum_{\text{all } x,y} (y - \mu_Y)^2 f_{X,Y}(x,y)$$
$$= (0 - 0.65)^2 \times (0.3 + 0.15 + 0.05) + (1 - 0.65)^2 \times (0.25 + 0.1) + (2 - 0.65)^2 \times 0.15$$
$$= 0.5275 \qquad \blacklozenge\blacklozenge$$

Note that the formulas for the expected value and variance of X and Y are equivalent to the formulas that we met in Chapter 4 for a single distribution. For example, in the discrete case, the marginal distribution of X is:

$$\Pr(X = x) = f_X(x) = \sum_{\text{all } y} f_{X,Y}(x,y)$$

Hence we have:

$$\mu_X = E[X] = \sum_{\text{all } x,y} x f_{X,Y}(x,y) = \sum_{\text{all } x} x \left(\sum_{\text{all } y} f_{X,Y}(x,y) \right) = \sum_{\text{all } x} x f_X(x)$$

So, we could have solved Example 8.5 by calculating the marginal distribution of Y:

$$\Pr(Y = 0) = 0.5 \quad \Pr(Y = 1) = 0.35 \quad \Pr(Y = 2) = 0.15$$

and by proceeding as for a single distribution.

Let's now look at three important theorems.

Theorem 8.1

For any two random variables, X and Y:

$$E[X + Y] = E[X] + E[Y]$$

Proof

Note: For this and subsequent theorems, we'll show the proof for the joint discrete case. The proof is similar for the continuous case.

$$E[X+Y] = \sum_{\text{all } x,y} (x+y) f_{X,Y}(x,y) = \sum_{\text{all } x,y} x f_{X,Y}(x,y) + \sum_{\text{all } x,y} y f_{X,Y}(x,y)$$

$$= E[X] + E[Y] \qquad \qquad \square$$

Theorem 8.2

If X and Y are independent random variables, then:

$$E[XY] = E[X]E[Y]$$

Proof

Recall that the independence of X and Y implies that:

$$f_{X,Y}(x,y) = f_X(x) f_Y(y) \qquad \text{for all } x,y$$

Hence, we have:

$$E[XY] = \sum_{\text{all } x,y} xy\, f_{X,Y}(x,y) = \sum_{\text{all } x,y} xy\, f_X(x) f_Y(y) = \left(\sum_{\text{all } x} x f_X(x) \right)\left(\sum_{\text{all } y} y f_Y(y) \right)$$

$$= E[X]E[Y] \qquad \qquad \square$$

A similar approach can be used to establish Theorem 8.3 (which we state without proof).

Theorem 8.3

If X and Y are independent random variables, and g and h are functions, then:

$$E[g(X)h(Y)] = E[g(X)]E[h(Y)]$$

Theorem 8.4

If X and Y are independent random variables, then:

$$\text{var}(X+Y) = \text{var}(X) + \text{var}(Y)$$

Proof

We have:

$$\text{var}(X+Y) = \sum_{\text{all } x,y} \big((x+y) - (\mu_X + \mu_Y)\big)^2 f_{X,Y}(x,y)$$

$$= \sum_{\text{all } x,y} \Big((x - \mu_X)^2 + (y - \mu_Y)^2 + 2(x - \mu_X)(y - \mu_Y) \Big) f_{X,Y}(x,y)$$

$$= \sum_{\text{all } x,y} (x - \mu_X)^2 f_{X,Y}(x,y) + \sum_{\text{all } x,y} (y - \mu_Y)^2 f_{X,Y}(x,y)$$

$$+ \sum_{\text{all } x,y} 2(x - \mu_X)(y - \mu_Y) f_{X,Y}(x,y)$$

Let's look at the third term in this expression:

$$\sum_{\text{all } x,y} 2(x-\mu_X)(y-\mu_Y)f_{X,Y}(x,y) = \sum_{\text{all } x,y} 2(x-\mu_X)(y-\mu_Y)f_X(x)f_Y(y)$$

$$= 2\left(\sum_{\text{all } x}(x-\mu_X)f_X(x)\right)\left(\sum_{\text{all } y}(y-\mu_Y)f_Y(y)\right)$$

But:

$$\sum_{\text{all } x}(x-\mu_X)f_X(x) = \sum_{\text{all } x} x f_X(x) - \mu_X \sum_{\text{all } x} f_X(x) = \mu_X - \mu_X = 0$$

Hence, we have:

$$\sum_{\text{all } x,y} 2(x-\mu_X)(y-\mu_Y)f_{X,Y}(x,y) = 0$$

and finally:

$$\text{var}(X+Y) = \sum_{\text{all } x}(x-\mu_X)^2 f_X(x) + \sum_{\text{all } y}(y-\mu_Y)^2 f_Y(y) + 0$$

$$= \text{var}(X) + \text{var}(Y)$$

□

Example 8.6

Using the information in Table 8.1, calculate the total expected payment by an insurance company that pays 10 in respect of every tornado in country P and 20 in respect of every tornado in country Q.

Solution

Using Theorem 8.1, and remembering that expectation is a linear operator, the total expected payment is:

$$E[10X + 20Y] = E[10X] + E[20Y] = 10E[X] + 20E[Y]$$

$$= 10 \times (0 \times 0.25 + 1 \times 0.43 + 2 \times 0.32)$$

$$+ 20 \times (0 \times 0.30 + 1 \times 0.36 + 2 \times 0.27 + 3 \times 0.07)$$

$$= 10 \times 1.07 + 20 \times 1.11 = 32.9$$

◆◆

It is also possible to define a **joint moment generating function** of two random variables.

Joint moment generating function

The **joint moment generating function** of random variables X and Y is defined as:

$$M_{X,Y}(s,t) = E\left[e^{sX+tY}\right]$$

for all values of s and t for which the expectation exists.

For a joint discrete distribution, the joint moment generating function is defined as:

$$M_{X,Y}(s,t) = \sum_{\text{all } x,y} e^{sX+tY} f_{X,Y}(x,y)$$

For a joint continuous distribution, the joint moment generating function is defined as:

$$M_{X,Y}(s,t) = \int_{-\infty}^{\infty} \int_{-\infty}^{\infty} e^{sX+tY} f_{X,Y}(x,y) \, dy \, dx$$

Example 8.7

The random variables X and Y are uniformly distributed on the region $0 < x < y < 1$.

Identify the joint moment generating function of X and Y.

Solution

The joint probability density function is defined over a triangle with corners at $(0,0)$, $(0,1)$ and $(1,1)$. This triangle has an area of 0.5. Since the joint probability density function must integrate to 1 over this area, the joint probability density function is therefore equal to 2, *ie*:

$$f_{X,Y}(x,y) = 2 \qquad \text{for } 0 < x < y < 1$$

The joint moment generating function is:

$$M_{X,Y}(s,t) = \int_{y=0}^{1} \int_{x=0}^{y} e^{sx+ty} f_{X,Y}(x,y) \, dx \, dy$$

$$= 2 \int_{y=0}^{1} e^{ty} \int_{x=0}^{y} e^{sx} \, dx \, dy$$

$$= \frac{2}{s} \int_{y=0}^{1} e^{ty} \left(e^{sy} - 1 \right) dy$$

$$= \frac{2}{s} \left(\frac{e^{(s+t)y}}{s+t} - \frac{e^{ty}}{t} \right) \Bigg|_{0}^{1}$$

$$= \frac{2 \left(e^{s+t} - 1 \right)}{s(s+t)} - \frac{2 \left(e^{t} - 1 \right)}{st} \qquad\qquad ◆◆$$

The following properties are simple to deduce from the definition of the joint moment generating function:

Properties of the joint moment generating function

(1) $M_{X,Y}(s,0) = M_X(s)$

(2) $M_{X,Y}(0,t) = M_Y(t)$

(3) $M_{X,Y}(t,t) = M_{X+Y}(t)$

We'll conclude this section by verifying a result that we stated without proof in Chapter 4.

Theorem 8.5

If X and Y are independent random variables, and $Z = X + Y$ then:

$$M_Z(t) = M_X(t)M_Y(t)$$

Proof

From the definition of the moment generating function, we have:

$$M_Z(t) = E\left[e^{tZ}\right] = E\left[e^{t(X+Y)}\right]$$

$$= E\left[e^{tX}e^{tY}\right]$$

$$= E\left[e^{tX}\right]E\left[e^{tY}\right] \qquad \text{by Theorem 8.3 and independence}$$

$$= M_X(t)M_Y(t) \qquad\qquad\qquad\qquad \square$$

8.4 Conditional moments

We have seen how to calculate conditional probabilities for a joint distribution. In this section, we'll apply these techniques to calculate the conditional expected value and the conditional variance of a random variable X given an event F.

For example, in an insurance setting, suppose that an insurer sells automobile insurance policies to low-risk, medium-risk and high-risk policyholders. We may want to calculate:

- the expected total claims arising from a policy, given that the policyholder is a high-risk individual

- the expected size of a claim arising from a policy, given that the claim exceeds $1,000

- the expected number of claims arising from a policy, given that the policyholder is a low-risk individual

- the expected size of a claim arising from a policy, given that the policyholder made exactly one claim

- the variance of the number of claims arising from a policy, given that the policyholder is a medium-risk individual.

The conditional expectation of a random variable is defined in much the same way as the expected value, except that we use a conditional probability function or conditional probability density function $f_X(x|F)$ in place of $f_X(x)$.

Conditional expectation

The **conditional expectation of X given that event F has occurred** is denoted $E\left[X|F\right]$.

For a discrete distribution, the conditional expectation is defined as:

$$E\left[X|F\right] = \sum_x x f_X\left(x|F\right)$$

For a continuous distribution, the conditional expectation is defined as:

$$E\left[X|F\right] = \int_x x f_X\left(x|F\right)dx$$

For example, suppose that four hospital patients in a study weigh 140, 161, 175, and 188 pounds respectively. Let X be the weight of a randomly selected patient in the study.

The expected weight of a randomly selected patient in the study is:

$$E[X] = 140 \times \frac{1}{4} + 161 \times \frac{1}{4} + 175 \times \frac{1}{4} + 188 \times \frac{1}{4} = 166$$

Let event F be the event that the patient weighing 175 pounds leaves the study. The conditional probability that each of the 3 remaining patients is randomly selected is $1/3$.

The conditional expected weight of a randomly selected patient in the study (given F) is:

$$E\left[X|F\right] = 140 \times \frac{1}{3} + 161 \times \frac{1}{3} + 188 \times \frac{1}{3} = 163$$

Conditional variance is defined is a similar way.

Conditional variance

The **conditional variance of X given that event F has occurred** is:

$$\mathrm{var}\left(X|F\right) = E\left[\left(X - E\left[X|F\right]\right)^2 \bigg| F\right]$$

The conditional variance can also be calculated as:

$$\mathrm{var}\left(X|F\right) = E\left[X^2|F\right] - \left(E\left[X|F\right]\right)^2$$

In our example of the study of hospital patients, we have:

$$E\left[X^2|F\right] = 140^2 \times \frac{1}{3} + 161^2 \times \frac{1}{3} + 188^2 \times \frac{1}{3} = 26{,}955$$

$$\Rightarrow \mathrm{var}\left(X|F\right) = E\left[X^2|F\right] - \left(E\left[X|F\right]\right)^2 = 26{,}955 - 163^2 = 386$$

So far we've looked at the conditional expectation and the conditional variance of a random variable Y given that an event F has occurred. Event F may relate to:

- information about a related (*ie* dependent) random variable Y, or

- information about the variable X itself.

To illustrate this, let's consider again the example relating to the distribution of tornadoes in countries P and Q. We'll repeat Table 8.1 below for your convenience.

Table 8.1

Joint probability function		Annual number of tornadoes in country Q			
		0	1	2	3
Annual number of tornadoes in country P	0	0.12	0.06	0.05	0.02
	1	0.13	0.15	0.12	0.03
	2	0.05	0.15	0.10	0.02

As before, let X be the number of tornadoes in country P in a given year, and let Y be the number of tornadoes in country Q in the same year.

We may wish to calculate $E[X|Y = 1]$, *ie* the expected number of tornadoes in country P given that there has been exactly one tornado in country Q. Here event F relates to information about the related (*ie* dependent) random variable Y.

Alternatively, we may wish to calculate $E[X|X > 0]$, *ie* the expected number of tornadoes in country P given that there has been at least one tornado in country P. Here, event F relates to information about the variable X itself.

Whatever the form of event F, the first step in the calculation of a conditional expectation or conditional variance is to calculate the conditional probability function (for a discrete distribution) or conditional probability density function (for a continuous distribution).

Example 8.8

Using the information in Table 8.1, calculate:

(i)   the expected number of tornadoes in country Q if there is one tornado in country P

(ii)   the expected number of tornadoes in country Q if there is at least one tornado in country Q.

Solution

(i)   We require $E[Y|X = 1]$. In order to calculate this conditional expectation, our first step is to calculate the conditional probability function:

$$f_Y\left(y|X = 1\right) = \frac{f_{X,Y}\left(1, y\right)}{f_X\left(1\right)} \quad \text{where} \quad f_X\left(1\right) = 0.13 + 0.15 + 0.12 + 0.03 = 0.43$$

Hence the conditional probabilities (which sum to 1) are:

$$f_Y\left(0|X = 1\right) = \frac{0.13}{0.43} \qquad\qquad f_Y\left(1|X = 1\right) = \frac{0.15}{0.43}$$

$$f_Y\left(2|X = 1\right) = \frac{0.12}{0.43} \qquad\qquad f_Y\left(3|X = 1\right) = \frac{0.03}{0.43}$$

We can now calculate $E[Y|X = 1]$ as:

$$E\left[Y|X = 1\right] = \sum_{y=0}^{3} y\, f_Y\left(y|X = 1\right)$$

$$= 0 \times \frac{0.13}{0.43} + 1 \times \frac{0.15}{0.43} + 2 \times \frac{0.12}{0.43} + 3 \times \frac{0.03}{0.43} = 1.116$$

(ii)   We require $E[Y|Y > 0]$. Once again, we'll calculate the conditional probability function:

$$f_Y\left(y|Y > 0\right) = \frac{f_Y\left(y\right)}{\Pr\left(Y > 0\right)} \quad \text{where} \quad \Pr\left(Y > 0\right) = 1 - 0.12 - 0.13 - 0.05 = 0.70$$

Hence the conditional probabilities (which sum to 1) are:

$$f_Y(1|Y>0) = \frac{0.06+0.15+0.15}{0.70} = \frac{0.36}{0.70}$$

$$f_Y(2|Y>0) = \frac{0.05+0.12+0.10}{0.70} = \frac{0.27}{0.70}$$

$$f_Y(3|Y>0) = \frac{0.02+0.03+0.02}{0.70} = \frac{0.07}{0.70}$$

Finally:

$$E[Y|Y>0] = \sum_{y=1}^{3} y\, f_Y(y|Y>0)$$

$$= 1 \times \frac{0.36}{0.70} + 2 \times \frac{0.27}{0.70} + 3 \times \frac{0.07}{0.70} = 1.586$$

Theorem 8.6   (The double expectation theorem)

For any two random variables X and Y :

$$E[Y] = E\Big[E[Y|X]\Big]$$

Proof

First notice that $E[Y|X=x]$ is a function of x .

From the basic definition of conditional expectation, we have:

$$E[Y|X=x] = \sum_y y\, f_Y(y|X=x)$$

Hence:

$$E\Big[E[Y|X]\Big] = E\left[\sum_y y\, f_Y(y|X=x)\right]$$

$$= \sum_x \sum_y y\, f_Y(y|X=x) f_X(x)$$

$$= \sum_{x,y} y\, f_{X,Y}(x,y) = E[Y]$$

The double expectation theorem is particularly useful when X and Y are quite different distributions, *eg* when X is a discrete distribution that models the number of claims and Y is a continuous distribution that models the total amount of claims given X . In this situation, the double expectation theorem allows us to calculate the expected total amount of claims, even though the number of claims is also uncertain.

A similar result gives a useful result for calculating variance. It is stated without proof in Theorem 8.7.

Theorem 8.7

For any two random variables X and Y:

$$\text{var}(Y) = E\left[\text{var}(Y|X)\right] + \text{var}\left(E[Y|X]\right)$$

Proof

From the basic definition of variance, we have:

$$\text{var}\left[Y|X\right] = E\left[Y^2 \mid X\right] - (E[Y \mid X])^2$$

Hence:

$$\text{var}\left[E[Y|X]\right] = E\left[(E[Y \mid X])^2\right] - \left[E(E[Y \mid X])\right]^2$$
$$= E\left[(E[Y \mid X])^2\right] - E^2[Y]$$

$$E\left[\text{var}[Y|X]\right] = E\left[E\left[Y^2 \mid X\right] - (E[Y \mid X])^2\right]$$
$$= E\left[E\left[Y^2 \mid X\right]\right] - E\left[(E[Y \mid X])^2\right]$$
$$= E[Y^2] - E\left[(E[Y \mid X])^2\right]$$

So:

$$E\left[\text{var}(Y|X)\right] + \text{var}\left(E[Y|X]\right)$$
$$= E[Y^2] - E\left[(E[Y \mid X])^2\right] + E\left[(E[Y \mid X])^2\right] - E^2[Y]$$
$$= E[Y^2] - E^2[Y] = \text{var}(Y) \qquad \qquad \square$$

Let's illustrate both of these results with a numerical example.

Example 8.9

45% of the participants in a clinical trial are male. For the male participants, the average height is 70 inches and the standard deviation is 3 inches. For the female participants, the average height is 65 inches and the standard deviation is 4 inches.

An individual is randomly selected from the group. Determine the expected value and variance of the individual's height.

Solution

Let X denote height for an individual randomly selected from this group.

We'll also define an indicator variable I to differentiate between male participants ($I = 1$) and female participants ($I = 2$).

Let's use these symbols to express the information given in the question:

$$\Pr(I = 1) = 0.45 \qquad \qquad \Pr(I = 2) = 0.55$$

$$E\left[X|I = 1\right] = 70 \qquad \qquad E\left[X|I = 2\right] = 65$$

$$\text{var}\left(X|I = 1\right) = 3^2 = 9 \qquad \text{var}\left(X|I = 2\right) = 4^2 = 16$$

Using the double expectation theorem (Theorem 8.6), the expected height of a randomly selected individual from this group is:

$$E[X] = E\big[E[X|I]\big] = \sum_{i=1}^{2} E\big[X|I=i\big]\Pr(I=i) = 0.45\times 70 + 0.55\times 65 = 67.25$$

Let's now compute $\mathrm{var}(X)$ using Theorem 8.7.

We have:

$$E\big[\mathrm{var}(X|I)\big] = \sum_{i=1}^{2}\mathrm{var}(X|I=i)\Pr(I=i) = 0.45\times 9 + 0.55\times 16 = 12.85$$

and:

$$\mathrm{var}\big(E[X|I]\big) = E\Big[\big(E[X|I]\big)^2\Big] - \big(E\big[E[X|I]\big]\big)^2 = 0.45\times 70^2 + 0.55\times 65^2 - (67.25)^2 = 6.1875$$

Finally, we have:

$$\mathrm{var}(X) = E\big[\mathrm{var}(X|I)\big] + \mathrm{var}\big(E[X|I]\big) = 12.85 + 6.1875 = 19.0375$$

Note that the formula for $\mathrm{var}(X)$ comprises two sources of variance:

- the first term represents the average variance *within* the male group and female group

- the second term represents the variability *between* the groups, in terms of the variance of the means of each group.   ◆◆

8.5 *Covariance and correlation*

For a joint distribution of two random variables X and Y, it is often useful to know how the values of X and Y are correlated with each other.

The **covariance** of two random variables, X and Y, is a measure of the tendency of the random variables to vary together. It characterizes the correlation between two random variables, *eg* whether X and Y tend to take high values simultaneously and low values simultaneously, or whether there is no discernible linear association between the values taken by X and Y.

Covariance

The **covariance** of the two random variables X and Y is defined as:

$$\mathrm{cov}(X,Y) = E\big[(X-E[X])(Y-E[Y])\big]$$

The covariance can also be calculated as:

$$\mathrm{cov}(X,Y) = E[XY] - E[X]E[Y]$$

The second version of the covariance can be proved as follows:

$$\text{cov}(X,Y) = E\left[\left(X - E[X]\right)\left(Y - E[Y]\right)\right]$$
$$= E[XY - YE(X) - XE(Y) + E(X)E(Y)]$$
$$= E[XY] - E[YE(X)] - E[XE(Y)] + E[E(X)E(Y)]$$

But $E[X]$ and $E[Y]$ are just constants, so:

$$\text{cov}(X,Y) = E[XY] - E[YE(X)] - E[XE(Y)] + E[E(X)E(Y)]$$
$$= E[XY] - E[Y]E[X] - E[X]E[Y] + E[X]E[Y]$$
$$= E[XY] - E[Y]E[X]$$

Example 8.10

Using the information in Example 8.5, calculate the covariance of X and Y.

Solution

From the solution to Example 8.5, we have:

$$E[Y] = 0.65$$

The expected value of X is:

$$E[X] = \sum_{\text{all } x,y} x f_{X,Y}(x,y)$$
$$= 0 \times 0.3 + 1 \times (0.25 + 0.15) + 2 \times (0.05 + 0.1 + 0.15) = 1$$

and we can calculate $E[XY]$ as:

$$E[XY] = \sum_{x,y} xy \, f_{X,Y}(x,y)$$
$$= \underbrace{0 \times (0.3 + 0.15 + 0.05)}_{x=0 \text{ or } y=0} + \underbrace{1 \times 0.25}_{x=1, y=1} + \underbrace{2 \times 0.1}_{x=2, y=1} + \underbrace{4 \times 0.15}_{x=2, y=2}$$
$$= 1.05$$

Hence the covariance of X and Y is:

$$\text{cov}(X,Y) = E[XY] - E[X]E[Y]$$
$$= 1.05 - 1 \times 0.65 = 0.4 \qquad \blacklozenge\blacklozenge$$

Note that the covariance of two random variables can be positive or negative. To see why, let's look more closely at the definition of covariance:

$$\text{cov}(X,Y) = E\left[\left(X - E[X]\right)\left(Y - E[Y]\right)\right]$$

This formula will produce a positive result if values of X that are greater than $E[X]$ occur at the same time as values of Y that are greater than $E[Y]$, and if values of X that are less than $E[X]$ occur at the same time as values of Y that are less than $E[Y]$.

An example would be if X represents the number of ice-creams sold on a certain day, and Y is the temperature on the same day. High values of X (*ie* high sales of ice-cream) tend to occur at the same time as high values of Y (*ie* hot days). We might say that sales of ice-cream are **positively correlated** with good weather.

Similarly, the formula will produce a negative result if values of X that are greater than $E[X]$ occur at the same time as values of Y that are less than $E[Y]$, and if values of X that are less than $E[X]$ occur at the same time as values of Y that are greater than $E[Y]$.

An example would be if X represents an adult's age, and Y is that individual's VO2 max, a common measurement of athletic fitness. High values of X tend to occur at the same time as lower values of Y (*ie* older people tend to be less fit than young adults). We might say that age is **negatively correlated** with VO2 max.

We can also derive the following properties from the definition of covariance.

Properties of the covariance function

(1) $\quad \text{var}(X) = \text{cov}(X, X)$

(2) $\quad \text{cov}(X, Y) = \text{cov}(Y, X)$

(3) $\quad \text{cov}(aX + bY, Z) = a\,\text{cov}(X, Z) + b\,\text{cov}(Y, Z)$

(4) $\quad \text{cov}(X, Y) = 0$ if X and Y are independent

(5) $\quad \text{var}(aX + bY) = \text{cov}(aX + bY, aX + bY) = a^2\,\text{var}(X) + b^2\,\text{var}(Y) + 2ab\,\text{cov}(X, Y)$

Property 4 follows directly from Theorem 8.2. Note that the converse of Property 4 is not always true, *ie* a covariance of zero does not necessarily imply that X and Y are independent.

Using Property 5 and setting $a = 1, b = 1$, we have:

$$\text{var}(X + Y) > \text{var}(X) + \text{var}(Y) \quad \text{if } \text{cov}(X, Y) > 0$$

Intuitively, if X and Y are positively correlated (*ie* X is large when Y is large, and small when Y is small) then the sum of X and Y should have a larger variance, since the large and small values are exaggerated.

We also have:

$$\text{var}(X + Y) < \text{var}(X) + \text{var}(Y) \quad \text{if } \text{cov}(X, Y) < 0$$

Intuitively, if X and Y tend to take opposing values (*eg* X is small when Y is large, and vice versa) then the sum of X and Y should have a lower variance, since the large and small values tend to cancel each other out.

Since the magnitude of covariance can vary greatly, we commonly use a measure of covariance known as the **correlation coefficient**. The correlation coefficient of two random variables, X and Y, is calculated from the covariance but is standardized in order to take values between –1 and 1.

Correlation coefficient

The **correlation coefficient** of X and Y is denoted ρ (rho) and is defined as:

$$\rho = \frac{\text{cov}(X, Y)}{\sigma_X \, \sigma_Y}$$

The correlation coefficient is a "unitless" measure, *ie* it is a pure number.

Example 8.11

Using the information in Examples 8.5 and 8.10, calculate the correlation coefficient of X and Y.

Solution

From the solution to Examples 8.5 and 8.10, we have:

$$E[X] = 1$$
$$\sigma_Y^2 = 0.5275$$
$$\text{cov}(X,Y) = 0.4$$

The variance of X is calculated as follows:

$$E\left[X^2\right] = \sum_{\text{all } x,y} x^2 f_{X,Y}(x,y) = 0^2 \times 0.3 \ + \ 1^2 \times (0.25 + 0.15) \ + \ 2^2 \times (0.05 + 0.1 + 0.15) = 1.6$$

$$\Rightarrow \sigma_X^2 = E\left[X^2\right] - (E[X])^2 = 1.6 - 1^2 = 0.6$$

Hence the correlation coefficient of X and Y is:

$$\rho = \frac{\text{cov}(X,Y)}{\sigma_X \sigma_Y} = \frac{0.4}{\sqrt{0.6} \times \sqrt{0.5275}} = 0.7110 \qquad\qquad \blacklozenge\blacklozenge$$

The correlation coefficient has the following important properties:

Properties of the correlation coefficient

(1) $-1 \le \rho \le 1$

(2) $\rho = 0$ if X and Y are independent (but the converse is not always true)

The correlation coefficient has another important property. If we take a number of random sample values from a joint distribution of the form (x,y) and plot these on a graph, we can explore the relation between the pairs of outcomes by drawing a "best-fit" line. A common way to define the best-fit line is the line that minimizes the total of the squared vertical distances between the points on the graph and the line. If we further constrain the best-fit line to pass through the point (μ_X, μ_Y), then the best-fit line is found to be:

$$y = \mu_Y + \rho \frac{\sigma_Y}{\sigma_X}(x - \mu_x)$$

In other words, the gradient of the best-fit line depends on the correlation coefficient.

When $\rho = 1$, the random variables X and Y are said to be **perfectly positively correlated**. X and Y take high values simultaneously and low values simultaneously.

This is shown in the graph on the right.

When X and Y are perfectly positively correlated, we can predict the value of one variable with certainty if we know the value of the other variable.

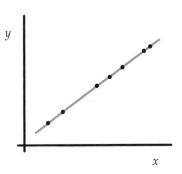

When $\rho = -1$, the random variables X and Y are said to be **perfectly negatively correlated**. When X takes a high value, Y takes a low value, and vice versa.

This is shown in the graph on the right.

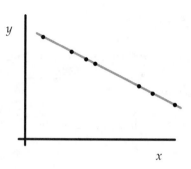

Again, when X and Y are perfectly negatively correlated, we can predict the value of one variable with certainty if we know the value of the other variable.

When $\rho = 0$, the random variables X and Y are said to be **uncorrelated**. There is no discernible linear association between the variables. When X takes a high value, Y may take a high value or a low value.

This is shown in the graph on the right.

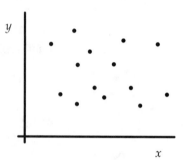

When X and Y are uncorrelated, we may not be able to predict the value of one variable with certainty if we know the value of the other variable.

Note that the correlation coefficient measures the strength of *linear* relationship between X and Y. It is possible for $\rho = 0$ but for X and Y to be dependent, *eg* if they are related in a nonlinear manner such as $Y = a + bX^2$.

8.6 *The bivariate normal distribution*

We'll conclude this chapter by looking at an important joint continuous distribution.

The continuous random variables X and Y follow a **bivariate normal distribution** if the joint probability density function is:

$$f_{X,Y}(x,y) = \frac{1}{2\pi\sigma_X\sigma_Y\sqrt{(1-\rho^2)}}\exp\left[-\frac{z^2}{2(1-\rho^2)}\right] \quad \text{for } -1 < \rho < 1$$

where:

$$z^2 = \left(\frac{x-\mu_X}{\sigma_X}\right)^2 - 2\rho\left(\frac{x-\mu_X}{\sigma_X}\right)\left(\frac{y-\mu_Y}{\sigma_Y}\right) + \left(\frac{y-\mu_Y}{\sigma_Y}\right)^2$$

$$\rho = \frac{\text{cov}(X,Y)}{\sigma_X\,\sigma_Y}$$

Although this joint distribution looks very complicated at first sight, it has some remarkably simple and important properties.

First, the marginal distributions of X and Y are normal with:

$$X \sim N\left(\mu_X, \sigma_X^2\right)$$

$$Y \sim N\left(\mu_Y, \sigma_Y^2\right)$$

Further, the conditional distributions of X and Y are normal with:

$$X|Y = y \sim N\left(\mu_X + \rho\frac{\sigma_X}{\sigma_Y}(y-\mu_Y) \; , \; \sigma_X^2(1-\rho^2)\right)$$

$$Y|X = x \sim N\left(\mu_Y + \rho\frac{\sigma_Y}{\sigma_X}(x-\mu_X) \; , \; \sigma_Y^2(1-\rho^2)\right)$$

We may use the bivariate normal distribution to model two associated random variables, which are each distributed normally.

For example, we may wish to measure the levels of LDL ("bad cholesterol") and HDL ("good cholesterol") in a group of individuals. If we define X and Y to be the levels of LDL and HDL respectively for an individual, and:

$$\mu_X = 130 \qquad \sigma_X^2 = 625 \qquad \mu_Y = 40 \qquad \sigma_Y^2 = 100 \qquad \rho = 0.2$$

Then if we find that an individual has an HDL equal to 58 (*ie* $Y = 58$), the conditional distribution of X given Y, is normal with mean:

$$E[X|Y = 58] = \mu_X + \rho\frac{\sigma_X}{\sigma_Y}(y-\mu_Y) = 130 + 0.2\times\frac{25}{10}\times(58-40) = 139$$

and variance:

$$\mathrm{var}(X|Y = 58) = \sigma_X^2(1-\rho^2) = 625(1-0.2^2) = 600$$

The bivariate normal distribution has an important property when $\rho = 0$. Remember that in general for two random variables, a correlation coefficient of zero does not necessarily imply that X and Y are independent. For the bivariate normal distribution, however, when $\rho = 0$, then X and Y are independent, since:

$$f_{X,Y}(x,y) = \frac{1}{2\pi\sigma_X\sigma_Y}\exp\left[-\frac{(x-\mu_X)^2}{2\sigma_X^2} - \frac{(y-\mu_Y)^2}{2\sigma_Y^2}\right]$$

$$= \left(\frac{1}{\sigma_X\sqrt{2\pi}}\exp\left[-\frac{(x-\mu_X)^2}{2\sigma_X^2}\right]\right)\left(\frac{1}{\sigma_Y\sqrt{2\pi}}\exp\left[-\frac{(y-\mu_Y)^2}{2\sigma_Y^2}\right]\right)$$

$$= f_X(x)f_Y(y)$$

Finally, there is a special case of the bivariate normal distribution if X and Y follow a standard normal distribution, with means equal to 0 and variances equal to 1. In this case, the joint probability distribution of X and Y is a called a **standard bivariate normal distribution**, and it has a simplified pdf of:

$$f_{X,Y}(x,y) = \frac{1}{2\pi\sqrt{(1-\rho^2)}}\exp\left[-\frac{\left(x^2 - 2\rho xy + y^2\right)}{2(1-\rho^2)}\right] \qquad \text{for } -1 < \rho < 1$$

The conditional distributions of X and Y also simplify as follows:

$$X|Y = y \sim N\left(\rho y, 1-\rho^2\right)$$

$$Y|X = x \sim N\left(\rho x, 1-\rho^2\right)$$

Example 8.12

An actuary measures the height in inches (X) and weight in pounds (Y) of a group of patients in a clinical trial for a new drug. The actuary finds that:

$$\mu_X = 68 \qquad \sigma_X^2 = 16 \qquad \mu_Y = 172 \qquad \sigma_Y^2 = 225 \qquad \rho = 0.6$$

If (X,Y) follows a bivariate normal distribution, calculate:

(i)   the probability that a randomly chosen individual is more than 64 inches tall

(ii)   the expected weight of a randomly chosen individual who is 72 inches tall

(iii)   the probability that a randomly chosen individual who is 72 inches tall weighs more than 199 pounds.

Solution

(i)   The marginal distribution of X is:

$$X \sim N(68,16)$$

Hence the required probability is:

$$\Pr(X > 64) = 1 - \Pr(X < 64) = 1 - \Pr\left(\frac{X-68}{\sqrt{16}} < \frac{64-68}{\sqrt{16}}\right)$$

$$= 1 - \Phi(-1) = \Phi(1) = 0.8413$$

(ii)   The expected weight of a randomly chosen individual who is 72 inches tall is:

$$E[Y|X=72] = \mu_Y + \rho\frac{\sigma_Y}{\sigma_X}(x - \mu_X)$$

$$= 172 + 0.6 \times \frac{15}{4} \times (72 - 68) = 181$$

(iii)   To calculate the probability that a randomly chosen individual who is 72 inches tall weighs more than 199 pounds, we must first find the conditional variance:

$$\text{var}(Y|X=72) = \sigma_Y^2(1-\rho^2) = 225 \times \left(1 - 0.6^2\right) = 144$$

Hence the conditional distribution of $Y|X=72$ is:

$$Y|X=72 \sim N(181,144)$$

and the required probability is:

$$\Pr(Y > 199|X=72) = 1 - \Pr(Y < 199|X=72)$$

$$= 1 - \Phi\left(\frac{199-181}{\sqrt{144}}\right)$$

$$= 1 - \Phi(1.5)$$

$$= 1 - 0.9332 = 0.0668$$

◆◆

Chapter 8 Practice Questions

Free online solutions manual

You can download detailed worked solutions to every practice question in this book free of charge from the BPP Professional Education website at **www.bpptraining.com**. You'll also find other useful study resources here.

Question 8.1

Two discrete random variables, X and Y, have the following joint probability function:

		\multicolumn{4}{c}{X}			
		0	**1**	**2**	**3**
	1	0.05	0.18	0.13	0.07
Y	**2**	0.09	0.14	0.08	0.06
	3	0.11	0.03	0.04	0.02

Calculate the probability that $X + Y \leq 3$.

Question 8.2

Using the information in Question 8.1, calculate the marginal probability function of X.

Question 8.3

Using the information in Question 8.1, calculate the conditional probability function of Y given that $X = 2$.

Question 8.4

Let T_1 and T_2 represent the times until failure in years of two linked components in a security system. The joint probability density function for T_1 and T_2 is constant over the region defined by $0 \leq t_1 \leq t_2 \leq 2$. Calculate the probability that the lifetime of the second component is more than twice the lifetime of the first component.

Question 8.5   *SOA/CAS*

An insurance company sells two types of auto insurance policies: Basic and Deluxe. The time until the next Basic Policy claim is an exponential random variable with mean two days. The time until the next Deluxe Policy Claim is an independent exponential random variable with mean three days. What is the probability that the next claim will be a Deluxe Policy claim?

Question 8.6   *SOA/CAS*

An insurance policy is written to cover a loss X where X has density function:

$$f(x) = \begin{cases} \dfrac{3}{8}x^2 & \text{for } 0 \le x \le 2 \\ 0 & \text{otherwise} \end{cases}$$

The time in hours to process a claim of size x is uniformly distributed on the interval from x to $2x$. Calculate the probability that a randomly chosen claim on this policy is processed in three hours or more.

Question 8.7   *SOA/CAS*

The future lifetimes (in months) of two components of a machine have the following joint density function:

$$f(x,y) = \begin{cases} \dfrac{6}{125{,}000}(50 - x - y) & \text{for } 0 < x < 50 - y < 50 \\ 0 & \text{otherwise} \end{cases}$$

Identify the range over which the pdf should be integrated in order to calculate the probability that both components are still functioning 20 months from now.

Question 8.8   *IOA/FOA*

The table below shows a bivariate probability distribution for two discrete random variables X and Y.

	$X = 0$	$X = 1$	$X = 2$
$Y = 1$	0.10	0.20	0.30
$Y = 2$	0.20	0.15	0.05

Calculate the value of $E\big[X \mid Y = 1\big]$.

Question 8.9

For a certain insurance policy, X is a loss amount claimed by an insured and Y is the amount of the loss that is allowed by the claim adjuster. The joint density of X and Y is modeled by:

$$f(x,y) = \begin{cases} \dfrac{8xy}{100^4} & 0 \le y \le x \le 100 \\ 0 & \text{otherwise} \end{cases}$$

Calculate the expected amount allowed on a claimed amount equal to 50.

Question 8.10

A diagnostic test for the presence of a disease has two possible outcomes: 1 for disease present and 0 for disease not present. Let X denote the disease state of a patient, and let Y denote the outcome of the diagnostic test. The joint probability function of X and Y is given by:

$$P(X = 0, Y = 0) = 0.800 \qquad P(X = 1, Y = 0) = 0.050$$
$$P(X = 0, Y = 1) = 0.025 \qquad P(X = 1, Y = 1) = 0.125$$

Calculate $\mathrm{var}(Y \,|\, X = 1)$.

Question 8.11

The future lifetime (measured in years) of a newborn child, Y, is assumed to follow a uniform distribution on the interval $[0, 100]$. Calculate the conditional variance of the age at death given that the individual survives to age 25.

Question 8.12

The random variables X and Y are uniformly distributed on the region $0 < x < y < 1$. Identify the moment generating function of $X + Y$.

Question 8.13

The random variable $X \,|\, Y = y$ follows a gamma distribution with parameters $\alpha = y$ and $\theta = 10$, where Y follows a uniform distribution on the interval $(5, 8)$. Calculate $E[X]$.

Question 8.14

The number of claims, N, which arise under a group of policies in a year has a Poisson distribution with mean 200. The claim amounts are independent of one another and of N, and are distributed normally with mean \$250 and standard deviation \$40. Calculate the standard deviation of the total claim amount arising from this group of policies in a year.

Question 8.15

Let X be a random variable with mean 34 and standard deviation 8, and let Y be a random variable with mean 41 and standard deviation 10. Let the covariance between X and Y be $\mathrm{cov}(X, Y) = -20$. Let $L = 4X - Y + 80$. Calculate the standard deviation of L.

Question 8.16

Using the information in Question 8.1, calculate the covariance of X and Y.

Question 8.17

Consider two random variables X and Y with covariance $\text{cov}(X,Y) = 24$, correlation coefficient $\rho = +0.8$, and with variances such that $\text{var}(X) = 4\,\text{var}(Y)$. Calculate the variance of X.

Question 8.18

Let X and Y denote the values of two stocks at the end of a five-year period. X is uniformly distributed on the interval $(0,12)$. Given $X = x$, Y is uniformly distributed on the interval $(0,x)$. Determine $\text{cov}(X,Y)$ according to this model.

Question 8.19

The random variables X and Y follow a bivariate normal distribution with:

$$\mu_X = 12 \qquad \sigma_X^2 = 9 \qquad \mu_Y = 20 \qquad \sigma_Y^2 = 25 \qquad \rho = 0.8$$

Calculate $E\left(X|Y = 17\right)$.

Question 8.20

Using the information in Question 8.19, calculate $\Pr\left(Y < 30|X = 15\right)$.

9

Transformations of Random Variables

In this chapter, we'll consider the situation where a random variable Y is defined as a function (or transformation) of another random variable X, or perhaps several random variables $X_1, X_2, \cdots$. We have already seen how to calculate some simple probabilities and moments of transformed variables in Chapters 4 and 7.

We'll look at the theory of transformations in general, for both discrete and continuous distributions, and we'll pay particular attention to three transformations with applications to the insurance industry:

- when insurance losses are subject to inflation from one year to the next

- when insurance losses are subject to a deductible

- when insurance losses are subject to a policy limit.

Finally, we'll conclude this chapter with a study of order statistics.

9.1 Transformations of a discrete random variable

Suppose that X is a discrete random variable and that $Y = g(X)$ is a function of X. Then how is the probability function of Y related to the probability function of X?

If the transformation $y = g(x)$ is 1-1, then it should be clear that for each x and y such that $y = g(x)$, we have:

$$f_Y(y) = \Pr(Y = y) = \Pr(Y = g(x)) = \Pr(X = x) = f_X(x)$$

However, if there are n values $x_1, x_2, \cdots, x_n$ such that $g(x_1) = g(x_2) = \cdots = g(x_n) = y$ then:

$$f_Y(y) = \sum_{x_i : g(x_i) = y} f_X(x_i)$$

Let's illustrate this with a simple example.

Example 9.1

Let X be a discrete random variable with:

$$f_X(-1) = 0.2 \qquad f_X(0) = 0.5 \qquad f_X(1) = 0.3$$

Determine the probability function of Y if:

(i) $Y = 2X$

(ii) $Y = X^2$

Solution

(i)   If $Y = 2X$, then the transformation is 1-1 and it is simple to see that:

$$f_Y(-2) = 0.2 \qquad f_Y(0) = 0.5 \qquad f_Y(2) = 0.3$$

(ii)   If $Y = X^2$, then note that $(-1)^2 = 1^2 = 1$, hence:

$$f_Y(0) = 0.5 \qquad f_Y(1) = f_X(-1) + f_X(1) = 0.2 + 0.3 = 0.5 \qquad\qquad \blacklozenge\blacklozenge$$

The cumulative distribution function of Y can be defined in a similar way as:

$$F_Y(y) = \Pr(Y \le y) = \sum_{x_i : g(x_i) \le y} f_X(x_i)$$

Once a discrete random variable has been transformed, expectations and variances can be calculated from $f_Y(y)$ in the usual fashion. However, they can also be calculated directly from $f_X(x)$ and the transformation $y = g(x)$ using:

$$E\left[Y^k\right] = \sum_x \left(g(x)\right)^k f_X(x)$$

For example, with $k = 1$ and $Y = X^2$ as above, we have:

$$E[Y] = \sum_x x^2 f_X(x) = (-1)^2 \times 0.2 + 0^2 \times 0.5 + 1^2 \times 0.3 = 0.5$$

or using $f_Y(y)$:

$$E[Y] = \sum_y y f_Y(y) = 0 \times 0.5 + 1 \times 0.5 = 0.5$$

As you can see, transformations of discrete random variables are quite straightforward. Let's work through another numerical example before we look at the more complicated area of transformations of continuous random variables.

Example 9.2

A tropical island is frequently affected by hurricanes. The total amount of damage caused by the hurricanes in a given year is:

Damage ($m)	50	250	500	1,000
Probability	0.2	0.3	0.4	0.1

The government of the island is considering whether or not to buy an insurance policy to cover hurricane damage. The policy will pay 80% of the annual damage in excess of $100m, subject to a maximum total payment of $500m.

Calculate the expected payment from the policy.

Solution

Let X be the total amount of damage, and let Y be the annual payment from the policy.

If $X = 50$ then $Y = 0$, since the damage does not exceed $100m.

For $X > 50$, we have:

$$Y = \min\{0.8(X - 100), 500\}$$

The payments are shown in the table below.

Damage ($m)	50	250	500	1,000
Payment ($m)	0	120	320	500
Probability	0.2	0.3	0.4	0.1

Hence the expected payment is:

$$E[Y] = \sum_y y f_Y(y) = 0 \times 0.2 + 120 \times 0.3 + 320 \times 0.4 + 500 \times 0.1 = 214$$

So, the expected payment from the policy is $214m.

♦♦

9.2 *Transformations of a continuous random variable*

If X is a continuous random variable and $Y = g(X)$ is a transformation of X, then there are two main methods for calculating the probability density function of Y:

- the **method of transformations**

- the **method of distribution functions**.

The best method in a particular situation will usually depend on the nature of the transformation and the information available.

The method of transformations

Suppose that the transformation $y = g(x)$ is 1-1 and differentiable. Let $x = g^{-1}(y)$ denote the inverse transformation that is obtained by solving $y = g(x)$ for x in terms of y.

Then:

$$f_Y(y) = f_X\left(g^{-1}(y)\right)\left|\frac{dg^{-1}(y)}{dy}\right|$$

Example 9.3

The random variable X has an exponential distribution with mean 1,000. If $Y = 1.1X$, then identify the distribution of Y.

Solution

The pdf of X is:

$$f_X(x) = \frac{1}{1,000}e^{-x/1,000} \qquad \text{for } x > 0$$

Now, if $Y = g(X) = 1.1X$, we have a 1-1 differentiable transformation.

The inverse transformation is:

$$X = Y/1.1$$

So, using the method of transformations:

$$f_Y(y) = f_X\left(\frac{y}{1.1}\right)\left|\frac{d(y/1.1)}{dy}\right| = \left(\frac{1}{1,000}e^{-y/1,100}\right) \times \frac{1}{1.1}$$

$$= \frac{1}{1,100}e^{-y/1,100} \qquad \text{for } y > 0$$

We can see that Y has an exponential distribution with mean 1,100.   ◆◆

The method of distribution functions is a two-step process that—unlike the method of transformations—does not require that the transformation be 1-1.

The method of distribution functions

Step 1: Relate the distribution function of Y to the distribution function of X.

Step 2: Differentiate both sides of this relation to obtain a relation of density functions.

For example, suppose that $Y = X^2$. Then we have:

$$F_Y(y) = \Pr(Y \leq y) = \Pr(X^2 \leq y) = \Pr(-\sqrt{y} \leq X \leq \sqrt{y}) = F_X(\sqrt{y}) - F_X(-\sqrt{y})$$

Differentiating both sides of this relation with respect to y, and using both $F_X'(x) = f_X(x)$ and the chain rule, we have:

$$f_Y(y) = f_X(\sqrt{y}) \times \frac{1}{2\sqrt{y}} - f_X(-\sqrt{y}) \times \left(-\frac{1}{2\sqrt{y}}\right)$$

 ## Example 9.4

The random variable X has an exponential distribution with mean 1,000. If $Y = 1.1X$, then identify the distribution of Y using the method of distribution functions.

Solution

We have:

$$F_Y(y) = \Pr(Y \leq y) = \Pr(1.1X \leq y) = \Pr(X \leq y/1.1)$$

$$= F_X(y/1.1) = 1 - e^{-(y/1.1)/1,000} = 1 - e^{-y/1,100}$$

We can easily confirm that Y has an exponential distribution with mean 1,100.

We can also calculate the pdf of Y as:

$$f_Y(y) = F_Y'(y) = \frac{1}{1,100} e^{-y/1,100} \qquad\qquad ♦♦$$

 ## Example 9.5

The random variable X has a normal distribution with parameters μ and σ^2. If $Y = e^X$, obtain $f_Y(y)$ using the method of distribution functions.

Solution

We have:

$$F_Y(y) = \Pr(e^X \leq y) = \Pr(X \leq \ln y) = \int_{-\infty}^{\ln y} f_X(x)\, dx = \int_{-\infty}^{\ln y} \frac{1}{\sigma\sqrt{2\pi}} \exp\left(-\frac{(x-\mu)^2}{2\sigma^2}\right) dx$$

Substituting $s = e^x$, the upper limit on the integral changes to $e^{\ln y}$, the lower limit changes to 0, $x = \ln s$, and we have:

$$\frac{dx}{ds} = \frac{d \ln s}{ds} = \frac{1}{s} \Rightarrow dx = \frac{1}{s} ds$$

Hence we have:

$$F_Y(y) = \int_0^y \frac{1}{\sigma s \sqrt{2\pi}} \exp\left(-\frac{(\ln s - \mu)^2}{2\sigma^2}\right) ds$$

Finally, differentiating we obtain:

$$f_Y(y) = \frac{1}{\sigma y \sqrt{2\pi}} \exp\left(-\frac{(\ln y - \mu)^2}{2\sigma^2}\right) \qquad \blacklozenge\blacklozenge$$

(This is actually the pdf of a named continuous distribution called the lognormal distribution.)

Note that we have used the method of distribution functions once before in this textbook, in the proof of Theorem 7.1. You may like to look back at this proof now that we have formally named and defined this method. In the next example, we'll show an equivalent proof of Theorem 7.1 using the method of transformations.

Example 9.6

If $X \sim N(\mu, \sigma^2)$ and $Z = \dfrac{X - \mu}{\sigma}$, show that $Z \sim N(0,1)$.

Solution

The pdf of X is:

$$f_X(x) = \frac{1}{\sigma \sqrt{2\pi}} \exp\left[-\frac{(x - \mu)^2}{2\sigma^2}\right]$$

The inverse transformation is:

$$X = \mu + Z\sigma$$

Hence:

$$f_Z(z) = f_X(\mu + z\sigma)\left|\frac{d(\mu + z\sigma)}{dz}\right|$$

$$= \frac{1}{\sigma \sqrt{2\pi}} \exp\left[-\frac{((\mu + z\sigma) - \mu)^2}{2\sigma^2}\right] \cdot \sigma$$

$$= \frac{1}{\sqrt{2\pi}} \exp\left(-\frac{z^2}{2}\right)$$

which we recognize as the pdf of the standard normal distribution. $\blacklozenge\blacklozenge$

Moments of $Y = g(X)$ can be calculated in the usual fashion using the probability density function of Y, or they can also be calculated from the probability density function of X and the transformation:

$$E\left[Y^k\right] = \int (g(x))^k f_X(x)\,dx$$

9.3 Common transformations in the insurance industry

We'll now look at 3 specific transformations with common applications in insurance.

-   We may wish to model the cost of insurance claims if we assume that losses increase in each year due to **inflation**.

-   We may wish to model the cost of insurance claims if we apply a **deductible** to each loss. This means that the insurance company will pay zero if a loss is below the deductible, and will otherwise make a claim payment equal to the loss *less* the deductible.

-   We may wish to model the cost of insurance claims if we apply a **policy limit** to each loss. This means that every claim payment made by the insurance company is restricted to a maximum of the policy limit.

In the following, X is a continuous random variable that represents the loss to an insured party.

Claims inflation

Suppose that losses are subject to $100\,r\,\%$ inflation next year. For example, if losses are subject to 5% inflation, $r = 0.05$. Let Y represent the loss distribution for next year.

The transformation is thus $Y = (1+r)X$, which is 1-1 and differentiable. So, we can find the probability density function for next year's losses using the method of transformations.

Let $y = g(x) = (1+r)x$, then:

$$g^{-1}(y) = y/(1+r)$$

and the pdf is calculated as follows:

$$f_Y(y) = f_X\left(g^{-1}(y)\right)\left|\frac{dg^{-1}(y)}{dy}\right| = f_X\left(\frac{y}{1+r}\right)\left|\frac{d(y/(1+r))}{dy}\right| = \frac{1}{1+r} f_X\left(\frac{y}{1+r}\right)$$

Example 9.7

In 2005, a random loss X is distributed uniformly on the interval $[0,1000]$. If insurance losses are expected to rise by 4% inflation per year, identify the pdf of the loss in 2006.

Solution

The pdf of X is:

$$f_X(x) = \frac{1}{1,000} \qquad \text{for } 0 < x < 1,000$$

The transformation is $Y = 1.04X$, which is 1-1 and differentiable, so we can find the probability density function for 2006 using the method of transformations.

Let $y = g(x) = 1.04x$, then $g^{-1}(y) = y/1.04$ and the pdf of Y is calculated as follows:

$$f_Y(y) = \frac{1}{1+r} f_X\left(\frac{y}{1+r}\right) = \frac{1}{1.04} \times \frac{1}{1,000} = \frac{1}{1,040} \qquad \text{for } 0 < y < 1,040$$

ie Y is distributed uniformly on $[0, 1040]$.   ♦♦

Deductible

Let Y represent the claim payment made by an insurance company that applies a deductible d to each loss X. Then:

$$Y = (X-d)_+ = \max\{(X-d), 0\} = \begin{cases} 0 & 0 < X \le d \\ X-d & X > d \end{cases}$$

We can calculate the expected value of the claim payments as:

$$E[Y] = \int g(x) f_X(x) dx$$

$$= \int_0^d 0 \times f_X(x) dx + \int_d^\infty (x-d) f_X(x) dx$$

$$= \int_d^\infty (x-d) f_X(x) dx$$

and we can calculate the variance using $\operatorname{var}(Y) = E[Y^2] - (E[Y])^2$ where:

$$E\left[Y^2\right] = \int (g(x))^2 f_X(x) dx$$

$$= \int_0^d 0^2 \times f_X(x) dx + \int_d^\infty (x-d)^2 f_X(x) dx$$

$$= \int_d^\infty (x-d)^2 f_X(x) dx$$

Hence:

$$\operatorname{var}(Y) = \int_d^\infty (x-d)^2 f_X(x) dx - \left(\int_d^\infty (x-d) f_X(x) dx\right)^2$$

Example 9.8

A random loss X is distributed uniformly on the interval $[0, 1000]$. Calculate the expected claim payment if a deductible of 100 is applied to each loss.

Solution

Let Y be the claim payment net of the deductible. Then the expected claim payment is:

$$E[Y] = \int_{100}^{1,000} (x - 100) f_X(x) dx$$

$$= \int_{100}^{1,000} (x - 100) \frac{1}{1,000} dx$$

$$= \frac{1}{2,000} (x - 100)^2 \Big|_{100}^{1,000}$$

$$= \frac{1}{2,000} \times 900^2 = 405 \qquad\qquad ◆◆$$

Policy limit

Let Y represent the claim payment made by an insurance company that applies a policy limit L to each loss X.

Then:

$$Y = X \wedge L = \min(X, L) = \begin{cases} X & 0 < X < L \\ L & X \geq L \end{cases}$$

We can calculate the expected value of the claim payments as:

$$E[Y] = \int g(x) f_X(x) dx$$

$$= \int_0^L x f_X(x) dx + \int_L^\infty L f_X(x) dx$$

$$= \int_0^L x f_X(x) dx + L(1 - F_X(L))$$

and we can calculate the variance using $\text{var}(Y) = E[Y^2] - (E[Y])^2$ where:

$$E[Y^2] = \int (g(x))^2 f_X(x) dx$$

$$= \int_0^L x^2 f_X(x) dx + \int_L^\infty L^2 f_X(x) dx$$

$$= \int_0^L x^2 f_X(x) dx + L^2 (1 - F_X(L))$$

 ### Example 9.9

A random loss X is distributed uniformly on the interval $[0, 1000]$. Calculate the expected claim payment if a policy limit of 500 is applied to each loss.

Solution

Let Y be the claim payment. Then the expected claim payment is:

$$E[Y] = \int_0^{500} x \frac{1}{1,000} dx + \int_{500}^{1,000} 500 \frac{1}{1,000} dx$$

$$= \left. \frac{x^2}{2,000} \right|_0^{500} + 500(1 - F(500))$$

$$= \frac{(500)^2}{2,000} + 500 \times \left(1 - \frac{500}{1,000} \right)$$

$$= 125 + 250 = 375$$

9.4 *Transformations of several continuous random variables*

Suppose that $Y = g(X_1, X_2)$ is a function of two continuous random variables. How can the pdf of Y be determined from the joint density function of X_1 and X_2? We solve this problem by applying an extension of the method of distribution functions.

The method of distribution functions for a joint continuous distribution

Step 1 Identify the region $\{(x_1, x_2) : g(x_1, x_2) \le y\}$ in the $X_1 \times X_2$ plane.

Step 2 Calculate $F_Y(y) = \Pr(Y \le y) = \Pr(g(X_1, X_2) \le y)$ from a double integral over this region.

Step 3 Calculate $f_Y(y)$ by differentiating $F_Y(y)$.

Example 9.10

A satellite has two independent power systems. The lifetime of the primary system is distributed exponentially with mean 10 years. The lifetime of the backup system is distributed exponentially with mean 5 years. Calculate the pdf of Y, the total time that the power system will remain functional, if the backup system is operated continuously as soon as the primary system fails.

Solution

Let $Y = X_1 + X_2$ where X_1 and X_2 are the lifetimes of the primary and backup systems.

The joint density of X_1 and X_2 is:

$$f(x_1, x_2) = f(x_1) f(x_2) = 0.10 e^{-0.10 x_1} \times 0.20 e^{-0.20 x_2} \qquad \text{where } x_1, x_2 > 0$$

Step 1: The region in the $X_1 \times X_2$ plane defined by the inequality $X_1 + X_2 \le y$ is a triangular region in the first quadrant below the line $X_1 + X_2 = y$.

Step 2: The cdf of Y is calculated as:

$$F_Y(y) = \Pr(X_1 + X_2 \le y) = \int_{x_2=0}^{y} \int_{x_1=0}^{y-x_2} 0.10\, e^{-0.10x_1}\, 0.20\, e^{-0.20x_2}\, dx_1\, dx_2$$

$$= \int_{x_2=0}^{y} 0.20\, e^{-0.20x_2}\left(1 - e^{-0.10(y-x_2)}\right) dx_2$$

$$= \int_{0}^{y} 0.20 e^{-0.20x_2}\, dx_2 - 2e^{-0.10y} \int_{0}^{y} 0.10 e^{-0.10x_2}\, dx_2$$

$$= \left(1 - e^{-0.20y}\right) - 2e^{-0.10y}\left(1 - e^{-0.10y}\right) = 1 + e^{-0.20y} - 2e^{-0.10y}$$

Step 3: Differentiate this to obtain the density function of Y:

$$f_Y(y) = F_Y'(y) = 0.20\left(e^{-0.10y} - e^{-0.20y}\right) \qquad \blacklozenge\,\blacklozenge$$

9.5 Order statistics

Let's finish this chapter by studying an important application of the theory we studied in the previous section.

Suppose that $X_1, X_2, \cdots, X_n$ are independent, identically distributed continuous random variables, from which we observe a sample $\{x_1, x_2, \cdots, x_n\}$. We might want to calculate quantities such as:

- the probability that the largest value in the sample exceeds 100

- the expected value of the k-th largest value in the sample.

In this situation, we are much more interested in the relative size of the values $\{x_1, x_2, \cdots, x_n\}$ than the order in which the n independent values are observed. To calculate probabilities associated with the relative size of the values, we'll start by ordering the sample by increasing size. We'll do this by making the following definition:

$$y_i = \text{the } i\text{-th smallest value in the sample } \{x_1, x_2, \cdots, x_n\} \text{ for } i = 1, 2, \cdots, n$$

So, y_1 is the smallest value in the sample, and y_n is the largest.

Since the X_i are continuous random variables, we can also reasonably assume that each value in the original sample is unique, *ie*:

$$x_i \ne x_j \quad \text{for all } i \ne j$$

Hence we have:

$$y_1 < y_2 < \cdots < y_n$$

The reordering allows us to restate probabilities and associated quantities more succinctly, in terms of Y_i $(i = 1, \cdots, n)$, the random variables associated with the i-th smallest value observed in the sample, known as **order statistics**.

For example, the probability that the largest value (in a sample of size n) exceeds 100 is:

$$\Pr(Y_n > 100)$$

and we can easily see that this probability is equivalent to:

$$1 - \Pr(Y_n \le 100) = 1 - \Pr\left(\{X_1 \le 100\} \cap \{X_2 \le 100\} \cap \cdots \cap \{X_n \le 100\}\right)$$

$$= 1 - \prod_{i=1}^{n} \Pr(X_i \le 100)$$

More generally, we can use this approach to derive the distribution function of Y_i:

$$F_{Y_i}(y) = \Pr(Y_i \le y)$$

This is equal to the probability that at least i values in the sample $\{x_1, x_2, \cdots, x_n\}$ are no greater than y. Exactly j values can be selected from the sample of size n in ${}_nC_j$ ways, so we have:

$$F_{Y_i}(y) = \Pr(Y_i \le y) = \sum_{j=i}^{n} {}_nC_j \left(F_X(y)\right)^j \left(1 - F_X(y)\right)^{n-j}$$

We can then identify the pdf of Y_i by differentiating the cdf. Let's work through an example.

Example 9.11

Claims are assumed to follow a uniform distribution on the interval $[0, 500]$. If 3 claims are observed, calculate the probability that:

(i)   the largest claim exceeds 450

(ii)   the middle claim is less than 240.

Solution

(i)   The probability that a single claim is no greater than 450 is:

$$\Pr(X_i \le 450) = F_X(450) = \int_0^{450} \frac{1}{500} dx = 0.9$$

Hence, the probability that the largest claim exceeds 450 is:

$$1 - \Pr(Y_3 \le 450) = 1 - \Pr\left(\{X_1 \le 450\} \cap \{X_2 \le 450\} \cap \{X_3 \le 450\}\right)$$

$$= 1 - \left(F_X(450)\right)^3 = 1 - 0.9^3 = 0.271$$

(ii)   The probability that a single claim is no greater than 240 is:

$$\Pr(X_i \le 240) = F_X(240) = \int_0^{240} \frac{1}{500} dx = 0.48$$

The middle (*ie* the 2nd-smallest) claim is less than 240 if either 2 or 3 claims are below 240. Hence the required probability is:

$$\Pr(Y_2 < 240) = \Pr(2 \text{ claims} < 240) + \Pr(3 \text{ claims} < 240)$$

$$= {}_3C_2 \left(F_X(240)\right)^2 \left(1 - F_X(240)\right)^1 + \left(F_X(240)\right)^3$$

$$= 3 \times 0.48^2 \times 0.52 + 0.48^3 = 0.4700 \qquad \blacklozenge\blacklozenge$$

Example 9.12

Using the information in Example 9.10, calculate the pdf of the amount of the middle claim.

Solution

The distribution function of Y_2 is:

$$\Pr(Y_2 \le y) = {_3}C_2 \left(F_X(y)\right)^2 \left(1 - F_X(y)\right)^1 + \left(F_X(y)\right)^3$$

$$= 3 \times \left(\frac{y}{500}\right)^2 \times \left(\frac{500-y}{500}\right) + \left(\frac{y}{500}\right)^3$$

$$= \left(\frac{1}{500}\right)^3 \left(1,500y^2 - 2y^3\right) \qquad \text{for } 0 < y < 500$$

Hence the pdf is:

$$f_{Y_2}(y) = F'_{Y_2}(y) = \left(\frac{1}{500}\right)^3 \left(3,000y - 6y^2\right) \qquad \text{for } 0 < y < 500 \qquad \blacklozenge\blacklozenge$$

It is possible to derive a general result for the pdf of the i-th smallest value in the sample, Y_i, by differentiating the general result for the cdf.

After simplification, we find that:

$$f_{Y_i}(y) = F'_{Y_i}(y) = \frac{n!}{(i-1)!(n-i)!} \left(F_X(y)\right)^{i-1} \left(1 - F_X(y)\right)^{n-i} f_X(y)$$

Intuitively, the event that $Y_i = y$ occurs if $(i-1)$ values in the sample are below y, one value in the sample is equal to y, and $(n-i)$ values in the sample are greater than y.

For example, we can calculate the solution to Example 9.11 as follows (with $i = 2$, $n = 3$):

$$f_{Y_2}(y) = \frac{3!}{1!1!} \left(F_X(y)\right)\left(1 - F_X(y)\right) f_X(y)$$

$$= 3! \left(\frac{y}{500}\right)\left(\frac{500-y}{500}\right)\left(\frac{1}{500}\right)$$

$$= \left(\frac{1}{500}\right)^3 \left(3,000y - 6y^2\right) \qquad \text{for } 0 < y < 500$$

Example 9.13

Claims are assumed to follow a distribution defined by:

$$f(x) = 3x^2 \qquad \text{for } 0 < x < 1$$

If 10 claims are observed, identify the pdf of the 4th smallest claim.

Solution

The distribution function of X is:

$$F_X(x) = \int_0^x f_X(s)ds = s^3 \Big|_0^x = x^3 \qquad \text{for } 0 < x < 1$$

Hence the pdf of Y_4, the 4th smallest claim is:

$$f_{Y_4}(y) = \frac{10!}{3!6!}(F_X(y))^3 (1-F_X(y))^6 f_X(y)$$

$$= 840 \times \left(y^3\right)^3 \times \left(1-y^3\right)^6 \times 3y^2$$

$$= 2,520y^{11}(1-y^3)^6 \qquad \qquad \blacklozenge\blacklozenge$$

Of course, once we identify the pdf of an order statistic, we can also calculate associated probabilities and properties such as the expected value and variance. Let's look at this idea in the final example in this chapter.

 ## Example 9.14

Claims are assumed to follow a distribution defined by:

$$f(x) = 3x^2 \qquad \text{for } 0 < x < 1$$

If 10 claims are observed, calculate the expected value of the 2nd largest claim.

Solution

First, note that the 2nd largest of 10 claims is the 9th smallest.

From Example 9.12, we saw that the distribution function of X is:

$$F_X(x) = x^3 \qquad \text{for } 0 < x < 1$$

Hence the pdf of Y_9, the 9th smallest claim is:

$$f_{Y_9}(y) = \frac{10!}{8!1!}(F_X(y))^8 (1-F_X(y))^1 f_X(y)$$

$$= 90 \times \left(y^3\right)^8 \times \left(1-y^3\right) \times 3y^2$$

$$= 270y^{26}(1-y^3) = 270(y^{26} - y^{29})$$

Hence, the expected value of Y_9 is:

$$E[Y_9] = \int_0^1 y f_{Y_9}(y) = \int_0^1 y 270(y^{26} - y^{29})dy$$

$$= \int_0^1 270(y^{27} - y^{30})dy = 270\left(\frac{y^{28}}{28} - \frac{y^{31}}{31}\right)\Bigg|_0^1$$

$$= 270\left(\frac{1}{28} - \frac{1}{31}\right) = 0.9332 \qquad \qquad \blacklozenge\blacklozenge$$

Order statistics

If Y_i represents the i th smallest value in a sample of n values, then:

$$F_{Y_i}(y) = \Pr(Y_i \leq y) = \sum_{j=i}^{n} {}_nC_j \left(F_X(y)\right)^j \left(1 - F_X(y)\right)^{n-j}$$

$$f_{Y_i}(y) = F'_{Y_i}(y) = \frac{n!}{(i-1)!(n-i)!} \left(F_X(y)\right)^{i-1} \left(1 - F_X(y)\right)^{n-i} f_X(y)$$

In particular, Y_1 represents the **smallest** or **minimum** value in a sample, and:

$$F_{Y_1}(y) = \Pr(Y_1 \leq y) = 1 - \left(1 - F_X(y)\right)^n$$

$$f_{Y_1}(y) = F'_{Y_1}(y) = nf_X(y)\left(1 - F_X(y)\right)^{n-1}$$

Also, Y_n represents the **largest** or **maximum** value in a sample, and:

$$F_{Y_n}(y) = \Pr(Y_n \leq y) = \left(F_X(y)\right)^n$$

$$f_{Y_n}(y) = F'_{Y_n}(y) = nf_X(y)\left(F_X(y)\right)^{n-1}$$

Chapter 9 Practice Questions

Question 9.1
IOA/FOA

The number of demands made on a computer service team each day has a Poisson distribution with mean 2. Under current arrangements the service team can handle no more than 3 demands each day. No demands are carried forward. Calculate the expected number of demands handled by the service team each day.

Question 9.2
IOA/FOA

For each group of policyholders the number of claims, Y, occurring in a period of one year is modeled by the following modified Poisson random variable, which incorporates a reluctance to claim with probability α:

$$\Pr(Y=0) = \alpha + (1-\alpha)\Pr(X=0)$$
$$\Pr(Y=r) = (1-\alpha)\Pr(X=r) \quad \text{for } r=1,2,3,\cdots$$

where X follows a Poisson distribution with mean μ.

Determine an expression for the variance of Y.

Question 9.3

The random variable X has the following pdf:

$$f(x) = e^{-x} \quad \text{for } x > 0$$

Identify the probability density function of $Y = X^2$.

Question 9.4

The random variable X follows a gamma distribution with parameters α and θ. Identify the distribution of $Y = cX$.

Question 9.5
IOA/FOA

Suppose that the distribution of a physical coefficient, X, can be modeled using a uniform distribution on $(0,1)$. A researcher is interested in the distribution of Y, an adjusted form of the reciprocal of the coefficient, where:

$$Y = \frac{1}{X} - 1$$

Identify the probability density function of Y.

Question 9.6   SOA/CAS

A device that continuously measures and records seismic activity is placed in a remote region. The time to failure of this device, T, is exponentially distributed with mean 3 years. Since the device will not be monitored during its first 2 years of service, the time to discovery of its failure is $X = \max(T, 2)$. Determine $E[X]$.

Question 9.7   SOA/CAS

Let T denote the time in minutes for a customer service representative to respond to 10 telephone inquiries. T is uniformly distributed on the interval with endpoints 8 minutes and 12 minutes. Let R denote the average rate, in customers per minute, at which the representative responds to inquiries.

Identify the density function of the random variable R.

Question 9.8

The lifetime X of a 25-year-old is assumed to follow the uniform distribution on the interval $[0, 75]$.

Calculate the length of time (in years) that the 25-year-old can expect to live in the next 10 years.

Question 9.9

An insurance policy reimburses a loss in excess of a 250 deductible. The policyholder's loss, X, follows an exponential distribution with mean 1,000.

What is the expected value of the benefit paid under this insurance policy?

Question 9.10   SOA/CAS

A manufacturer's annual losses follow a distribution with density function:

$$f(x) = \begin{cases} \dfrac{2.5(0.6)^{2.5}}{x^{3.5}} & x > 0.6 \\ 0 & \text{otherwise} \end{cases}$$

To cover its losses, the manufacturer purchases an insurance policy with an annual deductible of 2. What is the mean of the manufacturer's annual losses not paid by the insurance?

Question 9.11

An insurance loss for the year 2002 is modeled using the random variable X, with the following density function:

$$f_X(x) = \frac{2 \times 1,000^2}{(x + 1,000)^3} \quad 0 < x < \infty$$

Losses are assumed to increase by 5% over the next year.

Calculate the density function of Y, the random insurance loss for the year 2003.

Question 9.12

A satellite has two independent power systems. The lifetime of the primary system is distributed exponentially with mean 20 years. The lifetime of the backup system is distributed exponentially with mean 10 years. Calculate the pdf of Y, the total time that the power system will remain functional, if the backup system is operated continuously as soon as the primary system fails.

Question 9.13

Claim amounts X (in $000s) for a certain insurance policy are independent random variables for which:

$$\Pr(X > x) = \left(\frac{50}{x+50}\right)^2$$

Identify the pdf of the 3rd largest claim from a sample of 25 claims.

Question 9.14

Claim amounts (in $000s) for a certain insurance policy are independent random variables that each follow an exponential distribution with mean 10.

If five such claims are made, calculate the expected value of the fourth largest of the five claims.

Question 9.15   *SOA/CAS*

Claim amounts (in $000s) for wind damage to insured homes are independent random variables with common density function:

$$f(x) = \begin{cases} \dfrac{3}{x^4} & x > 1 \\ 0 & \text{otherwise} \end{cases}$$

Suppose 3 such claims will be made. Calculate the expected value of the largest of the three claims.

Review questions

Question 1

You are given the following information:

$$\Pr(A \cap B) = 0.2$$
$$\Pr(B) = 0.85$$

If A and B are exhaustive events, calculate $\Pr(A)$.

(A)   0.15

(B)   0.30

(C)   0.35

(D)   0.50

(E)   0.55

Question 2

The loss, X, for an insurance company this year has the probability density function:

$$f(x) = \frac{32}{(x+4)^3} \quad x > 0$$

Next year's losses are expected to be 7% higher than this year's losses.

The probability density function, $f(y)$, of next year's losses is given by:

(A) $f(y) = \dfrac{36.64}{(y+4.28)^3}$

(B) $f(y) = \dfrac{41.95}{(y+4.5796)^3}$

(C) $f(y) = \dfrac{92.48}{(y+6.8)^3}$

(D) $f(y) = \dfrac{34.24}{(1.07y+4)^3}$

(E) $f(y) = \dfrac{41.95}{(y+4.28)^4}$

Question 3

This morning four new claims arrived at an insurance office. There is a team of 10 people who can deal with claims, three of whom are considered experts. One of the new claims is a difficult case and can only be allocated to an expert. There are no restrictions on how the other claims can be allocated. Nobody is allowed to take on more than one new claim.

Calculate the total number of ways that the claims can be allocated.

(A)   252

(B)   507

(C)   1,008

(D)   1,512

(E)   5,040

Question 4

The lifetime of a circuit is modeled by a random variable with probability density function:

$$\frac{1}{32}x^7 e^{-\frac{x^8}{256}} \quad x > 0$$

Calculate the interquartile range of the lifetime of a circuit.

(A)   0.1974

(B)   0.3718

(C)   0.5213

(D)   2.024

(E)   281.2

Question 5

X is the amount of an insurance claim, with mean 245. $\ln X$ is normally distributed with variance 0.99841.

Calculate the probability that a randomly selected claim exceeds 300.

(A)   0.241

(B)   0.260

(C)   0.433

(D)   0.567

(E)   0.772

Question 6

Claim amounts for a particular insurance company follow a gamma distribution with probability density function:

$$f(x) = \frac{1}{16}x^2 e^{-\frac{1}{2}x} \quad x > 0$$

When the claim amount exceeds the value "mean plus 2 standard deviations", the claim is assessed by a specialist panel.

Calculate the proportion of claims assessed by the panel.

(A)   0.0088

(B)   0.0442

(C)   0.1491

(D)   0.5268

(E)   0.7792

Question 7

Policies are classified as Type I, II or III and all policies are independent. The number of claims per week for a Type I policy or a Type II policy has moment generating function $e^{2(e^t-1)}$, but for a Type III policy, the moment generating function is $e^{3(e^t-1)}$.

If a claim is made, Type I policies pay out $100, Type II policies pay out $200 and Type III policies pay out $300.

Calculate the moment generating function of the total pay out in a week.

(A) $\exp\left\{1,500e^t - 1,500\right\}$

(B) $\exp\left\{2e^{100t} + 2e^{200t} + 3e^{300t} - 1\right\}$

(C) $\exp\left\{7e^t - 7\right\}$

(D) $\exp\left\{15e^t - 15\right\}$

(E) $\exp\left\{2e^{100t} + 2e^{200t} + 3e^{300t} - 7\right\}$

Question 8

Claim amounts follow an exponential distribution with probability density function:

$$0.005e^{-0.005x} \quad x > 0$$

The insurance company introduces a deductible of 75 onto all policies, so that they pay out an amount Y.

Calculate the percentage reduction in $E[Y]$ compared to $E[X]$.

(A)   24.8%

(B)   31.3%

(C)   37.5%

(D)   45.5%

(E)   62.5%

Use the following information for questions <u>9 and 10</u>

A random variable has probability density function:

$$f(x) = \frac{\alpha 4^{\alpha}}{(x+4)^{\alpha+1}} \quad x > 0$$

Question 9

If the mean of X is $\dfrac{4}{3}$ calculate α.

(A)   2

(B)   3

(C)   4

(D)   5

(E)   6

Question 10

Calculate the skewness of X.

(A)   7.07

(B)   8.89

(C)   10.8

(D)   13.3

(E)   47.4

Question 11

The time taken in hours to process a claim has an exponential distribution with mean 8.

Calculate the probability that it will take more than 12 hours to process a claim given that it has already taken 7 hours.

(A)   0.223

(B)   0.417

(C)   0.535

(D)   0.583

(E)   0.777

Use the following information for questions 12 and 13

A random variable, X , has probability density function:

$$f(x) = \frac{288x^3}{(x^4 + 6)^3} \quad x > 0$$

Question 12

Calculate the median value of X .

(A)   0.557

(B)   1.26

(C)   2.85

(D)   2.97

(E)   3.42

Question 13

Calculate the absolute difference between the mode and the 80th percentile of X .

(A)   0.066

(B)   0.461

(C)   0.917

(D)   1.19

(E)   2.44

Use the following information for questions 14 and 15

The joint probability density function of random variables X and Y is:

$$f(x,y) = a(25 - x - 2y) \qquad 0 < x < 25 - 2y < 25$$

Question 14

Calculate the expected value of Y.

(A)   1.563

(B)   3.125

(C)   6.250

(D)   9.375

(E)   10.94

Question 15

Calculate the $\text{var}[X \mid Y = 5]$.

(A)   3.05

(B)   3.24

(C)   5.00

(D)   12.5

(E)   37.5

Use the following information for questions 16 and 17

A bag contains red, blue and green discs. There is one red disc and twice as many blue discs as green ones.

The probability of picking three discs of the same color is $\dfrac{7}{40}$.

Question 16

Calculate the number of blue discs in the bag.

(A)   3

(B)   4

(C)   6

(D)   8

(E)   10

Question 17

Calculate the probability that the third disc picked is a green given that the first two discs are the same color.

(A)   0

(B) $\dfrac{1}{48}$

(C) $\dfrac{1}{3}$

(D) $\dfrac{351}{748}$

(E) $\dfrac{39}{77}$

Question 18

The annual charges levied by fund managers on a particular fund are uniformly distributed over the range (a,b).

You are told that the mean charge is $150 and the variance of the charges is $\$^2 1{,}875$.

On a particular fund, the managers inform you that the charges exceed $120.

Calculate the probability that the charges are, in fact, greater then $170.

(A)   0.180

(B)   0.239

(C)   0.428

(D)   0.524

(E)   0.615

Question 19

There are 30 red balls and 26 blue balls in a bag. A sample of 8 balls is drawn out of the bag.

Calculate the probability that exactly 5 of them are red.

(A)   0.0373

(B)   0.0441

(C)   0.0442

(D)   0.2473

(E)   0.2608

Question 20

For a particular insurance policy, the claim amounts can be 1, 2, 3, 4 or 5 (in units of $000s) with probabilities 0.4, 0.3, 0.15, 0.1 and 0.05 respectively.

The number of claims received in a week follows a Poisson distribution with mean 3. The number of claims and the claim amounts are independent.

Calculate the probability that the total claim amount received in a week is less than $4,000.

(A)   0.127

(B)   0.224

(C)   0.231

(D)   0.237

(E)   0.281

Question 21

The random fraction of medical tests that give an incorrect result is modeled by X, which has probability density function:

$$ax(1-x)^4 \quad 0 < x < 1$$

If the fraction falls outside the range "mean plus or minus 3 standard deviations" then the medical test is reclassified and is withdrawn for further trials.

Calculate the probability that a test is reclassified.

(A)   0.0035

(B)   0.0586

(C)   0.2966

(D)   0.3362

(E)   0.9414

Question 22

The annual number of claims against a household policy has a negative binomial distribution with parameters r and $p = 0.58$.

The only additional information that you are given is that $\Pr(X = 8) = 0.3465\,\Pr(X = 6)$.

In a group of 10 independent policies, calculate the probability that the total annual number of claims is exactly 27.

(A)   0.0006

(B)   0.0009

(C)   0.0049

(D)   0.0383

(E)   0.0568

Question 23

A continuous random variable can take values between 100 and 600. The probability density function over this region is constant.

The probability that the random variable lies within t standard deviations of the mean is 0.9.

Calculate t.

(A)   0.406

(B)   0.594

(C)   1.56

(D)   2.12

(E)   3.12

Question 24

The number of claims received per day at an insurance company has a Poisson distribution with mean 3.

Calculate the probability that the company receives fewer than 1,000 claims in 2006.

(A)   0.0013

(B)   0.0015

(C)   0.0017

(D)   0.0019

(E)   0.0021

Use the following information for questions <u>25 to 28</u>

You are given the following joint probability distribution for X and Y (but your colleague has spilt his latte on the paper so some of the figures are unreadable):

		X	
		2	3
	2	*	0.4
Y	4	*	0.15
	6	*	0.05

You know that $\Pr(Y = 6) = 0.15$ and that the mean of Y is 3.4.

Question 25

Calculate $\Pr(X = 3 \mid Y = 2)$.

(A)   0.111

(B)   0.125

(C)   0.400

(D)   0.615

(E)   0.889

Question 26

Calculate $\text{var}[Y \mid X = 2]$

(A)   1.44

(B)   2.40

(C)   4.42

(D)   5.75

(E)   19.5

Question 27

Calculate $\text{var}[2X + 2Y]$

(A)   4.56

(B)   6.40

(C)   8.66

(D)   9.12

(E)   75.01

Question 28

Calculate the correlation coefficient of the random variables X and Y.

(A)   −0.992

(B)   −0.694

(C)   −0.526

(D)   −0.486

(E)   −0.340

Question 29

A group of 15 university graduates all age 22 have a party. The Math graduate has calculated that the probability that any individual in the group will not survive to age 60 is 0.17, independent of any other member of the group.

The group agrees to have a reunion when they reach 60, which they will definitely attend if they are alive.

Calculate the probability that more than 13 of the graduates will attend the party.

(A)   0.061

(B)   0.074

(C)   0.249

(D)   0.421

(E)   0.518

Question 30

Individual insurance losses at a particular insurance company have mean 12,500 and standard deviation 16,137.

Using a normal approximation, calculate the probability that the sum of 100 such claims exceed 1.6 million.

(A)   0.0150

(B)   0.0431

(C)   0.4141

(D)   0.9569

(E)   0.9850

Question 31

A catering company charges $28 per hour plus a standing charge of $48.

Laura wants them to cater for a conference she is organizing and she feels that the mean number of hours that she requires the company for is 16 with a standard deviation of 5.

Calculate the variance of the charge for catering.

(A)   496

(B)   700

(C)   3,920

(D)   3,968

(E)   19,600

Question 32

The number of telephone calls per day received by an insurance company's switchboard has a Poisson distribution with mean λ.

The probability that the number of telephone calls received in a week is 20 is 1.72 times the probability that it is 15.

Calculate the probability that exactly 5 calls are received in a randomly chosen day.

You may assume that the office shuts at weekends.

(A)   0.091

(B)   0.115

(C)   0.156

(D)   0.175

(E)   0.208

Question 33

A discrete random variable X can take the values 1, 2, 3, 4 and 5. You are given the following information:

$$E[X] = 3$$

$$\text{var}[X] = \frac{28}{11}$$

$$\Pr(X \geq 4) = \frac{5}{11} = \Pr(X \leq 2)$$

Calculate the probability that $X = 4$ given that it is greater than 2.

(A) $\dfrac{1}{4}$

(B) $\dfrac{1}{3}$

(C) $\dfrac{7}{19}$

(D) $\dfrac{7}{12}$

(E) $\dfrac{3}{4}$

Question 34

It has been discovered that 20% of the population has a recessive gene that makes the person with the gene more susceptible to heart attacks. An insurance company has 450 single-life policies in force.

Calculate the probability that more than 100 policyholders have the recessive gene.

(A)   0.108

(B)   0.119

(C)   0.126

(D)   0.134

(E)   0.146

Question 35

A plumber charges $50 per hour plus a call-out charge of $60.

The number of hours that the plumber works on a job has a normal distribution with mean 6 and variance 4.

Calculate the probability that the charge for a job exceeds $400.

(A)   0.3384

(B)   0.3446

(C)   0.4129

(D)   0.6554

(E)   0.6616

Question 36

A student passes an exam with a probability of 0.6.

Calculate the probability that she will fail at least four exams before she passes an exam given that each attempt is independent.

(A)   0.0102

(B)   0.0154

(C)   0.0256

(D)   0.0778

(E)   0.1296

Question 37

The number of claims per day has a Poisson distribution with moment generating function:

$$M_N(t) = e^{\lambda(e^t - 1)}$$

You are told that the ratio of $\Pr(N = 3)$ to $\Pr(N = 2)$ is 2.

Calculate the skewness of N.

(A)   0.028

(B)   0.408

(C)   0.577

(D)   0.707

(E)   1

Question 38

Patients of a chest specialist at a hospital are surveyed about their smoking habits. The results are as follows:

The probability of a patient with heart disease being a smoker is 0.6.

The probability of a patient with lung cancer being a smoker is 0.7.

The probability of a patient with emphysema being a smoker is 0.55.

28% of the patients have lung cancer and 5% have emphysema. The rest have heart disease.

Patients have only one of these diseases at any one time.

A randomly chosen patient is a smoker. Calculate the probability that they have lung cancer.

(A)   0.044

(B)   0.196

(C)   0.286

(D)   0.313

(E)   0.378

Use the following information for questions 39 and 40

An applicant for auto insurance is classified according to the risk of their age, type of car and home address. A sample of 100 applicants revealed the following data:

(i)   28 were classified as high risk due to their age

(ii)   53 were classified as high risk due to their home address

(iii)   6 were classified as high risk due to their age and home address but not type of car

(iv)   20 were classified as high risk due to their type of car but not age and not home address

(v)   15 were not classified as high risk under any category

(vi)   15 were classified as high risk due to their age and type of car

(vii) 17 were classified as high risk due to their home address and type of car

Question 39

Calculate how many were classified as high risk under all three categories.

(A)   10

(B)   11

(C)   12

(D)   13

(E)   14

Question 40

Calculate how many were classified as high risk under exactly two categories.

(A)   10

(B)   15

(C)   18

(D)   28

(E)   48

Question 41

The moment generating function of a random variable is:

$$M_X(t) = \frac{e^{100t} - 1}{100t}$$

Calculate the variance of X.

(A)   833

(B)   1,670

(C)   2,100

(D)   3,280

(E)   3,330

Question 42

An insurance company has a sample of 50 claims, 13 of which are for amounts known to be greater than $1,000.

15 claims are selected at random from this sample.

Calculate the probability that 8 are for claim amounts less than $1,000.

(A)   0.0059

(B)   0.0294

(C)   0.0373

(D)   0.0498

(E)   0.1164

Question 43

An insurance company introduces a policy limit of $5,000 to each loss.

Losses have an exponential distribution with mean $4,000.

Calculate the mean of the amount paid out after the limit has been applied.

(A)   1,000

(B)   2,854

(C)   4,854

(D)   4,989

(E)   6,854

Question 44

A man takes part in a game in which a biased coin is tossed 20 times and the number of times it falls heads is counted. A prize is paid equal to $e^{0.25X}$, where X is the number of heads thrown.

If the probability of landing heads on any throw is 0.4, and all throws of the coin have independent outcomes, calculate the expected amount of prize money the man will receive.

A   7.39
B   8.58
C   8.60
D   20.09
E   23.27

Question 45

The random variables X and Y follow a bivariate normal distribution with parameters:

$$\mu_X = 200 \quad \sigma_X^2 = 800 \quad \mu_Y = 150 \quad \sigma_Y^2 = 500$$

You are told that $E[X \mid Y = 175] = 225$.

Calculate the covariance of X and Y.

(A)   −500

(B)   −0.79

(C)   0.79

(D)   500

(E)   1,012

Question 46

Claim amounts follow a Pareto distribution with cumulative distribution function:

$$1 - \left(\frac{50}{x+50}\right)^4 \qquad x > 0$$

A random sample of 5 claims is taken.

Calculate the probability that the largest value in the sample is greater than 30.

(A)   0.0001

(B)   0.4370

(C)   0.5630

(D)   0.8474

(E)   0.9999

Use the following information for questions <u>47 and 48</u>

The random variables X and Y have the following joint probability density function:

$$ky(x+y) \qquad 0 < y < 10, \quad 0 < x < 2y$$

Question 47

Calculate $\Pr(X < Y)$.

(A)   0.125

(B)   0.250

(C)   0.375

(D)   0.500

(E)   0.625

Question 48

Calculate $\text{cov}(X,Y)$.

(A) $-1 < \text{cov}(X,Y) \le 0$

(B) $0 < \text{cov}(X,Y) \le 1$

(C) $1 < \text{cov}(X,Y) \le 2$

(D) $2 < \text{cov}(X,Y) \le 3$

(E) $3 < \text{cov}(X,Y) \le 4$

Solutions to practice questions

Chapter 1:   Introduction to Probability Theory

Q1.1:   (i)   {3,5,7}

(ii) {2,3,4,5,6,7,8,10}

(iii) {4,6,8,10}

Q1.2:   See online solutions manual

Q1.3:   0.55

Q1.4:   0.4

Q1.5:   0.5

Q1.6:   0.1

Q1.7:   0.6

Q1.8:   0.16

Q1.9:   0.05

Q1.10: 0.53

Q1.11: 0.20

Q1.12: 1/3

Q1.13: 0.5286

Q1.14: (i)   1/24

(ii) 5/8

(iii) 3/4

Q1.15: 0.64

Q1.16: 0.18

Q1.17: 17

Q1.18: 0.7

Q1.19: 0.0062

Q1.20: 4

Chapter 2:   Counting Techniques

Q2.1:   (i)   48

(ii)   16

(iii) 24

Q2.2:   (i)   1,000

(ii)   720

(iii) 860

Q2.3:   24,360

Q2.4:   16

Q2.5:   (i)   5,040

(ii)   2,520

(iii) 64,864,800

Q2.6:   17,153,136

Q2.7:   0.50

Q2.8:   0.0845

Q2.9:   (i)   0.2413

(ii)   0.0264

Q2.10: 0.4968

Q2.11: 0.4702

Q2.12: 0.65

Q2.13: 0.5323

Q2.14: 0.4326

Q2.15: 0.4471

Q2.16: 0.6759

Q2.17: 7

Q2.18: 0.3878

Q2.19: 0.0186

Q2.20: 0.0488

Chapter 3: Conditional Probability and Bayes' Theorem

Q3.1:	0.25	Q3.9:	0.0296
Q3.2:	0.3	Q3.10:	0.8922
Q3.3:	5/9	Q3.11:	0.2922
Q3.4:	0.7561	Q3.12:	0.4667
Q3.5:	0.34375	Q3.13:	0.2174
Q3.6:	0.4244	Q3.14:	0.4
Q3.7:	0.1583	Q3.15:	0.4545
Q3.8:	0.6319		

Chapter 4: Introduction to Random Variables

Q4.1: See online solutions manual

Q4.2: See online solutions manual

Q4.3: 0.2154

Q4.4: $-1/3 \le \theta \le 1/4$

Q4.5: See online solutions manual

Q4.6: 0.04

Q4.7: See online solutions manual

Q4.8: 1.4

Q4.9: $1 - 1{,}000(x+10)^{-3}$

Q4.10: 0.2394

Q4.11: 0.1317

Q4.12: See online solutions manual

Q4.13: 0.7931

Q4.14: 1.95

Q4.15: 0.5

Q4.16: 34.66

Q4.17: 1.3219

Q4.18: 0.75

Q4.19: 2,500

Q4.20: 51.52 and 1.3764

Q4.21: 1.057

Q4.22: 1.154

Q4.23: 4.8676

Q4.24: −0.4082

Q4.25: 1.8

Q4.26: 110

Q4.27: 200

Q4.28: $\dfrac{19}{27} + \dfrac{8}{27}e^t$

Q4.29: 10,560

Q4.30: 0.2251

Chapter 5: Common Discrete Distributions

Q5.1: 0.1798

Q5.2: 0.0401

Q5.3: 10.6, 2.232

Q5.4: See online solutions manual

Q5.5: 33.417 million

Q5.6: 0.9245

Q5.7: 985

Q5.8: 0.3828

Q5.9: 0.13824

Q5.10: See online solutions manual

Q5.11: 0.83692

Q5.12: 0.5470

Q5.13: 6.6923

Q5.14: 0.2817

Q5.15: (i) 1.25
       (ii) 0.8640
       (iii) 0.2215

Q5.16: 0.1404

Q5.17: 0.5649

Q5.18: 2

Q5.19: 699

Q5.20: $e^{-4\lambda}(1+4\lambda)$

Chapter 6: Common Continuous Distributions

Q6.1: 0.479

Q6.2: 1,840 and 1,918

Q6.3: 5.772

Q6.4: 1,000

Q6.5: 0.5781

Q6.6: 4.5

Q6.7: 0.0498

Q6.8: 0.4349

Q6.9: 0.3778

Q6.10: 0.1223

Q6.11: 0.3012

Q6.12: 600

Q6.13: 0.1464

Q6.14: 18

Q6.15: $2/\sqrt{\alpha}$

Q6.16: 0.1337

Q6.17: 240 and 3,974,400

Q6.18: 0.6065

Q6.19: 0.0943

Q6.20: 1,000

Chapter 7: The Normal Distribution

Q7.1: (i)   0.0010
       (ii) 0.0808
       (iii) 0.3307
       (iv) 0.3761

Q7.2: See online solutions manual

Q7.3: $X \sim N(-12,16)$

Q7.4: (i)   0.3821
       (ii) 0.7698
       (iii) 0.1070

Q7.5: 0.2882

Q7.6: 0.3772

Q7.7: 16

Q7.8: 0.8396

Q7.9: 0.1815

Q7.10: 0.3328

Q7.11: 0.1587

Q7.12: 1,128.20

Q7.13: 0.7698

Q7.14: 0.9729

Q7.15: 0.0113

Q7.16: 1.786

Q7.17: 22,915

Q7.18: 10,619.56

Q7.19: 0.0238

Q7.20: 0.1587

Chapter 8:   Multivariate Distributions

Q8.1:   0.7

Q8.2: $f_X(0) = 0.25, f_X(1) = 0.35,$
        $f_X(2) = 0.25, f_X(3) = 0.15$

Q8.3: $f_Y(1|X = 2) = 0.52, f_Y(2|X = 2) = 0.32$
        $f_Y(3|X = 2) = 0.16$

Q8.4:   0.5

Q8.5:   0.4

Q8.6:   0.172

Q8.7: $\dfrac{6}{125,000} \int_{20}^{30} \int_{20}^{50-x} (50 - x - y)\, dy\, dx$

Q8.8:   1.333

Q8.9:   33.33

Q8.10: 0.2041

Q8.11: 468.75

Q8.12: $(e^{2t} - 2e^t + 1)/t^2$

Q8.13: 65

Q8.14: 3,581

Q8.15: 35.83

Q8.16: −0.181

Q8.17: 60

Q8.18: 6

Q8.19: 10.56

Q8.20: 0.9772

Chapter 9:   Transformations of Random Variables

Q9.1:   1.782

Q9.2: $\text{var}(Y) = (1 - \alpha)\mu(1 + \alpha\mu)$

Q9.3: $e^{-\sqrt{y}} \times \dfrac{1}{2\sqrt{y}}$

Q9.4:   Gamma with parameters $\alpha,\ c\theta$

Q9.5: $(1 + y)^{-2}$

Q9.6: $2 + 3e^{-2/3}$

Q9.7: $5/2r^2$

Q9.8:   9.333

Q9.9:   778.80

Q9.10: 0.9343

Q9.11: $\dfrac{2 \times 1,050^2}{(y + 1,050)^3}$

Q9.12: $0.1\left(e^{-0.05y} - e^{-0.10y}\right)$

Q9.13: $\dfrac{2.15625 \times 10^{14}}{(y + 50)^7} \times \left[1 - \left(\dfrac{50}{y + 50}\right)^2\right]^{22}$

Q9.14: 4.5

Q9.15: 2.025 (thousand)

Review questions

Q1:	A	Q9:	C	Q17:	C	Q25:	E	Q33:	B	Q41:	A
Q2:	C	Q10:	A	Q18:	D	Q26:	A	Q34:	A	Q42:	B
Q3:	A	Q11:	C	Q19:	E	Q27:	B	Q35:	B	Q43:	B
Q4:	D	Q12:	B	Q20:	E	Q28:	D	Q36:	C	Q44:	C
Q5:	B	Q13:	B	Q21:	A	Q29:	C	Q37:	B	Q45:	D
Q6:	B	Q14:	B	Q22:	E	Q30:	A	Q38:	D	Q46:	C
Q7:	E	Q15:	D	Q23:	C	Q31:	E	Q39:	A	Q47:	C
Q8:	B	Q16:	C	Q24:	D	Q32:	C	Q40:	C	Q48:	E

Bibliography

DeGroot, Morris. "Probability and Statistics." Addison Wesley, 1986.

Goldberg, Samuel. "Probability: An Introduction." Dover, 1986.

Grimmett, Geoffrey and David Stirzaker. "Probability and Random Processes." Oxford University Press, 3rd edition, 2001.

Hogg, Robert and Elliot Tanis. "Probability and Statistical Inference." Prentice Hall, 6th edition, 2001

Ross, Sheldon. "A First Course in Probability." Prentice Hall, 6th edition, 2003.

Index